FOREI~~C~~

Richard Hughes was Australian by birth. He died in Hong Kong in 1984 aged seventy-seven. From 1972 he was Hong Kong correspondent for *The Times* and easily the most well-known and colourful newspaper man in the Far East. In a career spanning half a century he was the shrewdest of China-watchers and the Far East from Singapore to Korea became his 'beat'.

In 1956 Hughes achieved a spectacular coup when he obtained exclusive interviews with Burgess and Maclean in Moscow.

He was equally famous as a personality, if not an institution. His legend lives on in fiction as he has been immortalised both by John le Carré as the character of Craw in his novel *The Honourable Schoolboy*, and by Ian Fleming as Dikko Henderson in the novel *You Only Live Twice*.

An indication of his eminence lies in the fact that the Hong Kong Hilton displays a plaque bearing his name and image over his favourite table in the Grill Room. Furthermore in 1983 the Australian Government took the unprecedented step of paying him a pension even though he was not resident in the country of his birth.

In the author's own words, *Foreign Devil* consists of 'anecdotes and presumptions, excuses and reflections spread over thirty years of great events'.

FOREIGN DEVIL

Thirty Years of Reporting from the Far East

RICHARD HUGHES

CENTURY PUBLISHING
LONDON

LESTER & ORPEN DENNYS DENEAU
MARKETING SERVICES LTD
TORONTO

FOR MY SON

Contents

8 CONTENTS

V MYSTERY, CRIME – AND BARITSU

VI TRAVELLERS' TALES

L'Envoi

(at the wrong end, Japanese style)

Whene'er I take my walks abroad
What bloody fools I see;
But, such the justice of the Lord,
They think the same of me.

TRADITIONAL JAPANESE FOLKSONG,
Nara, circa AD 606.

Introduction

Alien Western newspapermen do not feel that they are always foreigners in Western foreign countries. But – like all Westerners – they know that they are foreigners, and remain foreigners, in the East. And foreign-devils, to boot. This doesn't mean that they are necessarily unpopular or unwelcome – outside communist states – or that they don't make and keep good friends among the Asians. On the contrary. (If they are lucky, they can win enchanting lovers or proud wives.) But they remain foreigners, outsiders, barbarians, devils – meaning alien, not necessarily satanic, intruders. It is not merely the Babel curse. Or the duration of expatriate residence. The hallmark of the so-called Old Hand, who has mastered the languages, and who often insensibly becomes more Asian than the Asians in his alien habits, superstitions and prejudices, is his self-knowledge and self-acceptance of his foreign-devil identity.

I first went to Asia, a virgin foreign-devil, in the year 1940, which (as all readers will instantly recall) was the Year of the Dragon. I borrowed £400 from my Sydney newspaper, and took a Japanese steam-packet, technically on long leave, to Japan. Only eighteen months before Pearl Harbour, there was not a solitary Australian diplomat nor a solitary Australian reporter on the scene.

I savoured briefly and enjoyed enduringly the Japan and Shanghai of those days, although I left, running hard, before 1941 (the Year of the Serpent, you will triumphantly shout). I thought Japan would be in the war in February, not December. But I was resolved to return.

After the Middle East war, I did return to the Far East, and there, with a brief interruption to cover Khrushchev's Twentieth Congress, I have remained ever since, to welcome a second and third Year of the Dragon (1952 and 1964) and, I hope, a fourth in 1976. Despite senility, I still enjoy being a foreign-devil on dragon-back.

It's a good, lively news-beat. Any working pressman who finds life dull in the Far East shouldn't be in the trade. And post-1940 has been the highwater news period for the foreign-devils. In those thirty years, colonialism has passed, China has stood up, Japan, broken and humiliated as only an Asian state can be broken and humiliated, has undergone the most amazing renaissance in history, and Asian communism – rather, aggressive and vengeful Asian nationalism – has arrived. The Dutch, the French and the British have gone. The Americans came and are now, in turn, getting out. The West is out. Asia is for Asia. And a damned good thing.

The reader is warned that there is no attempt at either earnest instruction or evangelism in these rambling notes and random memories of a foreign-devil's wanderings in Japan (pre-war and post-defeat), in China (pre-communist and post-communist), and in South-East Asia and Siberia. The economist, the specialist, the historian, the diligent student should replace this volume with a shudder on bookstall counter or library shelf. Here are, basically, anecdotes and presumptions, excuses and reflections – spread thinly over thirty years of great events.

In retrospect and mental decline, I believe it to be more rewarding to describe the Soviet colonel who changed his eye after every meal on the Siberian railway than to guess lyingly about Russian border troop deployments which were never glimpsed on the trek; more useful to recall in awe and alarm the fulfilled prophecy of the Blind Bonze of Luang Prabang than to speculate on the military highway which the Chinese are building into Laos.

The hell with portentous sermons and stale pontificating. Let us have some anecdotage. Dr Johnson (born in the Year of the Wild Boar) observed: 'I love anecdotes. I fancy mankind may come in time to write all aphoristically, except in narrative. I grow weary of preparation and connection and illustration, and all those arts by which a big book is made ... The word "anecdote" is now used after the French for a biographical incident; a minute passage of private life.'

So here come a foreign-devil's maundering anecdotes of the Years of the Dragon – dragons being, of course, notorious for their perverse, blundering, selfish, garrulous, snorting, incestuous and socially useless behaviour.

Could there really be some basis in fact for these Oriental superstitions? This is the inevitable question which every foreign-devil winds up asking himself. The foreign-devil pressman should never even whisper that question aloud; the immediate thundering echo from his Fleet Street office is: 'Bring him home! The bastard has been out there too long!'

And then – for me, personally – there is the other grim side of the coin: a tail for the head of the dragon. An anecdote.

On his last visit to Hong Kong, the formidable, percipient Premier of Singapore, Lee Kuan-yew, for whose ruthless judgment I have deep respect and fear, had half-a-dozen foreign-devil pressmen, who had known him since *merdeka*, to a reunion lunch at the Country Club. He was relating off-the-record impressions of his world tour and broke off with a rhetorical question: 'Are there any Australians present?'

Surprised and a trifle indignant, I raised my hand: 'You know very well, sir, there is one here.'

He turned to regard me silently for a few moments – in no way offensively, not even critically, but with a half-smile of indulgent good humour – and then remarked: '*You*, Richard! You an *Australian*? You are no longer an Australian, and no-one knows that better than you do.'

I could think of nothing to say. I still can't think of anything I should, or could, have said.

The foreign-devil can't win – no matter how many dragons he can ride, command or supplicate.

First Japanese Landfall

CHAPTER I

'You Better be Careful'

'We do not have the dirty words in Japanese, Hooje-*san*,' old bullet-headed Captain Yanagi of the good ship *Osaka-maru* confessed.

'So plis to teach us the Austlalian ones.'

It was a moment of mingled pride and relief for me. I was the only *gaijin* (foreigner) among the dozen-odd passengers Kobe-bound from Sydney in mid-1940, and I had feared that, involuntary prisoner of these sinister Orientals on a three-week journey, I might be subjected to subtle brain-washing, jujitsu humiliation, karate hazing or compulsory lessons in flower arrangement. Instead, most days I found myself presiding, after our Japanese-style lunches, in the smoking-room of the throbbing motor-ship, over an earnest study-group in pornographic semantics. They were polite and formal cultural sessions. The group comprised half-a-dozen Japanese wool-buyers, Captain Yanagi and his first mate, and a couple of consulate officials who had a useful working knowledge of adjectives and active verbs but were anxious to brush up on vocabulary.

I must own that I benefited personally from the exchanges, as the students pressed searching questions and offered novel theories and derivations – e.g.: 'C – A – T – H – O – U – S – E?' spelled out Akiyama-*san*, who listed his words alphabetically with a huge golden pencil in an ivory notebook. 'So? This is another name for brothel, like *Yoshiwara*? Why? Are the *joro* called cats?'

'The term originated in the United States,' I replied, somewhat at a loss.

'I have heard it often in San Flancisclo,' Captain Yanagi agreed. 'There, also, they could not tell me why. My girl flend, Marjalie, in Sydney did not know, too.'

The captain continually referred with great pride and tenderness to this Sydney companion, who seems to have been a woman of overpowering knowledge, patience and sympathy.

'Some of these words are very difficult,' Saito-*san* (who had mastered the precise use of 'l' and 'r') grumbled. 'Yesterday you told us that D – R – U – M was another word for brothel. But' – accusingly – 'you did not know why.'

'Perhaps,' suggested Akiyama, a methodical student, as he turned back a page or two of his book, 'perhaps because you can get a B – A – N – G there?'

This sally would have raised a snort of laughter at the old Marble Bar or the Press Club, but the Japanese class considered the theory soberly, with earnest frowns, pursed lips and mumbled asides and recorded the question and answer in careful detail. Once again – as I still do, after twenty-five years – I brooded over the unbridgeable gap between Western and Japanese humour. . . .

As I recall, my companions had agreed to like Australia and to ridicule the notion, eighteen months before Pearl Harbour, that Japan would ever go to war against us. They insisted that they had liked living in Australia; but they wanted to get back home; nonetheless, they would welcome a return visit – although some of the younger ones complained that Australian harlots often rejected them after discovering that they were Japanese: 'We thought you boys were Chows'. Greater rage hath no man than a Japanese mistaken for a Chinese, save perhaps a Chinese mistaken for a Japanese, or maybe a Korean mistaken for either.

Captain Yanagi, a kind mentor and a civilized man, made me learn basic Japanese words and warned me, apologetically and furtively, against likely brushes with Japanese army officers and all uniformed officials in Japan – 'because of the lelations between your countlee and mine.' A realist, he was clearly troubled by the prospects of war, but he never doubted that he would always be on the next turn-around run to Sydney and Marjalee. He once showed me a cherished snap of her taken at the Sydney Zoo – a very respectable, well-nourished, smiling figure, I thought, whom my dear mother would have welcomed at dinner in Melbourne. He also showed me – from the same wallet – a family picture of his wife, taken at the Tokyo Zoo: a frail ageing figure in kimono, surrounded by four shaven-headed teenage sons.

He taught me the words of 'China Nights', that nostalgic refrain which is still heard whenever Japanese fishing boats gather anywhere in the world. He had a genius for confusing 'r' and 'L' and he would sometimes substitute a noun for a verb – like using 'tear' for 'weep' – so that when he told me about the little girls weeping in 'China Nights', his fascinating reconstruction was: 'the rittle girls were tealing.'

Every morning we would assemble to listen to the world news in English on the ship's radio. Sometimes there were embarrassing moments. The Japanese would avoid my eyes when the reports carried the latest bellicose threats by Foreign Minister Matsuoka to the Americans and the West. I would avoid the Japanese eyes when Prime Minister John Curtin of Australia warned the Japanese Government. But we all looked the other way – the Japanese coming from Australia, and the Australian correspondent going to Japan – at the first bald announcement of the violent death of Jimmy Cox, Reuter correspondent, arrested in Tokyo for espionage. The Western press was deriding the Japanese claim that he had jumped to his death. I felt that the Japanese sympathized with me, and curiously I felt closer to them as we nodded silently together.

Captain Yanagi very correctly ran up a large, weather-beaten Rising Sun flag at the stern as we passed one stormy afternoon through the US territorial waters of Guam, a doomed, hump-backed silhouette against a dark sky. 'Japanese custom,' he told me.

By common unspoken consent, all the Japanese passengers changed dramatically into their dark *yukata*, the informal, deep-sleeved cotton robe, with black sash, on the sweltering afternoon when we tied up in Kobe. I was the only passenger in Western clothes. It is a tribute to the Japanese that I then realized, for the first time, that I was the *gaijin*, the stranger, the outsider, the putative enemy, the man whose girl-friends, way back in Australia, could confuse an honest Jap for a dirty Chow. The change in dress subtly transformed the speech, the bearing and the manner of my fellow passengers. There was no post-lunch class in dirty English that day. They were more relaxed, more confident, more assured, more decisive. In general conversation, they now discarded the English which they had considerately used in my presence. They knew they had come home. It was as simple as that.

'There is,' John Morris has pointed out, 'always a hint of the dark tiger about a Japanese in his *yukata*.' The simple elegant robe is the most admirable dress for comfort in the Far East. I wear it always. But *gaijin* are denied that hint of the dark tiger.

The relatives and friends and the firms' representatives rushed aboard, and I had my first sight of the Japanese hip-deep bows, *derrières* in formal command, sunken head beside sunken head, wary side-glance for the simultaneous rise and dip again. The Western handshake looks like a cheap hiccup in a drunken bar.

'Japanese custom,' whispered Captain Yanagi. We smiled together in esperanto. I realized, on the point of departure, with a sudden pang, how fond of him I had become. Marjalee, I decided, was a Sydney woman of great discernment; it was a thought that would have shocked my Australian prejudices three weeks earlier.

Sayonaras and visiting cards exchanged, I went to my cabin to get my typewriter and books and follow my trunk to the customs. On my bed was an orderly array of immaculately wrapped packages – a fan, a flag, a flute, a lecherous doll, chopsticks, a catalogue – each carrying a card of farewell and good luck, each a personal gift from my fellow passengers, now in hot and unimpassive confrontation with their hostile uniformed compatriots in the customs shed.

The Japanese official in charge of the book-examination of the Kobe customs office was wearing neither trousers nor coat, which hung on the wall behind him. Like all his colleagues in the crowded, oven-hot office, he was clad in the simple, revealing summer work-dress of the Kobe desk official: spectacles, open-neck shirt, gaping underpants, cotton socks with sexy brass suspenders, sandals, and a rich smokescreen of foul *daikon* breath. (*Daikon* is an aromatic type of Japanese turnip or pumpkin; never, *never*, eat it.)

We abominated each other at first glance. He grappled with my books, identified Gunther's *Inside Asia* and Chamberlain's *Japan Over Asia* with gratified rage, hurled them into a basket, told me that they were 'wicked and dirty' and would be returned to me only on departure. He questioned me closely about my visit, raising his voice for the benefit of his colleagues, grinning at their desks, and as stupid as all immigration and customs officials everywhere in the world – East and West, communist and non-communist.

'British journalist?' this son of a bitch hissed. He scrabbled for a Japanese newspaper, jabbed his filthy fingernail at a front-page story, tossed it at me. 'Jimmy Cox?' he snarled. 'You ever hear of him? He was British journalist. He wasn't careful. He dead now. You better be careful.'

It must have been Captain Yanagi's inspiration *in absentia*. 'We British are always careful, just as you Japanese, so your ambassador told me in Sydney, are always polite,' I declared unctuously. Even his ears reddened. He made a curious mewing noise like a baboon swallowing medicine. He wrote me a receipt for my books (duly honoured, I must concede, in December when I left); he rose, with a bow, and to the astonishment of his colleagues, put on his trousers – although he left the flies open – and escorted me to the door. His obscene mouth, with its decaying tombstone teeth, forced a smile and his eyes blazed with hatred as he inquired anxiously whether I knew my way to the Oriental Hotel. He bowed from the hips as I moved, with quiet dignity outside. But he couldn't help slamming the door behind me.

That same afternoon at the Oriental Hotel, I read, buried in a two-inch paragraph on page three of an English-language daily, an agency report of the death of Air Minister Fairbairn and another half-dozen close friends of mine in a stupid air crash outside Canberra. I went into the side saloon for a drink. Behind the half-moon bar there was a print of three fat monks fishing over the caption: 'Tomorrow will be Friday.' At one end of the bar was a drunken, florid, corpulent *gaijin*, surrounded by three silent, watchful Japanese civilians. He called to me offensively: 'Deutsch?' 'No,' I replied. 'But you will drink "Heil Hitler!" ' he demanded in English, lurching towards me. I could see the head-lines in Sydney: 'Australian Journalist Arrested In Kobe. Drunken Bar Brawl with German.' However, there was of course no choice. I told the kraut what he and Hitler could do, set my glass on the bar, and commended my soul to God – and the *kempei-tai*. Providentially the three watchful Japanese intervened. One apologized to me, the other two walked the German out, applying well-practised but respectful armlocks. The Japanese barman shrugged off my inquiries. I never found out who the German was, although the Japanese were clearly security police.

The ground shifted under my feet. Glasses and bottles rattled behind the bar. The barman picked his nose. It was my first Japanese earthquake. There was the reveille blast of a bugle in the outside lobby, which did surprise the barman. It was being quite a day. The barman accompanied me to the door in response to the bugle. Down the grand double staircase trotted in perfect precision twenty nazi youths in brown shirts and *lederhosen*, with swastikas on their arms and heavy knives against their buttocks. To the astonishment of the Japanese in the lobby, the young louts lined up facing huge Rising Sun and swastika flags draped on the stairway, raised their arms in the nazi salute, sang the Horst-wessel song, shouted 'Heil Hitler!' thrice and goose-stepped into the street.

Akiyama-*san* from the *Osaka-maru* had materialized beside me. 'Western custom?' he asked me enigmatically. Then: 'Come with me. I have a nice bar and pretty company – all Japanese – for dinner.' He was a good guide, God bless him.

All in all, the three weeks at sea and the half-day and night ashore in Kobe – always the best Japanese city for *gaijin* – had been an appropriate and instructive introduction for an innocent Australian to the new world, the New Order, and the new war.

Five years later, back in Japan, I made special and urgent inquiries to track down Captain Yanagi and my fellow-passengers on the *Osaka-maru*. I had treasured private and official addresses. The ship had been torpedoed and sunk with the captain and all hands in the Coral Sea. All the passengers – save two of the younger ones – had been killed in the air raids; the two who escaped the raids were posted 'missing' in the South Seas.

CHAPTER 2

So you Understand the Japanese?

Japan, of course, was a fascist police state in 1940. It was a hell of a place for a wretched foreign newsman to ply his simple trade. Despite the China Incident, curtain-raiser for their looming catastrophe, the Japanese had managed to retain at home some human pleasures and weaknesses. The Japanese had always endured and tolerated a measure of authoritarian discipline; *kodo* (the way of the Emperor) was linked with *bushido* (the way of the warrior), *shinto* (the way of the gods), and the traditional Japanese way of life, obedience and the pursuit of inhibitions and restraints.

In 1940, you could still see attractive women in Tokyo streets, although groups of vicious harridans, in *mampei* or bloomer-suits and patriotic sashes like women's lib fanatics turned commie, already crouched at *Ginza* corners to berate passing pretty, well-dressed girls as betrayers of the brave boys who were liberating the obstinate Chinese. The true fascist state, like the true communist state, does not welcome the attractions and distractions of pretty women. The first open signs that there was something rotten in the states of Czechoslovakia and Roumania were the mini-skirts.

The Son of Heaven was Japan's divine *Führer* – or infallible Chairman. Emperor worship was implacably enforced. As every crowded tram lurched past the 'double entrance' to the palace, the conductor barked a stern order and everyone arose and joined in a jostling obeisance, some with their *derrières* pointed inadvertently at the holy residence. On the rare occasions when the chrysanthemum-crested, maroon limousine passed, all traffic was halted and all pedestrians halted with their eyes cast to the ground. Every top-storey window was supposed to be screened so that no one might, even by accident, look down on the Son of Heaven.

The Emperor was always called 'Mr Charles Smith' or 'Charles'

or 'Big Charlie' by the foreign community. This pseudonym –
which was not intentionally disrespectful – permitted public
references to him without possible offence to Japanese within
hearing who regarded the use of the Emperor's name in general
conversation as impious. Even the Germans used the tag: 'Herr
Schmidt' or 'Grosser Karl'.

The friendly, intelligent, anti-military Akiyama-*san*, who was
Japanese consul-general in Sydney until he was shunted to
Mexico, had literally tears in his eyes when he apologetically
rebuked me for a newspaper story which I wrote about the
Emperor in early 1941. The tone of the article, which I had
composed with a prudent eye on Australian censorship, had been
mild and carefully inoffensive, but Akiyama-*san* was distressed
because I had had the temerity to describe the personal appearance
of the Emperor.

'Would an Australian Christian like a Japanese journalist to
describe the physical appearance of Jesus Christ if Jesus were
reigning, reincarnated, in Canberra?' he asked me seriously. 'The
Emperor is Japan's Jesus.' Today that reverence is incongruously
reminiscent of the Mao legend in China.

The Japanese High Command had to make a difficult choice
between reverence and realism during the first air-raid manœuvres
and air-defence tests over Tokyo in autumn 1940. The bombers
were supposed to attack every possible target in the capital and
reveal all weaknesses in the defences. But clearly there were
elements of blasphemy in a pretence by a Japanese plane to drop
a bomb on the moated, green-roofed palace, so nakedly the
answer to a bomber's prayer. And the Emperor had announced
his intention of observing the manœuvres from the palace
grounds, which meant that a pilot flying over the palace would be
able to look down on him.

After wrestling with its feelings, the High Command formulated
a typical Japanese compromise. No attempt was made to 'bomb'
the palace, but one day when the Emperor was absent a solitary
plane flew low over the palace grounds so that an anti-aircraft
post near the palace could fire and register a theoretical 'kill'.
Despite the Emperor's arranged absence, it was understood that
the air crew would keep their eyes as far as possible off the target.

As events transpired, the US planes carefully avoided the
palace in the systematic fire-bombing of Tokyo.

Japanese inhibitions and Japanese courtesy were often in confusing conflict under the cross-currents and shifting pressures of the 'New Order'. I was invited to address a luncheon by members of the sadly depleted Japan-Australia Friendship Society, of which Prince Tokugawa, who had been a popular first Japanese consul-general in Sydney, was then the President. I arrived to discover three long empty tables, formally set for thirty-six absent diners, and commanded by the solitary figure of the aristocratic President, with half-a-dozen waiters scratching their armpits in a puzzled group inside the door of the private room.

Prince Tokugawa greeted me warmly. There had been, he explained with a courtly bow and no hint of embarrassment, 'a slight misunderstanding', and all Society members had become somehow involved in 'another official meeting'. 'Governmental', he amplified, with a disdainful shrug.

'I must admit that I am selfishly grateful for the misunderstanding,' he continued, dismissing the waiters and taking me by the arm to a reserved table for two in the main dining-room. 'There are many matters of interest which we can better discuss between our two selves, without the distractions of a large, unfamiliar, uninformed company. These large official lunches, I am sure you agree, are tiresome and unrewarding affairs.'

It belatedly occurred to me, as we ordered lunch and reinforced *tan-san* bottles, that the signing of the tripartite pact between Japan, Germany and Italy had been announced the previous week, after my invitation, and that the tone of the Japanese press had dutifully swung against the British Commonwealth as well as the United States. Obviously the Japan-Australia Society had decided that the projected official meeting would be inconveniently timed.

Next day, a handsome malacca cane was delivered to my room, with a formal letter from the committee of the Society, thanking me warmly for the honour of my attendance at the luncheon, and expressing the deep appreciation of all members for my 'most helpful, illuminating and encouraging address', a full report of which, I was assured, had been 'preserved in the Society's records'. Prince Tokugawa's signature headed the personal signatures and formal chops of all committee members. I still have the malacca cane. But I would have to refer to the Society's records for the notes of my memorable address.

Mrs K, a charming but obstinate American resident of Tokyo, had learned enough fragmentary Japanese to be tempted to air and misuse it in public. Her maladroitness alarmed and depressed her sensitive bank-manager husband, but his nervous mumbled protests served only to inflame her to wilder verbal excesses.

At a formal dinner, the husband finally sought an ally. Mrs K brightly observed to a venerable Japanese scholar that the soup was *daijobu*. Mr K raised his voice to a distinguished if choleric British friend, Colonel P, whose Japanese was as fluent as his English. I was admirably sited to overhear the exchanges.

'Colonel,' Mr K said across the table. 'I have been trying for months to persuade my wife that she is wrong in saying *daijobu* in tribute to soup or food. I tell her that it means only that the soup is not poisoned or that the plate is quite clean. But she won't believe me. Perhaps she will believe you.'

The trapped colonel looked broodingly at the lady, who cried gaily: 'Of course I am right, aren't I, colonel? *Daijobu* is an honorific and a compliment.'

Colonel P, against his better judgment, assured the lady in gently disarming tones that her husband, alas, was right, and that *daijobu* was not a correct formal tribute to pay to the soup. Mrs K, bridling, resisted the colonel's correction as stoutly as she had already resisted her husband's. She carried her protest to the Japanese scholar, whose English was perfect, who was known and respected everywhere, and who was a close personal friend of Colonel P. He blinked benevolently through his spectacles at Colonel P, turned to the lady and said firmly: 'Of course you are right, madam. I fear that for once – ha, ha – Colonel P is wrong.'

Fortunately, the unsuspecting host, at the far end of the table, called at this explosive moment for a goodwill toast – 'to peace, coupled with the names of President Roosevelt, Prime Minister Churchill and Prince Konoye' – and I watched the enraged colonel swallow his fury with wordless movements of his lips. Later, unappeased by the excellent food and wine, he cornered his good friend, the scholar, with a ferocious demand for an explanation. I listened in awe.

'My dear colonel,' expostulated the surprised scholar, 'of course you were right. But of course I had to say you were wrong. I do not know the lady. But I know you are my friend. You, I knew, would understand and sympathize with me when I was compelled to say, wrongly, that you were wrong and she was right. Naturally, I cannot tell someone I hardly know that she is wrong when she is wrong, but happily I can always tell a close friend publicly that he is wrong when I know that he is right. Fortunately, you understand the Japanese.'

CHAPTER 3

The Untold Story of Richard Sorge

Richard Sorge, the greatest spy of them all, was hanged in Tokyo's Sugamo prison on 7 November, 1944, twenty-seventh anniversary of the Bolshevik revolution. Until the last, he believed that Stalin would save him by a swap. When the Japanese sentenced him to death on 29 September 1943, they also clearly believed – and probably hoped – that an exchange would be made. Two appeals were lodged, the sentence was confirmed in April, but execution was deferred for another seven months.

Sorge had to wait twenty years for posthumous credit and reward by the Soviet communists, whom he had served so faithfully, bravely and successfully. Then they made him a Hero of the Soviet Union. They printed a four-kopek stamp in his honour. They even gave a Moscow street and a Soviet tanker his name. Big deal. Fearless comrade pressmen wrote glowingly of his achievements, playing down the fact that the monster Stalin had ignored or dimissed his most valuable information.

Sorge's skeleton, with the shattered leg-bone that had left him with a perpetual limp and which he had suffered, ironically, fighting for the Kaiser's Germans against the Russians, is now buried in Tama cemetery outside Tokyo. His devoted Japanese mistress, the former Ginza bargirl, Hanako, lovingly extracted the gold filling from one of the teeth in his skull and wrought it into a ring which she still wears.

Much nonsense has been written about Sorge by people who should have known better. There are absurd stories that he was caught because of his careless lust for a beautiful Japanese 'dancer', who had been ordered by the Japanese secret police to surrender her honour in order to trap the *gaijin* spy. There are other absurd stories that Sorge was never hanged, that he was secretly exchanged for Japanese spies in Macao, Hokkaido, Shanghai and Mukden, that he screamed, 'To hell with all mankind!' on the gallows, that the 'dancer' who betrayed him was shot down in an alley outside a Shanghai nightclub – probably by Sorge himself.

Conversely, there have also been several excellent, painstakingly documented works written about Sorge – notably the definitive and indispensable *The Case of Richard Sorge* by two distinguished scholars, F. W. Deakin and G. R. Storry.

But the full story about Sorge has still not been told. There are too many gaps and contradictions. Sorge is still a mystery. Unlike the treacherous Philbys and Blakes and the professional Abels and Wynnes, he is not able himself to set his own record straight or gloss his crookedness prettily. Even when the Russians finally decided to acknowledge his services, they avoided some basic details and made a character-hero rather than a party-martyr out of him. The Germans fell into an uncomfortable silence, which they have never broken – save for some remarkable admissions by the late nazi security chief Schellenberg, which no one seems to have taken seriously. And the Japanese security men have chosen to hush up vital inner secrets about the Russo-German master spy and his Japanese traitors.

Every foreign newsman who has tried during the Occupation and since to tie up the loose ends that still clutter the Sorge case has only broken his fingernails. The Russian judge on the International Tribunal which tried the major Japanese war criminals refused implacably to allow any evidence about Sorge to be presented to the court. Ageing Japanese reporters who covered the original story insist that there is – or was – a secret Tokyo file about Sorge which was never released because it reviewed Tokyo's equivocal relations with both Moscow and Berlin. That was the belief also of the late Dr Harold Noble, the astute us operator who did the patient devilling for the first authoritative survey of the Sorge saga by General Willoughby, MacArthur's intelligence chief (*Shanghai Conspiracy: The Sorge Spy Ring*). And clearly Messrs Deakin and Storry ran into maddening dead-ends which even their exhaustive inquiries failed to breach.

Two unanswered questions are the heart of the Sorge story:

Why did the Russians allow Sorge to be hanged when the Japanese were prepared to exchange him?

Why did several suspicious nazis in Tokyo fail to unearth Sorge's notorious Communist Party record (readily available in the Berlin archives) while he, to their resentment, was being given the run of German secrets at the Tokyo Embassy and maintaining direct access to Nazi security authority in Berlin?

In my opinion, there is only one answer to these two basic questions. It is a simple answer, and once it is accepted all the gaps in the Sorge story are filled and all contradictions resolved.

I met and drank several times with Richard Sorge in Tokyo in 1940, when, as head of the Soviet spy ring in the Far East, he was officially a German newspaperman and a member of the Nazi Party, and technically press relations officer for the German embassy. Once he intervened – quite impersonally – to save me from a punch-up in Ketel's Nazi bar, the Rheingold, behind the Ginza. We met only by accident. We spoke together alone only once – and, in retrospect, his comment to me was wryly contemptuous. He never encouraged personal contacts with foreign correspondents; his urbane and courageous Yugoslav aide, Branko de Voukelitch, squeezed the useful information out of these fellow-*gaijin* reporters, just as his urbane and courageous Japanese right-hand, Hotsumi Ozaki, manipulated and milked Japanese reporters and diplomats. (Ozaki, like Sorge, was hanged; Voukelitch, broken physically but never morally or mentally by torture, was allowed to die in an icy Hokkaido prison.)

It would be gratifying to suggest that I – or other Western pressmen in Tokyo who had longer acquaintance with him – had at times a reservation or two about Sorge, that someone 'suspected'. It would also be utterly untrue. Sorge fascinated and repelled me as the prototype of The Nazi, tough, ruthless, arrogant, unscrupulous, bigoted, a bastard. He was a formidable, stocky – rather than large – man of forty-five, with the scarred face of a cruel gnome, bat's ears, bagged Oriental eyes which seldom smiled when his sensual mouth did. In a group, he was generally silent and coldly attentive, or else hectoring and in sardonic command of the conversation. He was by no means the giant he is usually said to have been. He stood 5 feet 11 inches at the most – tall by Japanese standards – and I reckon he would have boxed at around 180 lbs. He drank heavily but I never saw him drunk. He excelled at liar's dice. He had a habit of crumbling empty match-boxes and chewing toothpicks. He obviously kept himself in good physical condition, although by repute he performed most of his regular exercises indoors on his knees. More than enough has been written about his interest in women. He had two official wives – one divorced, the other mislaid, neither in Tokyo – but he was never a man to overwhelm one woman with the attentions which consoled so many.

At no time did he allow liquor or women to affect his judgment or distract him from his coldly efficient and audacious operations. He was, after all, a pro – probably the greatest of them all. His reflex guard, it seems, was never lowered. In all his drinking and writing, jesting and wenching, questioning and finangling, over nine tense years in Japan and Shanghai, he never once let slip a hint that he knew a word of Russian.

That there were reservations about him at the outset in Tokyo – but *only among Japanese* – is borne out by his own report that early Japanese contacts twice addressed him out of the air in Russian. He never understood. In turbulent Shanghai he was marked down as a Russian spy by the police, although significantly his Berlin letters of introduction assured him an immediate welcome at the consulate-general.

His Japanese achievement was, all agree, a triumph. A Western stranger to the Far East, a *kwai-lo* (foreign-devil) to the Chinese and a *gaijin* (foreigner) to the Japanese, he enlisted, directly and indirectly, a spy ring of sixteen men and women, Western and Japanese, which laboured and flourished for seven years in pre-war Japan. He had access to the innermost secrets of the German embassy, photographed codes and documents in an office inside the embassy, read despatches from Hitler and other nazi leaders and helped, at the respectful request of the non-nazi ambassador, ponderous General Ott, to draft replies. Ozaki, his top Japanese aide, was a confidant of the unhappy Prince Konoye, thrice Premier.

Sorge had been specially trained in Moscow. He maintained the most stringent precautions against discovery by the Japanese security police (*Tokko*) and military police (*Kempei*). But he never appeared at any time to be worried by the possibility of detection by the nazi authorities, whom he was betraying as smoothly as he was hoodwinking the Japanese.

The Sorge ring was finally uncovered, on the eve of Pearl Harbour, by chance – in the shape, ironically but perhaps appropriately, of a cowardly and disgruntled Japanese Communist

Party member, Comrade Ritsu Ito, who, for personal reasons and in blind spite, struck at the weakest link of the outer ring, unaware that this treachery would destroy the whole Sorge apparatus, of which he knew nothing.

Sorge had successfully accomplished his mission. From 1937 to 1941, Stalin had been informed in advance of every projected military move and policy shift by Japan, as well as all top-level details of German military and diplomatic policy and thinking in the Far East. Specifically, Sorge advised Russia of the intended nazi invasion a week in advance; he was able to give assurances that Japan would not attack Russia, at a time when there were desperate doubts in the Kremlin about the wisdom of trans-ferring crack Soviet troops from Siberia to halt the attack outside Moscow; he was finally able to advise that the Japanese would strike south into the Pacific when they went to war, and not west, and would respect the commitments of the Russo-Japanese neutrality pact, which Stalin eventually broke to be in at the kill after the atomic bombs.

Sorge then suggested – October 1941 – that, his mission having been fulfilled, his apparatus should be dissolved and that he should be recalled to Russia for more useful work. This message was found lying on his desk uncoded when he was picked up by the *Tokko* in bed – alone – in the early morning of Saturday, October 18.

To consider and speculate upon the untold Sorge story, it is necessary to recall personal facts, curiously blurred or con-veniently neglected, about his birth and bitter formative years. He was born in 1895 at Baku in Russia. His father was a German engineer, but his mother was Russian. His paternal – i.e., German – grandfather is said to have been the Adolf – happy coincidence – who was personal secretary to Karl Marx when the First International was founded. True, there is some dispute over that fact, but grandson Richard seems to have persuaded himself that it was true and cherished the notion, right or wrong, as a blood example and family goad throughout his Party life. His personal file – so strangely undiscovered in Himmler's archives until the search was ordered on a different level *after* Sorge's arrest – carried the claim to this proud ideological pedigree.

Richard was taken to Germany by his parents when he was an infant. He served the Kaiser bravely in the First World War, was wounded twice, won the Iron Cross – and then, like so many embittered young Germans, became a founding member of the first Communist Party in revolutionary Hamburg. He studied at Berlin, Kiel and Hamburg universities, and became a Doctor of Political Science. He worked as school teacher and coal miner in the Ruhr and also as a party organizer and subverter. He was, in fact, ordered to leave the Ruhr under threat of arrest by the Allied military government as a communist agitator. Such was his zeal and reputation that, in 1924, he was hand-picked for Party training in Moscow: he went openly to Russia, joined the One True Party in Russia (under Central Committee sponsorship) and became a Comintern agent.

The new Russian Sorge then had three years in the Scandinavian and British mission fields as a Comintern evangelist, using for the first time his cover as a journalist and shyly wearing the title of Doctor. He broke with the Comintern because, reputedly, he refused to accept the organization's dangerous combination of espionage and party operations. He was transferred, by his request, to the celebrated Fourth Bureau of the Red Army General Staff – then, as now, the most effective intelligence agency in the Soviet Union.

It cannot be stressed too strongly that most of this Sorge party record had been filed with Teutonic thoroughness by German security bureaucrats. As soon as official demands were made for the belated file check on Sorge, Himmler produced this dossier with its damning record and testimony for Ribbentrop (October 1942), adding that 'these inquiries have now been made for the first time, but had they been requested and carried out earlier, would have produced the same results'. Himmler remarked self-righteously: 'Since Sorge constantly obtained his information about Axis policy and its future policy from the best German sources, the Sorge case represents great political dangers.'

Why were no inquiries made previously? The Gestapo maintained ceaseless watch over German foreign embassies. Sorge was given a hero's welcome in Japan by the ambassador, General Ott, a heavy, honest, dull German of the old school, who disliked the nazis and detested the Gestapo. Sorge was a favourite of Mrs Ott, who had known him in Munich before her marriage to

Ott, and who, the malicious whispered, had radical leanings herself and had not been immune to Sorge's charm. Most of the German embassy staff, naturally enough, followed the lead of the ambassador and his wife, and were happy to help and indulge the cynical but well-informed, hard-drinking but hard-working foreign correspondent, who had won the Iron Cross in Germany's previous war and who had become unofficial 'adviser' to the embassy command in Germany's new war.

(When Sorge arrived in Shanghai, en route to Tokyo, with his references and letters from leading nazi writers, he became the immediate confidant of Dr H. Voigt, representative of Siemens, and an agent for Nazi intelligence.)

At the outset, some members of the German embassy in Tokyo did not warm to Sorge. The naval attaché in particular distrusted – or disliked – him. But his replacement from Berlin later became one of Sorge's close companions. It is difficult to believe that those officials who resented Sorge as a foreign correspondent operating with special dispensation out of the embassy did not transmit their doubts to Berlin friends, probing the Sorge background. There were many Nazi Party risks among the German community resident in Japan – as elsewhere.

ss Colonel Josef Meisinger, the Gestapo chief, who was later hanged for his atrocities as 'the Beast of Warsaw', and who had actually been director of internal Party Archives, arrived in Japan in 1940 (not 1941, as Deakin and Storry say) to work in liaison with the Japanese *Kempei* and the *Tokko* in maintaining anti-communist surveillance and, in particular, in scrutinizing the operations and loyalties of German officials and residents. He brought with him a run-down of the personal files of all German embassy officials.

Meisinger's personal unpopularity in the German embassy was an open secret in Tokyo. His abominable record in Vienna and Warsaw had preceded him and was in fact largely responsible for his transfer to Tokyo. We correspondents, sitting in the lobby of the old Imperial Hotel and waiting for the liquor to be turned on at 5 pm, had no difficulty in noting the cool welcome which he received when he joined the German embassy table there. The group went through the mountebankery of rising to greet each other solemnly with the nazi salute and reverent 'Heil Hitler!' Meisinger, a grinning, swashbuckling, donkey-faced scoundrel, liked to creep up on the table and, emerging from the shelter of a pillar, to thrust his forefinger, like a revolver, behind the ear of a surprised compatriot. This habit was not relished – either by the victim or his companions.

Meisinger boasted that he trusted no-one: 'Sometimes I have doubts about myself.' Yet Meisinger and Sorge became immediate – however superficial – friends. Had Meisinger not seen Sorge's file? Had someone shown him a fake file? Who and why? Sorge was then officially a Nazi Party member, but his membership card had followed him to Tokyo from Berlin. He was notoriously the 'outsider' with access to the embassy, a 'bohemian' newspaperman, a loner. He would have been amusingly obvious in a James Bond adventure.

Surely the conclusion is irresistible. If Sorge had had a clearance from nazi security in Berlin to work as a secret agent in Japan for *Germany*, this role known only to one or two top contacts there and in Berlin, the riddles of the untold Sorge story are answered. Indeed, if this hypothesis is accepted, it would appear that those top German contacts were rather clumsy or careless in preserving Sorge's cover.

The casting, too, would have been beautifully and precisely correct: no-one would have exulted more in the role of a double agent in these doubly tortuous circumstances than Richard Sorge. His cover was doubled; his deception was doubled; his range for mischief and for insight was doubled; his prestige was doubled; his value to Moscow was doubled; his potential damage to the nazis *and* the Japanese was doubled. An aura of reasonableness and conscious rectitude would purify his excesses. All his natural arrogance and even a calculated measure of indiscretion would be justified – and even desirable. Heady and dangerous encouragement for a gambler: he was, technically, a triple agent; in a three-handed poker game, he had *kibbitzers* looking over one opponent's shoulder, while the other opponent was showing him his true hand in trusting reciprocity for Sorge's marked cards.

Consider, now, this theory in the light of supporting and independent testimony. Walter Schellenberg, chief of nazi security says flatly (in the posthumous *Schellenberg Memoirs*): 'Richard Sorge's intelligence material grew more and more important to us, for in 1941 we were very keen to know more about Japan's plans concerning the US. . . . And at the beginning of our campaign in Russia, he warned us that in no circumstances would Japan denounce her nonaggression pact with the Soviet Union.'

Schellenberg also says categorically that in 1940 the nazi security apparatus, operating inferentially but clearly on a restricted but decisive level, protected Sorge from 'difficult' investigation by 'the Nazi Party', because of the value of Sorge's intelligence material. At this time, Schellenberg admits, Sorge was actually able to use the official German News Agency to transmit intelligence to him personally through the Agency's director, Wilhelm von Ritgen.

Remember, also, that Sorge returned to Moscow for discussions for three weeks in 1935, after having laid the foundations of his Tokyo spy ring. He made certain demands in the light of his experience. He says himself in his statement written inside Sugamo prison: 'I was then given permission to supply a certain amount of information to the German embassy in order to strengthen my connection there. It was left to my own judgment as to what information I should pass on and as to when it should be given.'

There is also a human and revealing anecdote, related by Sorge's sagacious Japanese cross-examiner, Mitsusada Yoshikawa (the Thought Department of Japanese security), of the first and only meeting between Sorge and Ambassador Ott, five days after Sorge's arrest. Yoshikawa obviously knows more than he disclosed. He has recorded the formal permissible exchange of inanities between Sorge, 'who looked completely exhausted,' and Ambassador Ott, 'who was in uniform' (a nice bit of Japanese reportage):

Ott: Well, how are you?
Sorge: I am quite well.
Ott: How about your food?
Sorge: It is sufficient.
Ott: Is there anything you need?
Sorge: No, thank you.

Then Sorge said: 'This is our last meeting.' Whereupon Ott was visibly moved. . . . In soldierly Prussian style, he saluted Sorge, who rose, bowed and reseated himself, placing his face in his hands, as Ott left the room.

I submit that Ott, whatever his protocol responsibilities, would never have saluted a former German soldier if he had then had any suspicion that that compatriot had been a calculating traitor, who had deceived him and (at least) embassy contacts for years, and whose unmasking in such circumstances would spell the ruin of Ott personally and diplomatically. Ott surely had received his undercover orders. Had he not been so deeply and secretly committed, he would by then have realized that Sorge had been fooling him. The fact that he insisted fiercely on the interview, compelling Prime Minister Tojo to override *Tokko* objections, is itself persuasive evidence. Then he donned his uniform for a purely symbolic meeting. What other explanation is there except that Ott saw himself as a German soldier paying tribute to another German soldier who had been trapped – as Ott honestly believed – in dedicated service to their common fatherland.

One is tempted to speculate on whether Comrade Sorge, the gambler who had lost after winning, had any reaction of personal remorse when the trusting Ott saluted him. Probably not: communism castrates all human sentiment, personal emotion and generous instinct. The only good communists are bad communists.

The Japanese Government was embarrassed by the evidence which was discovered amongst Sorge's papers and belongings. There was sufficient embarrassment over the arrest of a German master spy working for the Russians after the Japanese warlords had decided to strike south and maintain expediently their non-aggression pact with the Russians. But if – as many insiders believe – they discovered also that the master spy had been working against them on behalf of the nazis – on which priority? – their alarm must have been unbounded. The Caucasian nazis, after all, were their pledged allies in the West as they drove against the Americans, the British, the Dutch and the French in the East. Yet here, alas, were these inscrutable nazis, apparently, plotting against the honourable *samurai* and maybe preparing to discard those Oriental allies for a deal with their deadly communist enemies – just as those Oriental allies would be prepared in crisis to come to terms with the deadly communists against the Caucasian nazis. How could the anxious and bewildered Japanese trust anyone? As they ran their eyes down the impressive list of sixteen Sorge spies whom they had netted working for the Russians, they could detect not a single Russian among them:

all Germans and Japanese, plus a Yugoslav. The leader had never had ascertainable contact with the Soviet embassy in Tokyo; he was an official of the nazi embassy, a Nazi Party member, and he worked for German newspapers; he did not ask for intervention by the Soviet embassy until he had admitted his guilt and claimed that he had been working against the embassy which employed him, and deceiving the newspapers which featured his objective reports on the Japanese scene. What could an honest and sincere Japanese make of this *gaijin* duplicity?

Yoshikawa-*san* summed up the Japanese dilemma with cautious and even obscure restraint:

We were wondering whether Sorge was really a spy for Germany and using the communists in Japan but actually spying for the nazi régime. That was one question. The second question was whether Sorge was a double agent for both Berlin and Moscow. The third question was whether he was really a spy for Moscow pretending to be a nazi. Therefore we examined Sorge without preconceived opinion.

Three veteran Tokyo newspapermen whom I knew well during and after the Occupation – all dead now – swore privily that Yoshikawa-*san* and the *Tokko* passed on an inner file to the Government which proved conclusively that there had been deluded Gestapo backing, on rigorously restricted levels, for a Sorge who had cynically and adroitly manipulated this backing for the greater advantage of his only interest: the Fourth Bureau of Military Intelligence. This is the only theory that makes any sense to me. It is the untold story of Richard Sorge. It explains the confusion in both the German and Russian camps after Sorge was arrested. Double agents are lonely and distrusted people – even in their basic and original headquarters. They are always dispensable – or expendable. Their primary interest must always lie in the shadow of doubt. Their operations are known only to a clique in their chosen side.

There is no evidence that either Ozaki, Klausen (the wireless operator) or Voukelitch ever considered the possibility that Sorge might have been a double agent.

Sorge's two 'protectors' in the Fourth Bureau were General Berzin and Colonel 'Alex' Borovich. Both were executed during the Stalin purges. After they had been shot, he was on his own. There was no one in Fourth Bureau especially interested in arranging an 'exchange' to save him. There is evidence that some of his invaluable reports were being filed under the heading of 'doubtful misleading information'.

Both Berzin and Borovich were eventually 'rehabilitated', like Sorge, and awarded posthumous honours. Jolly good show.

Let me add some personal anecdotal trimmings to the untold Sorge story.

On the theory that a newspaper reporter should try to keep in touch with the enemy when he is in a neutral country in time of war, I drank often – and amiably enough – with Germans in Tokyo, Kobe, Osaka, Kyoto and Yokohama and at Hakone and Karuizawa in 1940, when the Goering blitz, in Japanese opinion, was softening-up a doomed Britain for invasion.

There were many anti-nazis – perhaps non-nazis would be more correct – among the Germans, especially those who dined at Lohmeyer's, the basement restaurant on a corner behind the Ginza. The nazis drank at Ketel's Rheingold restaurant-bar across the street. The front door was shaped like a giant Bavarian beer barrel and you turned the bung to open. Wilhelm Ketel was a German expatriate who, like so many *gaijin*, had found Japan a congenial haven for life and work. He had a red, corrugated face and white tangled hair and looked like a poor man's Beethoven with a hangover. (When he was questioned later about his association with Sorge, he asked disarmingly, 'What would I know of espionage? I am just a poor pork-butcher.')

On this night he was draped over the bar behind the trestles and forms where the nazi community was drinking *steins* of good Japanese draught beer, with their arms around the waists of the bargirls. There was a piano behind the bar covered with a swastika flag. A ladder in the far corner led to a large trapdoor in the ceiling. Half-a-dozen men were standing at the bar. They included a giant 'Student Prince' type and an eccentric one-armed drunk, who, I discovered later, was regarded as the Rheingold bore even by the nazis because he ceaselessly reminded them that he had lost his arm in obscure circumstances as a submarine officer in the service of the Kaiser. Talking quietly to Ketel was the man who was subsequently pointed out to me as Richard Sorge.

'I am an Australian,' I remarked fatuously. 'Is there anyone here who will drink with the enemy?'

Ketel summed me up, shrugged, pushed an already filled *stein* towards me. 'On the house,' he said. 'Prosit.' There was idle talk as we took one another's measure. They all spoke English. (The point should be made here that British and German embassies had warned their nationals that there was to be no brawling in front of the Japanese, that neutrality was to be preserved at all costs. The instruction generally was respected.)

Emboldened by Lohmeyer's Harbin vodka, I asked: 'How do you feel now that you are losing the war?' Not surprisingly, there was an explosive – if gibbering – response. One-arm literally jumped up and down. Ketel glared. The Student Prince aimed a punch at me. Sorge grabbed him, snarled at him in German, said to me reasonably: 'Be polite, please, if you drink with us.' 'Fair enough,' I replied. 'But I am not impolite. Germans in Lohmeyer's just told me Britain had lost the war. I return the compliment. Wait until the Russians are fighting with us. Hitler cannot win on both Fronts.'

It is curious, in retrospect, to recall that that was the first remark I ever made to Sorge – 'little knowing', as old reporters used to write in police leads. I do not recall any reply, but I would still like to know what he thought. One-arm, bouncing and gabbling, was restrained. Communication became non-political. I bought a round. Sorge withdrew to the fringe of the group. He spoke quietly but firmly to the Student Prince – a cheap drunk – and escorted him to the urinal where his grateful relief was audible to us all.

When I left, the Student Prince offered to accompany me. We strolled back under the moonlit elevated railway to the black peacock silhouette of the Imperial. He was in a serenade mood. I had become sobered in the dull aftermath of vodka and beer. Suddenly he pointed to the moon. 'Bomber's moon!' he cried. 'Bombs on London!' He turned to me, beginning to weep, and to my rage seized me by the lapels. 'Richard, I have a girl in London,' he sobbed. 'She is beautiful. True nordic. I met her in Bavaria just before the war. We are affianced. I have not heard from her. But she is in London tonight – do you hear me? – Under this moon and under the bombs.'

He was sodden with self-pity as I pushed him away, smoothing my lapels and detesting him. His mood changed. Now the Student Prince rampant, he drew himself up: 'But I still say –

"Bombs on London"!' Then, as God is my witness, he cried, 'Heil Hitler!' before he lumbered off, shaking his square head, pleading, expostulating, explaining in incoherent German some mystical message to someone who was not there.

I saw him by chance next morning, walking on the Ginza with Sorge. I waved and cried hello. The Student Prince's eye flickered recognition. Then he looked deliberately away and strode on with blank face and raised chin. Sorge gave me a curt nod and a queer smile. Later old press hands told me the Student Prince was a Gestapo officer who was being recalled; Sorge, the gossip ran, thought him 'unreliable'.

I saw Sorge several times later, after having learned who he was. He attended some of the weekly press briefings by the Gaimusho (Foreign Ministry) spokesman, fat oily Suma-*san*, with the pop eyes and squint. He occasionally joined groups of foreign pressmen in the Imperial lobby. Once or twice I saw him from a distance at the Fujiya Hotel in scenic Hakone – usually with a pretty girl. He sometimes dropped in at the white marble bar and British-club-like library in the old Tokyo Club.

He never asked questions at the press briefings in the Gaimusho: of course he had no need to ask any. He listened, abstracted or bored, and usually lingered behind to chat with the respectful Suma-*san* in private. He had a natural instinct for 'face'. In retrospect, he must have been vastly amused, behind his indifferent mask, at the excitement of the international press corps when, assembled by urgent phone calls, we heard officially of the signing of the Tripartite Pact between Germany, Italy and Japan on the warm evening of 27 September 1940. For months, as the honest patriotic German newsman and Nazi Party man, he had sat in, by invitation, as adviser with the Germans as they discussed Ribbentrop's plan to try at least to keep Japan's honourable foot inside the nazi door. His close association with the preliminary planning of the Pact, followed each night by secret progressive radio reports to Moscow, smacks of a Peter Sellers' farce.

Sorge was satisfied by then that Japan would not attack Siberia. With the signing of the Pact, he had the assurance of closer and more confidential and trustful talks between Germany and Japan in Tokyo, and therefore the prospect of more rewarding information for Moscow. Ott, in fact, wanted Sorge to attend the signing of the Pact, in gratitude for Sorge's advice, but Dr Heinrich Stahmer, the high-browed, bespectacled envoy from Ribbentrop (who replaced the disgraced Ott after the Sorge scandal broke), objected – not because of suspicion but because he didn't want too many witnesses. So Sorge went placidly along to the Gaimusho that night.

I had direct conversation alone with Sorge one night before I went on to Shanghai. We happened by chance to be leaving together from a press table in the Imperial. I made some fatuous remark, regretting the fact that our countries were at war. 'We Germans are really human, you must remember,' he replied with a straight face. 'We like music. We like wine. And we have a great love for flowers,' he added; leaving me briskly for his waiting Hanako-*san*, beautiful (I still remember) in a purple kimono, and bowing deeply to him as he advanced on her with the open arms of an uninhibited, non-party Cossack.

Some other loose ends of the Sorge story should be tied up. The authorities agree on the circumstances of his arrest and the break-up of the ring, but many people have been misled by the grotesque love-trap fabrication.

It was a Judas, not a Delilah, job. And it was a Judas job by proxy. Sorge probably never knew the vicious Japanese Communist Party member, Ritsu Ito, a one-time informer, who struck at the most useless member of the outer ring, a wretched little sewing-mistress and – of all things – Seventh Day Adventist and member of the Women's Christian Temperance Union, Mrs Tomo Kitabayashi. It is improbable that Sorge ever heard of her. Mrs Kitabayashi was enrolled, for reasons that can be only incredulously guessed at, by one of the Japanese members of the Sorge inner group, Okinawa-born artist Miyagi, who was tortured and died bravely before he was sentenced.

Miyagi knew Mrs Kitabayashi, who had improbably become a Communist Party member in the 'Little Tokyo' of Los Angeles in the thirties. Miyagi was recruited in Los Angeles for the Sorge apparatus and, when he later ran across Mrs K, with her sewing pupils and her Seventh Day Adventist nutfoods in bucolic Wakayama prefecture, decided to recruit her for the outer ring. The mind boggles over the nature of the 'secret information' which the wctu vegetarian was able to feed back bravely into

Sorge's secret headquarters. Why on earth did Miyagi pick her up? No Mata Hari she, poor woman. She was said to have pined for the lost delights of *gaijin* life in Los Angeles after her return to Japan with a curious husband, who seems to have known nothing of her absurd secret life.

Comrade Ito found her somehow and, in his expedient role as informer on parole, fingered her to the *Kempei-tai* as a Party member and spy. The cops kept her under surveillance, noted her visitors, picked up Miyagi and so followed, laboriously, toughly and inscrutably, the trail that led to Ozaki and Sorge. It should not be forgotten that, when Sorge learned later, in frustration and incredulity, of the events that led to his unmasking, he never criticized either Miyagi or the unhappy Mrs Kitabayashi. Nor should it be forgotten that the Russians in Tokyo, who – reflecting Stalin's cynical rejection of Sorge – did not respond to Sorge's direct approach at the time, took no punitive action whatever, then or later, either directly or indirectly, through the then submissive Japanese Communist Party against the probationary police pimp, but still Party member, Ito.

For the hard record, Miyagi was arrested in his Tokyo home on 11 October 1941; under ruthless interrogation, he tried to kill himself by throwing himself from a second storey window and broke his leg. His 'voluntary statement' came next day. (See later story on the death of Reuter's Jimmy Cox.)

Ozaki was arrested in his home on 15 October. He wrote in prison: 'A squad of procurators descended upon us. I had had an uneasy premonition for several days, and on that morning I knew that the final hour of reckoning had come. Making certain that Yoko had left for school, for I was anxious that my daughter should not be present, I left the house without looking at my wife and without any farewell speech. I felt that, with my arrest, everything had ended. . . . When I was interrogated that afternoon, it was – as I had expected – on the subject of my relationship with Sorge; I realized that the whole network was being exposed, and I said to myself that everything had ended.'

Sorge conferred uneasily in his Azabu home with Branko de Voukelitch, the Yugoslav, and Max Klausen, the German radio operator, on 17 October. They did not know of Ozaki's arrest. But he had not kept two appointments and a phone call to his office in the South Manchurian Railway building (opposite the us embassy) had been unanswered. Miyagi had also missed an appointment.

'Sorge, in bed, was drinking with Voukelitch when I arrived (7 pm)' Klausen wrote later. 'I joined the circle, opening the bottle of saké which I had brought. The atmosphere was heavy and Sorge said gravely – as if our fate were sealed – "Neither Joe (Miyagi) nor Otto (Ozaki) showed up to meet us. They must have been arrested." '

Sorge was arrested at 6 am on Saturday 18 October, and taken, in pyjamas, slippers and overcoat, angrily objecting, to the Toriizaka police station, within sight of his Azabu home. His servant, who did not live in, had not arrived. There was one female eyewitness of his arrest, but it was his caged pet owl – not, alas, the deceitful but noble, seduced but patriotic Ginza striptease dancer of legend.

The *Tokko* efficiently listed the material which they removed from Sorge's home. It included three cameras, us $1,782, a list of Nazi Party members in Japan, the German Statistical Year Book (the code source for incoming and outgoing messages) and the draft, in English, of his uncabled message to Moscow, proclaiming final success and urging immediate recall.

The original of this tragic message, partly in code in preparation for transmission, was found damningly in Klausen's home, when he, like Voukelitch, was also arrested in the dawn hours of the 18th.

But well-informed pressmen whom I knew closely in Tokyo in Occupation days agreed, in the well-lubricated intimacy, gossip and tradesmen's esperanto of newspaper reporters the world over, that a top-secret Sorge diary, recording partly in a Pepysian code his personal association with members of the German embassy, was also discovered but vanished mysteriously in the archives of the embarrassed Ministry of Justice, which wanted no awkward discussions with their nazi allies about indications of German espionage in Japan.

Appropriately enough, Prince Konoye, who had unwittingly passed on most of his successive governments' secrets to Ozaki and so to Sorge, had resigned two days before Sorge's arrest and the day after Ozaki's arrest. (Konoye, who was succeeded by Tojo, took poison after surrender to avoid arrest and trial as a major war criminal.)

There is not the slightest foundation for either of the two stories of Sorge's alleged outbursts on the gallows. He is supposed, by one account, to have cried out, just before the trap was sprung in the efficient death-house behind the Buddhist chapel: 'Long live the Union of the Socialist Soviet Republics!'; by another account, to have shouted, 'To hell with mankind!' Both reports are false. Either outburst would have been out of character. And, in any event, I tracked down the hangman, with the aid of an old Tokyo friend. The executioner, a bland elderly Japanese, then living in Oizumi-gakuen-cho (outside Tokyo), insisted that both Ozaki and Sorge died 'gently and sincerely'.

Sorge was hanged at 10.20 am on 7 November 1944, less than an hour after his Japanese right hand – 'my first and most important associate' – had been hanged. They both behaved with the dignity that would have been expected from their unfailingly correct behaviour under arrest and interrogation. They did not meet. Each thanked the prison chaplain and officials for 'all your kindnesses'. Ozaki knelt before the image of Buddha – with what communist beliefs still nurturing him, one wonders – burned incense and listened while the chaplain declared: 'Life and death are one and the same thing to one who has attained impersonal beatitude, which can be attained by entrusting everything to the image of Buddha,' and then recited the Three Promises of the Great Sutra of Constant Life. (What would Stalin and the Fourth Bureau have said?)

Sorge, the hangman reported, glanced impassively at the golden Buddhist altar as he passed directly to the gallows. He bowed his head silently and accommodatingly as the noose was fixed.

According to Professor Storry, who relates his interviews with Yoshikawa and Sorge's Hanako-*san*, Sorge's skeleton was salvaged only because of his girl's devotion. He had been buried among the vagrants' graves at the horrible Zoshigaya cemetery and someone had stolen the small name-sign on his grave for firewood. For two years Hanako-*san* persevered in her campaign to recover the remains, which are now buried in Tama graveyard next to the coffins containing the remains of Hotsumi Ozaki and Yutoku Miyagi. I guess the three of them would have approved that final arrangement and might have wished the bones of Voukelitch to have been in their company also.

Hanako-*san* was abused, spat upon and slapped around by the

unspeakable *Kempei-tai* after Sorge's arrest, but was invited by
the Russians in 1965 to holiday on the Black Sea Riviera, where
she saw a Russian play, *Press Attaché in Tokyo*, describing Sorge's
career in Japan. In the same year, Anastas Mikoyan, then President
of the Soviet Union, received and awarded Yoshiko, widow of
Voukelitch, a posthumous honour on behalf of her husband:
'Order of the Patriotic War, First Class'. One can only surmise
that Hanako-*san* didn't get an award because, after all, she wasn't
married to Sorge.

For reasons completely unconnected with espionage, I cannot
resist quoting the nine precepts which Ozaki – a far better
journalist than Sorge was, or thought he was – laid down as a
guide for intelligence agents:

1. Never give the impression that you are eager to obtain news:
men who are engaged in important affairs will refuse to talk to you if
they suspect that your motive is to collect information.
2. If you give the impression that you have more information than
your prospective informant, he will give with a smile.
3. Informal dinner parties are an excellent setting for the gathering
of news.
4. It is convenient to be a specialist of some kind. For my part, I am
a specialist on Chinese questions, and have always received inquiries
from all quarters. I was able to gather much data from men who came
to ask me questions.
5. My position as a writer for newspapers and magazines stood me in
good stead.
6. Because I was often asked to lecture in all parts of Japan, I had an
excellent chance to learn general trends of local opinion.
7. Connections with important organizations engaged in the collection of news are vital. I was affiliated with the *Asahi Shimbun* and later
with the South Manchurian Railway.
8. Above all, you must cultivate trust and confidence in you on the
part of those who you are using as informants in order to be able to
pump them without seeming unnatural.
9. In these days of unrest, you cannot be a good intelligence man
unless you yourself are a good source of information.

The reason I list the Ozaki precepts, with a respectful salute to
one communist at least who was an idealist as well as a realist, is
because they constitute a perfect guide to all young foreign
correspondents. Every successful foreign newsman I ever knew

followed and follows, consciously or instinctively, those same rules – especially Precepts 1, 2 and 9.

Sorge was no lady's man in the field of espionage. 'Women are absolutely unfit for espionage work,' he wrote in his arrogant post-arrest memoirs while confidently awaiting the Soviet spy-exchange which never came. 'They have no understanding of political and other affairs and I have never received satisfactory information from them. Since they were useless to me, I did not employ them in my group [Mrs Tomo Kitabayashi?]. . . . Even upper-class women have no comprehension of what has been said by their husbands and are, therefore, very poor sources of in-information [Madam Ott?]. . . . This does not apply only to Japanese women; in my opinion, no woman in the world has the aptitude for espionage work.'

He added chastely: 'I might add that cultivation of intimate relations with married women for purposes of espionage will arouse the jealousy of their husbands and hence react to the detriment of the cause.' (It would be instructive to have the class-conscious reaction to this sentiment of 'Old Faithful', Kim Philby, his latest wife and *her* husband, cuckolded Comrade Maclean, in permissive Moscow today.)

But Sorge was hardly grateful here. It was, after all, a staunch woman US party spy, Comrade Agnes Smedley, who selected and introduced to him in Shanghai, Hotsumi Ozaki. It was, also, a Baltic woman, the mysterious and beautiful Olga, who recruited Branko de Voukelitch, his other key assistant. They met and arranged future meetings in a Shanghai bookshop run by another Communist Party woman, an Irene Wiedemeyer, who had been married to a Chinese communist, Wu Sho-ku.

Sorge's Shanghai introduction to Tokyo has a poignant historic interest today. Sorge was just getting his Tokyo show on the road when the tough British police broke the Shanghai apparatus which ran the Far Eastern Comintern spy network in China and was the link between Moscow and the Chinese Communist Party. The chief operator was a Polish comrade, known as Hilaire Noulens, who had a dozen cover names and thoughtfully carried one Canadian and two Belgian passports. He had conferred with Sorge, who got out before the police picked up Noulens. The Japanese police in Shanghai did pick up a contact linking the Noulens ring and Ozaki, but they let him go. It was a narrow squeak for Sorge. The Russians – kinder to Noulens then than they were to Sorge a decade later – made an exchange to save Noulens from execution in Nanking.

No one knows what happened to Noulens after that, although it is presumed that, having escaped the Chinese Nationalists, he was liquidated by Stalin during the purges. Here is today's historic tie-up. Noulens' counterpart in his network's Hongkong branch was an Indo-Chinese, who was duly identified in party records seized at Noulens' headquarters in Nanking Road, Shanghai. This agent was held by the British in the colony, but for some stiff-upper-lipped British reason was never handed over to the French *Sûreté* in Saigon. He was known then as Nguyen Ai Quac. When he surfaced once more – mysteriously freed – his name was Ho Chi Minh.

Finally, we should spare an inch or two of space – with a sigh, or an oath – for one of the forgotten 'honourable' – if marginal – Japanese members of the Sorge machine. He is Kinkazu Saionji, disgraced aristocratic grandson-by-adoption of illustrious Prince Saionji, Japan's famous *genro* (elder statesman) of the early 1900s, who tried, in ageing retirement, to curb the Pearl Harbour warlords and to stiffen the Emperor's backbone.

Kinkazu Saionji, an Oxford graduate, acted as informant for Ozaki in betrayal of Prince Konoye, who trusted him as a *samurai*. He was arrested, tried and found guilty of espionage, but escaped with a 'suspended' sentence because of his shamed family connections. He went as a representative of the confused Japanese Communist Party to live in Peking in 1957 (when he was 50) and was there encouraged by the Chinese comrades to posture as 'unofficial Japanese ambassador,' living in Party luxury like a 'kept' eunuch in the former Italian embassy. He returned to Tokyo in 1970, can travel to and from Peking, and remains brazenly active as an open running-dog for the Chinese communists instead of a traitorous spy for the Russian communists. At the outset, he tried to strengthen the ties between the Japanese comrades and the Chinese comrades, while retaining his loyal affiliations with the Russian comrades. As the party winds of the ensuing decade blew hot and cold from Moscow and Peking around the anxious ankles of the Japanese comrades, Saionji in

Peking elected, not surprisingly, to go along with Peking's east wind. The ungenerous argue, not implausibly, that had he been in Moscow, he might have shown a preference for the bracing Russian wind.

Kinkazu has since been expelled from the Japanese Communist Party: 'For having submitted blindly to the guidance and control of a special foreign country and for having criticized the neutral foreign policy of the Japanese Party.' But surely he scores maximum marks for pragmatism: a volunteer traitor, first, on the Russian side against Japan; second, on the Japanese side for China; then on the Japanese and Chinese side against Russia; now on the Chinese side against Japan again. It is a beautiful communist circle. But he will certainly need to be very useful to the realistic Chinese to retain his present stance – if that word can be misused.

A jesting *Gaimusho* jingle about Kinkazu Saionji may be loosely translated:

> When you troll like Kinkazu,
> You twist before you think you do.

INSCRUTABLE POSTSCRIPT

Shortly after my 1940 arrival in Tokyo, I received an unknown visitor at the Imperial Hotel. My name and photograph had appeared in the Tokyo English-language press as a visiting Australian newspaper reporter – unique. It was known that a first Australian Minister, Sir John Latham, was arriving at the beginning of 1941.

My visitor was a Japanese lady, smart, handsome, statuesque; Western clothes, good English, no blandishments (alas), no sidelong glances – forty, I should guess, to my thirty-four (but the ripe fruit is ever the sweeter). She wouldn't drink, but sipped some tea with a formidable air on the quiet, semi-private verandah which overlooked the right-hand side-garden of the Imperial lobby. She told me she had been born in Tokyo but had been living for some time in Los Angeles, working as a seamstress and also as a private secretary. She wondered if I could recommend her for a secretarial post with the new Australian ambassador, whose impending arrival had delighted all peace-loving Japanese. She had references: she crackled a tremendous sheaf of red-ribboned documents at me.

I told her that I was not sure that I would be in Japan when Sir John arrived and that, in any event, I had no influence whatever. Would I be kind enough however, she pressed, to present her card to the Australian Trade Commissioner who was holding the fort until Sir John made Canberra's leisurely appearance? Of course, I said.

I passed the card on to 'Bunny' Hard (standing in for Sir Keith Officer, who was then in Canberra explaining to Sir John that Shanghai was not in Japan and that the Emperor did not sleep at the Grand Shrine of Ise). 'Bunny' shrugged and said that staff appointments were outside his jurisdiction also. He clearly suspected that I had placed an immoral price on my patronage.

Now, it happens that in those youthful, clear-eyed days I kept a diary of sorts. I scribbled down that lady's name and address. I know she never got the job. 'Bunny' Hard, alas, is dead, and I was never able to ask him if he submitted the card. The incident interested me only when I read the first list of arrested members of the Sorge spy ring. My strange visitor hadn't looked a scrap like the famous nonentity whose name and address had been on that card which I passed on. There was not the faintest resemblance between my visitor's formidable features and the homely, terrified full-face study of the original weak link in the Sorge chain. But the name and address of that obscure but vital victim were identical with the identification on the card of my strange visitor (in English and Japanese script on the reverse): Mrs Tomo Kitabayashi – Kokawa, Wakayama Prefecture.

So what do you make of that? I wonder how many members of the Sorge ring escaped.

CHAPTER 4

The Death of Reuter's Jimmy Cox

The mysterious death of Melville James Cox, who either jumped or was thrown to his death under interrogation by the Japanese *Kempei-tai*, is virtually forgotten today. It happened in 1940, after all, and although it was world headline news, only newspapermen, diplomats and foreigners who were in Japan at the time now recall the shock, the international reaction, and the continuing doubts over the cause of his violent death. Those who remember, however, can still become heated in argument when the mystery is raised in reminiscent discussion.

I believe that the mystery has been resolved. A responsible and unprejudiced eyewitness quietly testified to the Japanese Ministry of Justice in early 1960 (when he was dying of tuberculosis) that he saw Cox jump from the ledge outside an open third-storey window of the *Kempei-tai* headquarters. The witness was Yaroku Shimazu, a highly respected former reporter for the *Asahi Shimbun*, whom I knew during the Occupation, and who knew Cox personally and was covering *Kempei-tai* activities for his newspaper at that time.

He happened to enter the inner courtyard of the building from the front street just after lunch. 'There was a shout,' Shimazu said, 'and I looked up to see Cox climb out on the ledge. He looked calmly around him, raised his hands to his face, and deliberately jumped. He turned over as he fell but still shielded his face. He crashed to the asphalt courtyard only about fifty yards from where I was standing.'

Shimazu told me, with a shrug, that he did not report his evidence at the time because the violent death seriously embarrassed the *Kempei-tai*, and he had no particular reason or wish to help them by involving himself in the inquiry and acquitting them of suspected responsibility. On the contrary, like most Japanese civilians, he detested the *Kempei-tai*, in their uniform with red armband and two holstered revolvers.

It was a measure of the lack of general interest in the old mystery that, so far as I know, no Japanese newspaper published the Shimazu story. I was in Tokyo at the time and wrote the story, which my papers ran in abridged form in Australia and England, but there was no follow-up, and I am still surprised to discover how few people – even newspapermen – know the facts. The story should be known, I believe, because it helps to recapture the tense, explosive atmosphere of Japan in 1940; and because it is a tribute to a brave Englishman and a good newspaperman, who should not have a question mark over his grave.

Cox, forty, married, guardian of two adopted Japanese orphans, experienced and popular foreign correspondent, had been arrested – together with thirteen other Britishers in different parts of Japan – on 27 July on charges of espionage which have never been specified. He was not seen alive by any foreigner after he was taken to the *Kempei-tai* headquarters, a brownstone building whose windows surveyed – and still survey, because the building survived the bombings – the placid green moat and granite walls of the Imperial Palace. (This was the same building in which the survivors of the Doolittle raid were imprisoned, to be taken through a tunnel under the road to a military barracks on the opposite side of the road and then to their execution.)

The last friend to see him was a newspaper colleague, who met him leaving his apartment under arrest. A stolid, stockily-built man with thick, black-rimmed spectacles, he was pale and worried-looking, but he walked briskly between his two escorts, buttoning his coat, and gave his startled friend a forced smile and a jest about 'the Lord High Executioner' as he passed to the waiting car. His wife was politely assured by the gendarmes on the night of his arrest that he was confined in comfortable quarters but was permitted no callers. If she wished to leave the suitcase containing a change of clothing, tobacco, cigarettes and fruit, they would certainly see that it was delivered to him. Actually, Cox had been imprisoned in a small, mosquito-ridden, stone cell in the basement in which he could not stand erect and with only a plank bed to sleep on. When his widow called again to collect his belongings two days later, she saw the untouched suitcase standing behind the door of the office in which she had left it that night.

The gendarmes alleged that Cox leapt to his death through an open window while he was being interrogated. No violence –

they hissed and bowed – had at any time been used. They said that he was unconscious when picked up and that all desperate attempts to save him by certain injections failed. To these injections, of which Japanese doctors are still inordinately fond, they attributed the marks of a hypodermic needle found on his chest and leg. They produced an unsigned letter to his wife which they said they found in his pocket. They insisted that they had irrefutable evidence of his espionage guilt.

In the rambling, bamboo-and-paper Foreign Office, the spokesman, Mr Yakichiro Suma (later wartime ambassador to Spain, later purged, later peace-loving conservative member of the Upper House in the Diet), read aloud the following statement to representatives of the world press, all of them colleagues of the dead man:

According to a joint announcement by the Ministries of War and Justice, Melville James Cox, Reuter correspondent in Tokyo, one of those arrested on a charge of espionage, threw himself from a third-storey room of the Tokyo military police headquarters on July 29 at 2.05 pm in an attempt to commit suicide, although the guards tried to stop him. He died at 3.46 pm.

A note addressed to his wife was discovered on his person which read as follows:

See Reuter re rents.
See Cowley re deeds and insurance.
See Hgk Bank re balance and shares in London.
I know what is best
Always my only love
I have been quite well treated
but there is no doubt how matters are going.

[Note: This is the exact form in which the statement was typed in the official handout.]

In the light of the above note, it seems that, with the progress of the investigation, the deceased became aware of the fact that he could not escape conviction for his crime.

Despite this evidence and finding – maybe chiefly because of the evidence and finding – foreigners in Tokyo widely accepted the alternative theory that the gendarmes had so grievously maltreated Cox with drugs and baseball bats (which they specially favoured for inducing 'voluntary' statements) that the only way to disguise his broken condition was to fling him out of the window. Some of these, I daresay, would still reject Shimazu's belated testimony.

I arrived in Japan the week after Cox's death, which we had heard news of on the ship's radio at sea. I met and talked with most of his friends. Few doubted that he had been brutally killed. Maybe it was because I was a newcomer, and had not yet been affected by the heavy, brooding, insidious apprehension which oppressed most anti-Axis foreigners, that I leaned to the minority opinion that Cox must have jumped to his death.

Cox had been dispirited and melancholy for several months before his arrest. His friends were concerned about him. He had a gloomy tiffin daily at the American Club but otherwise saw few friends and had disengaged his wife and himself from bridge and other social engagements. He asked awkward and needling questions at the Foreign Office press briefings. He made no attempt to disguise a growing animosity towards all Japanese. He was worried about the prospect of Britain's defeat under *Luftwaffe* blitz.

Further, the last thing the gendarmes wanted was to have one of their prisoners die on their hands. They were in no hurry to extort a 'confession' or to illtreat senselessly and blindly. They liked to question and re-question – remorselessly, repetitively, maddeningly – hour after hour, day after day. Nor, my candid Japanese newspaper friends assured me, would the gendarmes use physical violence in such a short time as two days – far less fatal physical violence. If they did use violence, they had had sufficient experience to know when to stop for a breather and when to resume questions.

There was, it must be admitted, factual dispute about the letter allegedly found in Cox's pocket. Mrs Cox first identified the writing as her husband's. Later, private reports said that she denied this. It was pointed out that the letter was not signed. But death, torture or urgency aside, any husband will scribble a brief note to his wife and, for the very reason that it is for his wife, will not think it necessary to sign it. Nor does the note read like a Japanese forgery – except perhaps for the 'I have been quite well treated', and even this sounds too restrained for a Japanese military cop, who would surely have tried to lay it on more thickly and who would almost certainly have forged an initial.

In the outcome, the *Kempei-tai* gained nothing but lost a lot when Cox died. They wanted a badgered confession and if possible statements implicating others – especially from a press-man with important 'inside' contacts. They certainly did not want, within three days, a dead prisoner – silent and useless. Nor did the Japanese Government, acutely embarrassed after its loud proclamations of a broken spy ring. Following the international reaction, a board of inquiry was set up to exonerate the *Kempei-tai*. Foreign Minister Matsuoka, mercurial and unstable even when things were going well, became jittery. The gendarmes were pro-fusely on the defensive. Some of the other suspects were quietly released. So far as I know, none was ever tried.

But Jimmy Cox, a working correspondent in Japan in 1940, with his news files and notes, no matter how harmless, had no hope. Under the all-powerful *Kempei-tai*, Japan's emergency espionage 'laws' could be stretched to frame any pressman as an enemy and a spy. No court had authority over the *Kempei-tai*. A Japanese reporter pointed out to me seriously that, by buying a tourist handbook on Japan's feudal castles, I could be technically accused of espionage; the book had been formally proscribed by the Imperial Army, because it contained 'classified military secrets', but by some oversight it was still on display and sale at the Imperial Hotel bookstore.

Jimmy Cox, then, was a brave man when he jumped to his death. He knew that he had been chosen as press scapegoat in the espionage arrests. Under 'persuasion' over a long period, he might easily have incriminated others as innocent as himself. His persecutors wanted only the names of 'contacts', with forced and fabricated undertones. With the disinterested eye-witness testi-mony of Yaroku Shimazu, the Japanese Ministry of Justice, significantly restrained, quietly closed its files on the Cox case, with a firm verdict of suicide.

Legally, that is. But, morally, Jimmy Cox, taking his brave leap, was as surely murdered by the *Kempei-tai* as if they had flung him out of the window.

Mrs Cox left Japan with her husband's ashes. The two adopted Japanese orphans were taken away from her. No one has ever been able to trace them.

CHAPTER 5

The Escape of Reuter's Leslie Smith

There is a forgotten newspaperman's story about Jimmy Cox's luckier Reuter counterpart, Leslie Smith, in Tsingtao, northern China. It is a contemporary, but happier, footnote to the Cox tragedy.

Leslie heard Chamberlain's declaration of war against Hitler over the radio in the Reuter office in Shanghai. All the staff were on the scene, including those off-duty, like Leslie, who was officially on leave after two years' coverage of the Sino-Japanese war.

The international setup was of course even trickier and less 'neutral' in China than in Tokyo. Kenneth Selby Walker, Reuter's able and courageous Far Eastern manager, who vanished later in a Japanese prison camp in Java, was confronted at once with unhappy racial problems in the branch office in Tsingtao, a port-city and former German concession already under dictatorial Japanese control.

Walker told Leslie regretfully that he would now have to dismiss poor Gerti Boerter, then in charge of the Tsingtao bureau. 'She is a nice girl, you know,' said Walker, 'and we all like her and she does a good job. But, God help us, she is now technically an enemy alien. You must go up there tomorrow and take over the office until I can find an alleged neutral to relieve you. Play it safe, Leslie.'

Smith recalls the precariously balanced international press-reporting 'neutralism' in 1939-40 Tsingtao. The local English-language daily printed war news with the strictest impartiality from Britain, Germany and Japan. Each country's news agency was accorded precisely the same lineage on the front page, with identical display in parallel columns: the German Deutsch Nachrichten Buro (DNB), Japan's Domei and Reuter's. The editor, a middle-aged Briton with years of experience in Asia, continued to publish with masterly discretion, parrying week after week the sullen suspicious raids and queries by the Japanese naval security bosses.

'We had a staff of three radio operators – a stateless Russian and two Chinese assistants,' Leslie Smith says. 'They monitored Reuter by radio day and night, and we distributed the service to newspapers, banks and business-houses. The foreign community got on together well enough, united expediently in common defence against the Japanese overlords.'

Little did Leslie Smith know (as the old police-round reporters once ruminated), but he was innocently perched on a more exposed cliff-edge than was Jimmy Cox, on whom the Tokyo *kempei-tai* were then closing.

'The Japanese security headquarters ordered me one morning to present myself for interrogation,' Leslie recounts. 'The security chief was a naval officer, polite but formidable. He wanted to know all about our Reuter radio equipment. Did we have a radio transmitter? The Japanese knew that secret intelligence was reaching Chinese guerrillas.

'Of course not, I assured him. I was not a fool, I flattered myself. Even if Walker had not warned me, I had been around long enough in China to have sufficient sense to avoid security transgressions. I had already personally inspected our offices, accompanied by the Russian operator. We were taking no risks.

'I invited the security officer to visit and search our premises, without warning, day or night. We had only normal and approved receiving equipment.'

Twice again Leslie Smith was summoned to security head-quarters for increasingly suspicious interrogation. The intelligence leaks were continuing. Twice again Leslie ridiculed the sugges-tion: 'Come and see for yourselves. What madness it would be to operate a secret transmitter from Reuter's office, under' – a polite bow – 'such close, efficient and understandable surveillance.'

The Smith line was convincing. The Japanese never searched the office.

Then Smith the Englishman was replaced by a more 'neutral' chief, a Dane. Leslie took a Japanese ship back to Shanghai for reassignment. The day he returned to the central office in the International Settlement, he was handed a cable from Tsingtao, reporting a Japanese security raid on Reuter's office, just after his departure, and the discovery of a secret transmitter, well-hidden in a drawer in the radio-room. One of the Chinese operators was a Nationalist agent, who had been regularly using the set to communicate with guerrillas in the nearby hills.

The Danish manager, just arrived, escaped arrest for complicity.'

The *kempei-tai* dragged off the operator. He was never heard of again.

Leslie Smith, of course, would have had no hope.

CHAPTER 6

Sex Shop Sayonara

A dark quarter of a century has dustily unrolled, but I still nurture fresh and tender memories of the Honourable Sex Shop in pre-war Kobe, rightly esteemed by lonely mariners plying the China seas in the twenties and thirties. It was doomed, alas, to destruction by US fire bombings in 1944. In distant ports, I do not doubt, gnarled sea captains heard the tidings of its violent passing with bowed heads and a sentimental pang. It was like the news of the murder of an old friend, tried and trusted, however furtive.

My own affectionate and grateful tribute to the old cultural establishment harks back to December 1940, when I was departing rather hastily after an initial mission of gloomy reportage for Australian newspapers. In my alarm and despondency, I believed that the war would come in two rather than twelve months. The Honourable Sex Shop then rescued me from an embarrassing and even disastrous *sayonara*. And, what is more important, it demonstrated in the hectic war mood of those unhappy days that one touch of sex makes the whole world kin – East and West alike, suspicious security cops and even military gendarmes included. Further, at a time when Australians feared Japan, the Hon Sex Shop indirectly helped to warm the hearts of Sydney newspapermen towards Japanese newspapermen by fostering a fellow-tradesman's respect that was none the less real because it was completely illusory.

Kobe's Sex Shop was a modest, two-storied, clapboard structure in simple neo-Yedo style, which crouched with a discreet leer on a side street corner within kite-flying distance of Sannomiya station. The bright dome of the old Tor Hotel – also marked down for aerial destruction – loomed like a miniature Albert Hall above and behind the Shop's proud Rising Sun flag. The Shop was flanked by a barber's saloon and a *sushi* bar. The single uncompromising English word 'SEX' glared like a beacon in sunken white lettering on a scarlet board above the front swingdoors, where the three banners of nazi Germany, Mussolini Italy and Japan drooped dutifully from an entwined triangle of bamboo poles, which at street level constituted a popular and appropriate rendezvous for local dogs.

The Kobe Honourable Sex Shop sustained its commercial success largely by goodwill and word-of-mouth advertising. But it also published a catalogue – today, a rare collector's item – which was distributed widely and freely at Oriental seaports from Shanghai to Singapore, and which, despite picturesque infirmities and deficiencies in pidgin English, was sufficiently explicit to attract a regular and rewarding clientèle. From the street, the Shop's windows gave little clue to the specialized merchandise on sale within. There were dusty bottles of liniment and pills, anonymous tins and tubes and strange cardboard devices with Japanese caligraphy in one window, and non-committal posters vaguely evocative of a horse-doctor's clinic in the other.

A Rabelaisian Dutch shipping representative, long resident in Kobe and distinguished for his non-celibate mode of life, acted as my guide and interpreter on my *sayonara* visit to the Shop. (He subsequently died in a Kobe internment camp, despite the loving ministrations of his two faithful Japanese mistresses, who regularly brought him all the delicacies from their own rationed food.) In sentimental vein, I had explained to him that I proposed taking back on the good ship *Tokyo Maru* that night a handful or two of amusing kickshaws and trinkets from the Honourable Sex Shop as souvenirs to untravelled Australian friends. I thought it would be a harmless deception, which might serve to promote goodwill, were I to present one or two novel contrivances to the Australian Journalists' Association as alleged gifts from the Japanese Journalists' Union.

My friend, warmly agreeing, led me inside. In dramatic contrast to the reticent front-window display, large glass showcases in the cool saloon were crammed, like Fifth Avenue jewellery stores, with a glittering range of weird and wonderful appliances, baubles, knick-knacks and *apparatachi*, which, in their jumbled assortment of *caoutchouc*, tassels, tiny bells, feathers, ointments and diagrams, suggested a combination of toy emporium, surgery and Gestapo torture chamber rather than an Arabian Nights' entertainment. Instructive and astonishing posters, in lurid colour and brutal detail, embellished the walls.

My guide – at heart, I believe, a religious man – drew my attention to a thin silken screen which depended from the ceiling to within a foot of the sales counter. I gathered that this screen, rippling at our entrance, was a delicate Oriental stratagem designed to set a modest and possibly embarrassed Western customer at his ease when selecting *trivia d'amour* and associated gewgaws. Buyer and salesman could hear only each other's voices and see each other's hands. 'Just like a confessional,' my friend pointed out with reverent approval.

I must report that, when I began to make an eccentric selection of souvenirs and in particular to seek quotes for purchase of two of the more remarkable posters, the salesman, an elderly morose fellow with an appalling squint behind his huge horn-rimmed glasses, came out into the open to appraise me face to face. My companion evidently managed to reassure him, and we eventually left with an interesting armful of ingenious and diversified booty. Some esoteric objects listed in the catalogue – rhinoceros-horn powder, tiny wigs, implausible masks, a microscopic carillon, and the like – were not available, 'because,' the salesman explained gloomily and obscurely, 'of the China Incident.'

Back in the Oriental Hotel on the waterfront, I dumped these purchases on top of the clothing in my packed trunk, beside the three Axis flags which I had exuberantly raped from a parked German embassy car outside the Imperial when I left Tokyo the night before.

I did not know at the time, but it had been a providential last-minute shopping sally.

Aboard the *Tokyo Maru*, that dark evening, one hour before sailing-time, two figures of doom were grimly awaiting me: a corpulent *Tokko* security man in civilian clothes, who appeared not to have shaved for a week, and a tough *Kempei-tai* gendarme, with his customary armband, two revolvers and that omnipresent foul *daikon* breath.

I had had one or two or three plugs of *Tami* all-malt whisky (known generally to *gaijin* drinkers as 'White Walking Stick' brand because of its deleterious effect on the optical nerves) with my Dutch friend at a pleasant little bar outside the wharf. This stimulant had been reinforced by a lively interlude with a politically-minded German seaman from a Hamburg freighter, who, overhearing us speaking English, had interrupted to deliver himself of a magnificent denunciation first of Hitler, and then of 'you *dummkopf* Englanders!' for not having called Hitler's bluff in the Ruhr.

My exhilaration and excitement over departure suddenly drained out of me, leaving me empty and anxious, when the security cop instructed me, with a peremptory hiss, to open my trunk for examination. In my ignorance and stupidity, the possibility of a security check of my luggage on departure had not crossed my mind. It was a tricky emergency. The pockets of my two packed coats and the interior of my spare pair of shoes were now bulging with a formidable selection of news clippings and articles from the Tokyo and Shanghai English-language press, which I had patiently collected over the past months and left in the safe keeping of an embassy friend to foil the Wednesday afternoon searchers of my belongings in the Imperial. There was also a thick notebook, crammed with frank observations, useful dates and compromising names.

The nature of the cuttings and material – rice crop failure, shortages of gasoline and supplies, rural unrest, official criticism and admissions, critical conversations – could leave no possible doubt that unfriendly reports about Japan were in prospect. In any event, as already pointed out, under normal *Kempei-tai* interpretation of espionage in Japan at that time, any pressman with files of figures or facts in his possession, harmful or critical, was guilty until he had proved himself innocent, or the gendarmes had lost interest in him.

At the best, therefore, I was now confronted with the certainty of an intimidatory and humiliating interrogation at a police-station and confiscation of all my material; at the worst, I might be held for consultation with Tokyo and miss the ship. Also, it occurred to me belatedly, that a diplomatic complaint might have been lodged in Tokyo about my stupid theft of the Axis flags from the German embassy car.

So I slowly opened my trunk, which was in the corridor outside my cabin, and stood back with a foolish grin of appeasement. The two security men bent eagerly over the contents. The *Kempei-tai* man picked up the nazi, Italian and Japanese flags, unfurled them in surprise, and looked at me with grudging satisfaction. 'Perhaps your government not like these?' he suggested, blowing his nauseating fog at me. 'Maybe you better pliz put this in the pocket when you come Austlalia, so?' I acknowledged his friendly hint with a grateful bow.

But the *Tokko* man, his eyes gleaming and his unshaven chins trembling, was unrolling one of those posters. I guess he thought it was a secret map. It was, however, a graphic diagram of a unique, Heath Robinson apparatus with a pump-handle, designed – as the text explained in basic English and Japanese – for improbable bodybuilding exercises by a man with a marked feeling of sexual inferiority. 'Happiest Invention of the Century' was its proud title. The cop and the gendarme examined the contrivance with keen interest and animated comment and looked at me indulgently.

A ship's officer, bustling past, sighted the poster, halted unbelieving at first, joined our study circle and – I noted even in my confusion – privately jotted down the price (the equivalent of £10 sterling at that time).

The second poster, feverishly unrolled, proved disappointingly conventional by comparison, but it was picturesque and frivolous, with Oriental echoes of Port Said, and clearly lacking in any military or political significance. Then, by miraculous inadvertence, the hastily wrapped parcel of my Sex Shop souvenirs unfolded and sprang open like a trick jack-in-the-box, spilling its unequivocal treasure-trove on the floor. We all bent to recover the objects. My companions, now in completely relaxed spirits, held the more interesting articles aloft with cries of delight and gratification. The *Tokko* cop roguishly waggled one atrocious object in my face. Even the *Kempei-tai* man was chuckling and went so far as to perch one trophy on his head like a shameful hat.

At this moment, along the corridor came a fellow-passenger – an elderly and admirable Kobe missionary lady. She paused, peering cordially to share our interest and amusement, performed a slow and dreadful doubletake and, with compressed lips and fierce eyes, proceeded faltering on her way. She never spoke to me on the three-week passage.

This was the last touch. Uproarious laughter followed her down the corridor. The convulsed security men tenderly restored my belongings to the trunk, rejected further examination, urged me to relock it. I pressed one or two tokens of affection on them. We parted in hearty masculine goodwill. '*Banzai* the Sex Shop!' I shouted, as they passed, waving and crying '*Sayonara!*', down the gangway. I had gained tremendous face with the ship's captain and officers – if not with some of the passengers.

I managed to get the posters and a battered remnant of my souvenirs past the Australian customs and safely ashore in Sydney. A plague of seaborne ants, secreted mysteriously in the hold, discovered my trunk and devoured most of the *caoutchouc* and perishable material. I duly and lyingly presented the two posters and one ingenious contrivance – 'it is more better to fill with warm milk than warm water' – to the old Sydney Journalists' Club as a professional tribute from the Japan Journalists' Union. These souvenirs were gratefully accepted and, I believe, formally acknowledged. For some time they were on restricted display, among other cultural treasures, to members in good standing and pop-eyed VIP's. By common if misguided consent, it was agreed that they reflected the enduring camaraderie of pressmen and press clubs the world over. At the old curved bar and around the early poker machines, it was also agreed that their presentation, in dark and difficult days, refuted the delusion that the Japanese sense of humour somehow differed from ours.

Decrepit, I now publicly confess this youthful deception. It was in a good cause. *Banzai* Kobe's Honourable Sex Shop! *Mort au champ d'honneur!*

PART II

Return to Japan

CHAPTER 7

Occupation Hara-kiri

Hara-kiri is now supposed to be a vulgar, even four-letter, word. The proper term, the purists tell us, is *seppuku*. By any other name, however, a self-driven short sword into the belly to disgorge the bowels would strike as deep.

The honourable eyewitness of, and participant in, the solitary formal act of *seppuku*, which mourned Japan's surrender, preferred the four-letter word, when he told me the story for the first time in measured and brutal detail twenty years ago. He himself administered the *coup-de-grâce* to the throat of the unconscious but still living celebrant, who was his brother-in-law and the last Japanese leader to commit *hara-kiri*, or *seppuku*, correctly and sincerely.

The celebrant was General Korichika Anami, Minister of War in the Suzuki Cabinet which accepted surrender on the casting vote of the Emperor. He vainly opposed the decision – weeping on his knees. He ceremoniously expiated his 'grave offences' at dawn on 15 August 1945 (Year of the Rooster), and so did not hear the fateful broadcast of the Emperor's rescript, 'supporting the insupportable' and proclaiming unconditional surrender to his people. (It was General Anami who, foiled in his wish to fight on, contrived at least to insert the incredible lead into the imperial rescript: 'The war has developed not necessarily to Japan's advantage.' That was his last official act as Minister. He had dismissed himself as Minister before he dismissed himself as a person.)

My oldest and closest Japanese friend, 'Tiger' Saito, the *Asahi* war correspondent, brought along the earnest narrator, Colonel Masahiko Takeshita, to tell me the story in my modest villa in Shibuya – a detached annexe in the pleasant grounds of the Occupation hotel equivocally known as 'The Shibuya Riding Academy'.

To me, the Takeshita record is at once a vivid close-up of the classical Japanese response to shock and humiliation, and a cautionary reminder of Japanese resilience in transforming direct defeat into indirect victory. *Hara-kiri* is pride after a fall; atonement before restoration.

I hope that this *hara-kiri* story is an appropriate introduction to the following chapters about Occupied Japan – which of course attempt no serious history of that well-documented period but only continue the windy theme of personal reminiscence.

With 'Tiger' as interpreter, Takeshita's strange story was three hours in the telling. I heard that the colonel later wrote an account of the incident for a Japanese periodical, but I have never seen that version.

The circumstances of the Emperor's decision to accept the Potsdam Declaration, when his Supreme War Council remained hopelessly divided, have been frequently recorded. It may be briefly recalled that General Anami, supported by the chiefs of both the Imperial Army and Navy, steadfastly opposed a recommendation for acceptance by the Foreign Minister, the Navy Minister and the President of the Privy Council. Despite the two atom bombs, General Anami demanded four unshakeable and impossible conditions: (1) that the Japanese national polity should remain intact and the Emperor supreme; (2) that the Japanese forces abroad should not be disarmed at those points, but only by Japan on return home; (3) that there should be no occupation of Japan; (4) that no Japanese should be punished for responsibility for the war.

The Emperor's overriding decision was transmitted to the Allies, whose acceptance on 12 August confirmed that the Emperor must submit to, and obey, the Supreme Commander of the Allied Forces during the Occupation, but that his future status would be determined freely by the Japanese people. Then followed the attempted *coup* by desperate young army officers, who vainly searched the palace for the Emperor's recorded proclamation in the early morning of August 15, after murdering the commander of the Imperial bodyguard, General Mori, and his son-in-law, Colonel Shiraishi, for resisting the mutiny.

This was when General Anami was busy organizing his death, comforted – it appears from Colonel Takeshita's account – by the fact that the date coincided fortuitously with the anniversary of his father's death. 'Tiger' Saito, hearing the account for the first time, was visibly more moved in interpretation than the relaxed colonel was in recollection of the facts to us both over a slowly emptying bottle of Scotch.

The colonel had intruded on General Anami's elaborate *hara-kiri* preparations in his study at the War Minister's official residence. He was busy writing and at first resented the intrusion even of his wife's brother, but thawed, beamed and produced *saké* when Colonel Takeshita respectfully expressed his approval and admiration of the General's intentions. He had the consideration to forbear from telling Anami of the projected *coup*: 'I did not wish to disturb his mind or interfere with his timetable, and I also feared that he might have deemed it necessary to intervene personally at the palace and needlessly endanger his life.' ('Tiger' and I exchanged glances and drank in unison.)

Anami told Takeshita that he had not only written his resignation and will but also an unworthy verse for posthumous record. The short will was prefaced: 'I respectfully apologize to the Emperor for my grave offences by now committing suicide.' On the reverse side he wrote: 'With firm belief in the indestructibility of divine and eternal Japan.' His verse, which he read aloud with correct scorn but obvious gratification, ran:

> Basking in the Emperor's great favour in life,
> I have not a syllable of word
> To leave behind.

General Anami produced two short swords, razor sharp and freshly polished, and presented one to the colonel, ostensibly as a memento but clearly intended as a generous invitation to inflict the *coup-de-grâce*. Then unexpectedly a liaison officer arrived, carrying a dutiful report from the *coup* commanders, Majors Hatanaka and Shiizaki, of their abortive mutiny, together with an official expression of regret for the unfortunate necessity of having killed General Mori and his son-in-law aide. (The Emperor's recorded rescript had been safely locked in his personal safe.) General Anami was not as shocked as Colonel Takeshita had feared. (In reply to our question, Takeshita conceded that Anami might indeed have had word of the impending *coup*, and explained that his official responsibility would naturally have been in conflict with his personal sympathy.)

The general formally expressed his disapproval of the mutiny and his profound regret for the assassinations, and assured Takeshita that his *hara-kiri* farewell would include a sincere apology for the incident.

Another visitor was Colonel Ida of the War Office, a close friend, who also congratulated General Anami on his resolution, and – 'after a pleasant chat', as Takeshita put it – listened to the general read his poem, drank a farewell cup of *saké*, bowed, saluted and withdrew.

'General Anami stepped behind a screen and changed into a white shirt which the Emperor had graciously given him as a gift when the general was his aide,' Colonel Takeshita proceeded. 'He also donned full military uniform with decorations and then emerged to drink some more *saké*. He said that he would not die wearing any covering over the shirt, which the Emperor had worn only once, and removed his coat to place it in the *tokonoma* (alcove), with the sleeves folded in embrace around a photograph of his second son, who had been killed in the China Incident two years before. "I shall be leaving the world with him," he said. He then requested me to cover his body with the medalled coat after *hara-kiri*. He also asked me to convey a message to his wife (the colonel's sister), conveying sentiments of trust and gratitude, and another to his surviving son, instructing him to avoid rash behaviour and a hasty death. "He is inclined to be impulsive," he explained.'

It appears that the general did not deem it proper to disembowel himself indoors on the *tatami* (mat) and wished to avoid embarrassing the guards in the courtyard. He went on to the verandah in the dawn, bowed thrice in the direction of the palace, squatted, stabbed himself in the left lower side of the belly, drew the short sword across to the right, extracted it, and tried to apply it to the artery on the right side of his neck. Colonel Takeshita continued:

He was very skilful and unhurried. The entrails flowed out over his thighs. There was not much blood and no smell. I saw blood running from his throat. I moved from the rear and pointed my sword inquiringly at his throat. He managed to say no, and indicated that he wanted to be left alone, as he fell, losing consciousness, on his right side. I saluted and withdrew to telephone the Vice-Minister for War, now the new Minister. He acknowledged my report and told me that the palace mutiny was under control.

I hastened back to the verandah. The body was unconscious, but the limbs were twitching and the entrails were still oozing. I drove my sword deep into his throat.

'Tiger' and I drank – also deeply. The colonel complimented me on the quality of the Scotch, and then, speaking as a relative of General Anami, requested permission to correct a misleading impression which he felt existed about the nature of 'the grave offences' for which the general had apologized to the Emperor, and which had caused him to commit *hara-kiri*. These 'offences' were not only official culpability for the mutiny and his personal opposition to the Emperor's will, but also – it was necessary to stress – responsibility for the Imperial Army's 'mistaken course of action after the outbreak of the Manchurian Incident, which precipitated the Pacific war and led to defeat'.

The colonel had gone to the trouble of writing down these 'offences' in detail before he arrived with 'Tiger'. (He had referred to no other notes during his narrative.) He hoped that I fully understood the general's reasons: 'Some people mistakenly believed that he apologized only for having opposed the Emperor and for his official responsibility for the palace *coup* as commander. But he apologized also – please understand – for Japan's defeat.'

I asked 'Tiger' to assure the colonel that I quite understood. (We later sent him a transcript of his account.)

Of course, scores of other high-ranking Japanese officers followed Anami's example and killed themselves in their homes or in front of the Imperial Palace next day. But they shot or poisoned themselves – and some their wives also – and they did not commit formal *hara-kiri* or *seppuku*.

There has been only one case of ritualistic *hara-kiri* in Japan since 1945: the ceremonial disembowelling and subsequent beheading of the forty-five-year-old author and patriot, Yukio Mishima, in late 1970. General Anami is virtually unknown to the Mishima generation. But that generation will not forget Mishima's proud, theatrical revival of the tradition. The Mishima *hara-kiri* was a portent as well as a reversion. In Japanese history, a revolution is called a restoration.

Let the two following quotes by a celebrated Japanese father and son, effectively bridging the Japanese generation-gap, close this chapter on a less bloody, but equally sharp and decisive, Japanese note. One was Shigeru Yoshida, the last of the *genro*, Occupation Prime Minister and first Prime Minister of independent Japan; the other is Kenichi Yoshida, satirical genius in English and Japanese alike. Each is the unmistakable voice of enduring Japan, although neither was interested in the *hara-kiri* – or *seppuku* – sword.

Shigeru Yoshida: General MacArthur never issued orders to me. I discussed matters with him, and he then reached decisions. . . . Criticism of the Americans is a right accorded even to Americans. But in the enumeration of their faults, we Japanese cannot include their occupation of Japan.

Kenichi Yoshida: I believe that the Occupation has been of great value to Japan. For two reasons.

First, we Japanese are very proud. But we have never been humbled before. And there can be no true pride without some acquaintance with humility.

Secondly, not all of our people have had the opportunity, as I have had, of travelling abroad, and observing Western customs and culture at first hand. In the shock of defeat at the hands of a powerful and ruthless enemy, some of our young people might easily have mistaken military victory for superior culture. Happily, the American Occupation brought to Japan its own culture and living habits, and our people were able to study for themselves personally the behaviour of the West, and so reassure themselves gratefully of the enduring superiority of the Japanese way of life.

CHAPTER 8

Down and Out in Shimbun Alley

When I was down and out in Tokyo in 1947–8, I accepted the post
of manager of the Foreign Correspondents' Club. It is one of my
proudest boasts that I contrived to survive in that exposed and
vulnerable position for nearly two years at $80 a week (plus free
board and half-price drinks) without once bringing in the military
police, striking one of my colleague-employers, or going to jail.
This is an achievement which I seriously believe rivals General
MacArthur's record as Supreme Commander: after all, he had the
power and the glory and the military police. All I had, at the
outset, was a drunken and uproarious vote of endorsement from
the membership – when no-one, including myself, quite knew
what was happening; and then, subsequently, a slowly disinte-
grating administrative grasp – never practised or experienced – of
a near-insolvent establishment, which combined some of the
features of a makeshift bordello, inefficient gaming-house and
blackmarket centre, with the basic goodwill and bitter feuds
of any press hostelry anywhere, and the aspirations and pre-
tensions of an outpost of the 'free world' in a defeated oriental
state.

We had a mixed membership of war-weary correspondents, the
world's best reporters and combat photographers, liberal, conservative and radical commentators, and some of the world's most
plausible rogues and magisterial scoundrels. There were American
and British and French and Russian and Chinese and Australian
and New Zealand newspapermen, cameramen and radio broad-
casters. It was too early then for television.

It was, I suppose, the liveliest and least conventional residential
club in the world: a five-storied, brownstone building at No 1
Shimbun ('newspaper') Alley, which had been in pre-war days an
undistinguished and slightly sleazy Tokyo restaurant, with private
Japanese-style rooms upstairs and a tiny stone Shinto shrine on
the roof. (I had an anxious half-hour preventing one demented

correspondent from tipping this shrine into the alley as a dangerous symbol of Japanese feudalism.)

General MacArthur had approved the requisition of these dilapidated, rat- and cockroach-infested premises for the accommodation of the world press. The fond memories come crawling and crowding back to make an old, discredited manager's wounds suppurate. There is that familiar uproar of intellectual disputation, breaking glass, knuckle play and folk singing in the packed bar; there is the occasional crackle of random small-arms fire on the top floor, where some of the prickliest, gun-happy Pacific war veterans are holed up – two or three to each barricaded, liquor-stacked room; there is the tumult of the Japanese band playing its theme song *Sioux City Sue* in the dining-room; there is the smell of burned hamburgers, spaghetti and meat-balls rising greasily from the army kitchen in the basement; there is the rattle of the poker-machines and the surge of self-criticism by disappointed gamers; there is the constant back-fire and fender-jolting of jeeps forcing parking-space on the sidewalks of the narrow alley; there is the heavy tread of a unit of General Swing's paratroop boys arriving eagerly from distant Hokkaido for 'drinks on the club', pledged by transient members who were seldom in residence when their guests presented themselves; there is the frequent panic near the reception desk when the terrified occupant of one of the convenient retiring-rooms bursts out, screaming and *en déshabillé*, after a pulled chain has inexplicably released boiling water and hissing steam into the receptacle.

A blurred and blurring brewer's fog settles like an alcoholic fallout over those explosive early days in Shimbun Alley. The caravan has moved on, and I can't hear the dogs barking, but I can still imagine them lifting their legs.

Like most of the significant events in life, my improbable appointment as manager of the Press Club – as the FCC was invariably called – appears, in retrospect, to have caught me by surprise, to have reared up and bitten me in the rump like an act of God, unexpected and indeed not necessarily wanted. I had had a sordid subjective disagreement with my then newspaper employer in Sydney, who had wounded me with the tone of his recall summons ('I will deal with you when you return'). I guess I could have limped home and perhaps endured his gentle, sad-eyed reproaches, but I was young and headstrong and stupid, and I didn't want to go back to an executive newspaper post in Sydney, and I did want to stay in Tokyo. I cabled my resignation – which was accepted with speed and even relish.

And so there I was, unemployed, impoverished, emaciated, replete only with self-pity, on that stormy night in 1947, when the world press, assembled rampant in the Tokyo Press Club movie-theatre forum, which resembled an inebriated Tower of Babel, was demanding managerial reform and a new deal for discontented club members. In every press club, everywhere in the world, the manager of course is always a wretched downtrodden fellow, under unceasing fire and suspicion. He is, all agree, corrupt, lazy, inefficient, sharp and immoral. He drinks too much – or not enough. He rigs the poker-machines. He exercises unbridled *droit-de-seigneur* over all club waitresses and any girls in the bands or entertainment troupes which visit the club. He flogs the liquor, peddles drugs, and fiddles the books. He is both a libidinous Aunt Sally and a wish-fulfilment father figure for all those envious, poor-white members who have their own ideas of how they would manage a press club.

Anyway, at this historic Tokyo meeting a crazy contagious cry was suddenly taken up and stormily repeated – like Thurber's 'The dam has burst!' There is no record of the originator of the blind emotional clamour. I found myself hoarsely echoing the shouts without quite knowing what I was supporting. The hysterical demand was for the appointment of a newspaperman as manager, with dictatorial suzerainty over the gentlemanly Japanese manager, on the theory that a newspaperman would understand and anticipate colleagues' desires and problems, would smoothe or soothe professional and personal disputes, would have a typewriter in the pot and two jeeps in the garage for every needy press member in emergency, would gather spot-news releases, guide club management, convene press conferences and club luncheon-speakers; would ensure a supply of accessible women and unrationed liquor; would make water run uphill; would start a club library; and would even improve the club menu.

But who? Who would be Superman? Or Supermug? What half-wit or megalomaniac could be expected to accept this clownly crown? Again, mysteriously and anonymously, at first shyly and then thunderously, the cry was taken up: 'Dick Hughes!' Why, of course, old Dick, good old Dick – out of a job and on his arse.

I had it made. Warm, wet, shining faces surrounded me. Friendly hands hammered my back and spilled my whisky. I felt like an heroic volunteer for a suicide mission. Don't let the side down, buster! And why not? It was a job, after all.

Tokyo's No 1 Shimbun Alley had its first and last press manager.

The eccentric experiment endured for a couple of eccentric years, under three different executive committees and three different presidents. It was often harrowing but it was sometimes rewarding. I don't really believe that the club was seriously harmed by the Hughes stewardship. We pulled off a couple of smart 'developmental' deals – one involving a mild conspiracy with MacArthur personally – and we ran the show as essentially a pressman's reservation, inn, refuge, tabernacle and rookery, with traditional sanctions and conventions that – in honourable theory – were none the less binding because they were unwritten, but in Shimbun Alley application – were all the more fragile because only erratic vigilante self-discipline operated. I repeat, we never once were reduced to an appeal for intervention by the Occupation military police, although 'bouncing' tactics were unavoidable on many nights of crisis, when exhilarated or belligerent non-members rolled up, demanding refreshment, massage and amenable company at all hours. Japanese staff could not offer physical resistance even to violent intruders in MacArthur uniform; I, a timid man, leaned on the never-failing support of resident correspondent, Larry Tighe (RIP), good-humoured but formidable newsman with a Golden Gloves record.

Selfishly, I don't think I suffered as a reporter during that uneasy Jekyll-and-Hyde period. I still recall most early-Occupation happenings through a Press Club bar-glass, not always darkly. No one can pretend to be uninformed in a press club. News and revelation, scandal and fact – bizarre and blue-bolted – are always on tap at the bar – at first or second hand.

At No 1 Shimbun Alley I had the best Japanese manager in Tokyo, Kay Kawana; the best Japanese barkeep, Akimoto-*san*; the best club accountant, Chinese Ling; the only efficient bilingual telephone switchboard in the Occupation.

For me, the amorphous, tortuous and utterly undefined duties of club management always took top priority over part-time stringer coverage for substitute Australian news-services, *The Wall Street Journal*, *The Financial Times* (London), and other marginal free-lancing, until I managed to stow aboard *The Sunday Times* (London) and *The Economist*. But those strange labours also uncovered or discovered Japanese friendships and insights into Japanese behaviour, character and reactions.

In my ignorance and inexperience, I committed one egregious racial blunder which, to my shame, I was never able to correct, but which I have never forgotten. Happily, I never had to sack a newspaper reporter when I was a chief-of-staff in Sydney. But once I had to sack two Japanese kitchen-hands when I was manager of the Tokyo Press Club. Roast-beef was suddenly and unexpectedly 'off' half-way through a crowded lunch session – so a pretty and efficient little waitress told me in apologetic and obvious surprise. I went into the kitchen to detect two kitchen-servers – red-handed and greasy-handed – who had taken advantage of the temporary absence of the army mess supervisor, the admirable Sergeant Pfeiffer, to appropriate and secrete three joints of beef in a large container, which, I fear, had previously been used to smuggle similar contraband. They offered no defence. They remained expressionless and silent. I sacked them on the spot, and reported the incident to the committee – rather smugly, I fear, because I was bridling under some members' criticism of the manager's slack discipline.

After lunch, the little waitress approached me, in the company of the stolid dining-room captain, bowed humbly, expressed deep contrition for the affair, and announced that she was resigning. The captain repeated and reiterated to her my distracted and near-apoplectic assurances that no one suspected her of the faintest complicity, or even knowledge of the offence. Had she not reported the strange withdrawal of the beef to me herself? What the hell? But she left quietly and with great dignity, and I could never find out where she went, or what happened to her in a hostile city then singularly deficient in respectable employment for young women.

Of course she was right, and of course I was wrong. I was a goddam foreigner, a *gaijin*. She was a Japanese. I had sacked two Japanese, and she, a Japanese, had been involved, however inno-cently. 'It would have been okay if you had told me to sack them,' the Japanese captain told me with Japanese satisfaction.

The appended extracts from my managerial diary offer a contemporary Occupation newsreel of the passing Japanese scene as
then viewed from No 1 Shimbun Alley:

The unofficial 'rule', insisting that all visitors and guests, when being
entertained by residential members, must vacate bedrooms at 4 am,
was quietly rescinded at executive committee meeting (February 1947).
It was noted that it had already lapsed – unofficially – but it was decided
to abrogate it officially.

To escape technical liability for registration as an Occupation
'house of assignation', the club introduced this regulation in the
rough pioneering days of 1945–46, and so mustered a sullen,
yawning harem of towsled ladies, in varying stages of undress,
into the club lounge each morning to await the breakfast-gong,
which eventually signalled the dawn of another day and legiti-
matized return to the bedrooms.

It was, all agreed, an adroit Western stratagem – which confused the hell out of the club staff, as well as many trusting visitors
on their first incautious bivouac.

Carl Mydans, *Life* photographer, was persuaded after dinner to re-tell
the story in the club bar of Major James P. S. Devereaux, whose
defiant reported challenge, 'Send us more Japs!', won world headlines
when his tiny marine force was holding off the Japanese invasion of
Wake Island. Carl was present when Devereaux met the press early in
the Occupation at Radio Tokyo, after spending nearly four years in a
Japanese prison camp.

Devereaux (Carl recalled) was 'a surprisingly small, thin man, whose
uniform seemed too big all around him as he stood for a moment
blinking in the hot lights. But he had a commanding carriage, and on
his face was an unexpected pleasant, gentle look.'

'Major Devereaux,' a correspondent called out, beginning the
first question. Devereaux held up his hand, smiling. 'They just gave
me these,' he laughed, and he pointed to the colonel's eagles on his
collar.

'Colonel Devereaux,' the correspondent began again, 'with all
you've been through, it must seem pretty good to be in Tokyo tonight.
How do you feel we ought to treat the Japanese?'

'With fairness,' the colonel said. He turned to another correspondent,
who was signalling for attention.

'Colonel,' the next question came, 'do you think there are any good
Japanese?' 'Absolutely,' Colonel Devereaux answered.

Then another correspondent spoke up: 'During the height of the battle for Wake, it was reported how you sent a message saying: "Send us more Japs!" Would you tell us the circumstances of that message – why you sent that message?'

Colonel Devereaux looked perplexed for a moment. Then he said: 'I sent no such message.' A small smile crept over his face. 'As you can see, we had more Japs than we could contend with.' 'The room,' (Carl closed) 'broke into laughter and then applause. And Devereaux walked out of that meeting and back into history a bigger man and far greater hero than the small, thin officer who entered.'

Club president Tom Lambert (AP) and I called on General MacArthur today in his office re our frustrated attempts to induce Mitsubishi (as owners and landlords) to repair and renovate the club premises. It was the first time I had met MacArthur. He was sympathetic, but pointed out that Mitsubishi technically could insist that this work was a charge against tenants, not landlords.

He paced his small office, smoking reflectively, then said: 'It would, of course, be improper for me to intervene as Supreme Commander. But I don't see why I can't cover your flank. Set up a dinner at the club for the Mitsubishi brass and invite them to inspect the premises. I shall send along a colonel as an observer. Only an observer, you understand? Observers, I have found, can be very useful.'

'How much is the estimate? A quarter of milllion *yen*? Well, well.'

(Later) I escorted three polite Mitsubishi board-members on an intensive inspection of the premises after a cordial but spartan dinner, which the army mess had craftily and austerely prepared. Col K, commanding Eighth Army messing, casually stressed from time to time the Supreme Commander's special interest in the Press Club. By pre-arrangement, he questioned me closely about last week's explosion in the basement lavatory, which was not due to bomb sabotage but to some abnormality in the club's boiler and sanitation system – also manifest in the irregular diversion of scalding water and steam geysers to the lavatory toilets. Col K repeatedly drew attention with sharp disapproval to property disrepair, which he and I had noted in detail on an earlier inspection that afternoon. He made copious notes, groaning, whistling and shaking his head. He alarmed the visitors by an apparent heavy stumble on a defective step.

(Later again) Mitsubishi agreed to pay 285,000 *yen* for immediate club renovations. 'A good standover job by a good observer,' General MacArthur remarked when I telephoned him the good news.

Impressed drinkers in the club bar read a *haiku* (seventeen-syllable poem) which State Minister Tokuji Kanamori wrote to celebrate the passage through the Diet of the new 'democratic' constitution, which he introduced. Kanamori-*san*, who likes to paint pumpkins as a hobby, presented his poem to Bill Costello (CBS):

> The right of rest is provided in Article 28;
> So I enjoy lying under pumpkins,
> Listening to the drone of bees.

I have a waiting list of seven residents who wish to transfer to Room 7 on the fourth floor. This popular room overlooks the large windows of the showers and two bedrooms in the Soviet women's billet next door. The Russian girls seldom draw the blinds. As a reportorial note: There are more brunettes than blondes in the Soviet mission; few are statuesque.

Mess supervisor Sergeant Pfeiffer raised with me the question of the club's indulgent practice of allowing 'second' or 'return' serves of soup and sweets (custard or fruit salad) to all diners, without insisting on consumption at table of the second serve. We both know that certain resident correspondents, who maintain Japanese mistresses upstairs but are not prepared to pay for their meals, order the 'seconds' for delivery to the rooms, where presumably the girls themselves add hand-carried noodles or *sushi*.

Pfeiffer, an easygoing bloke normally, complains that these thrifty members are now scooping up bread, butter and sugar as they leave the dining-room tables for pantry stockpiling upstairs. Would we discourage this pilfering by curtailing generosity with the minor courses? 'Let the bastids pay for the extra soup and gook,' he argues. A nice point. Decision weakly deferred.

The new little Ginza singer with the club band introduced two new Tokyo dance-hits, *The Pine Tree* and *The Apple Tree*, the words of which suggest to some earnest correspondents political rather than arboreal significance.

The first is the song of a little pine tree which once sighed because it could not grow more quickly into a larger tree, but which, now that it has grown up, realizes that it must face and overcome the strong and angry winds which whistled far above its head when it was a small, safer and happier tree.

And the second song is about a rich red apple which everyone admired until it was plucked and found to be as rotten inside as it was fair outside.

Inspector Mitsuro Kimbara of the Metropolitan Police Board fascinated us at an informal press conference in the club bar before lunch. He was discussing the death sentences on two notorious sex-killers, 'Bluebeard' Kodaira and Tsuji, who had each murdered more than a score of women over a period of a year.

Yes, he agreed with a hearty laugh, sex crimes had recently shown a sharp increase throughout Japan. Was he not alarmed?

'No, no! I am of opinion that this increase in sex crimes is evidence that social conditions are returning to normalcy. When people have to carry around empty stomachs and are afflicted with hardships and unemployment, they have no time to think about sex or romance. More sex crimes mean less poverty. They are a tribute to the Occupation.' He bowed.

What was the policy of the police authorities for the restraint or correction of these encouraging crimes?

'We will, as in the past, do our best to effect the arrest of culprits in the early stages of their criminal careers,' Inspector Kimbara replied, adding with calm logic: 'If "Bluebeard" Kodaira and Tsuji had been arrested earlier, they would not have committed so many serious crimes.' Someone tried to protest that earlier arrests would delay the return to normalcy and stability and full employment. But it was all too baffling.

I joined Isoji Aso, Japanese wit and essayist, and Walt Simmons (Chicago *Tribune*) for lunch. We talked about the mysterious Japanese laugh, which is apt to confuse *gaijin* when used politely in moments of personal grief or shock. Aso-*san* explained that we must learn to distinguish between five special categories of Japanese laughter: *ahahi* (merry), *ihihi* (vulgar), *uhuhu* (derisive), *ehehe* (sycophantic), and *ohoho* (modest).

Walt said I had an *ihihi* laugh; I said he favoured the *ehehe*.

According to Aso-*san*, most Japanese laughter had originally been *ahahi*, but Buddhism with its threats of reward and punishment had confused and darkened the merriest Japanese laughter. However, the lusty and erotic 'pillow-book' humour of the Heian period – Walt and I nodded understandingly with an *ehehe* smile – had added a more delicate and allusive mood to Japanese humour.

I asked Aso-*san* which Japanese song made him laugh the most. He did not hesitate. 'Bassho's *haiku* written at the inn near Take-A-Piss Pass in Izu,' he declared with an *ahahi* guffaw, and quoted:

> Fleas and lice
> And at my pillow-side,
> A pissing horse.

That, I had to point out, didn't sound very humorous to the harassed manager of No 1 Shimbun Alley, who had to endure members' complaints. Aso-*san* was properly *ohoho* but Walt-*san* was characteristically *uhuhu*.

CHAPTER 9

The Death-Chair Christmas Card

The 1947 Christmas card, which was delivered to me from New York at the Tokyo Press Club in late January 1948, was a thoughtful, moving encyclical, although unconventional and even macabre in design and message. Airmailed economically without benefit of envelope, the tourist postcard was a simple but dramatic closeup in colour of the death-chair in Sing Sing prison. The typewritten sentiment on the back, clear for all to read, transmitted seasonal greetings for Christmas and the New Year with studied indirection and, some might think, execrable taste. It ran, to the best of my recollection:

THE LEE EXPORTING COY., NEW YORK   *December, 1947.*

Richard Hughes Esq
Posing as a Foreign Correspondent
Press Club
Shimbun Alley Tokyo.

Dear Sir: In response to your welcome inquiry, we have pleasure in submitting sample illustration of the type of goods which you wish to import to help democratise Japan. This is a sturdy but elegant model, easy on power, maintenance and the eye, if hard on the seat, and has given satisfaction to all users. Testimonials available. Pray advise numbers required as quantity will of course govern price (f.o.b., San Francisco – Yokohama.) With personal respects and greetings for Christmas and the New Year to both yourself and General MacArthur in your noble labours, (signed) Harry Lee, president and managing director.

Harry Lee – better known now as Alwyn – was a gifted colleague in documentary reporting in younger and happier days in Melbourne and Sydney, who became a distinguished writer on literary matters for *Time* but is now, God love him, dead. The brutal whimsy of his greeting did not surprise me. He is still remembered as the perpetrator of the most callous line in Australian news reportage; it managed to run through a carefree first-edition of a Melbourne paper (*circa* 1934) as a trimming to an imaginative review of the incidence and treatment of leprosy in Australia: 'Denouncing conditions in Australian lazarets as "abominable", a leading leper said today . . .'

I indulged a nostalgic smile, therefore, at the mystique of Christmas goodwill in his characteristic message, and attributed the one-month delay in delivery to the hazards of Occupation mail-handling. There was an enigmatic Japanese rubber-stamped chop beside my name and address, and later I discovered that a pencilled line had been drawn and erased under the Queens-berryian slur on my position. My initial reaction naturally was consideration of a suitable riposte for Lee at his New York office. Subsequent developments, however, were to cast instructive light on the mood and influence of Occupation operations and on Japanese reaction to Western persiflage.

An elderly Buddha-like Japanese, with the well-rubbed, heavily locked valise that was the Tokyo badge of bureaucratic authority, tapped on the door of my bedroom-office on the first floor of the Club. He was accompanied by a younger, less benevolent, sharply dressed Japanese, whom I dimly recalled having seen from a distance, exchanging mysterious parcels in confidential huddles with members in the Club lobby. They entered so ingratiatingly, bowed so deeply, and shook hands so warmly that I was immediately on my guard. Their cards bore no direct Occupation affiliation or official designation – another warning signal. We sat down, laughing watchfully together. They both spoke good English and accepted my suggestion of coffee with profound obeisance and shouts of ungovernable gratitude. After ten minutes of protocol compliments and backscratching, Buddha suddenly got down to business on a hearty man-to-man basis.

'Mr Hooje,' he explained, 'I am employed in humble capacity in postal department. There it is our duty and pleasure to hasten safe delivery of letters – ha, ha – to all important correspondents like yourself who have so kindly come to help Japan with your advice and experience to become free democratic country. Sometimes, however, we have unfortunate delays because of stupidity of young untrained men – ha, ha. I am afraid that we delayed important business communication to you, which was first sent by error to my good and discreet friend here, Mr Takahashi, who has advisory post with Occupation under Supreme Commander Mac-Arthur.' He bowed his head as if in prayer, and Mr Takahashi ducked his.

'I am part-time adviser to Occupation on trade, import and export licences, exchange allocations, and liaison with Japanese interests, etcetera and etcetera,' Mr Takahashi explained, with the soft, superior sneer of the 'inside' man.

'We refer, Mr Hooje,' Buddha lowered his voice, 'to the message and blueprint from Mr H. Lee's New York Corporation concerning your negotiations for import of electric chairs. The imbecile postal clerk, a *bakayara* (bloody fool) from the rural areas, read the message – harmlessly, ha, ha – and thought that it should have been addressed to businessman – not foreign correspondent. He referred it, all good faith, you understand, but incorrectly – we apologize deeply, Mr Hooje – to Mr Takahashi, thinking absurdly that he would have your import licence number. It is, as you know, sometimes unusual for newspaper correspondent to hold also import licence under Occupation law – ha, ha.' (It was, as Buddha well knew, downright illegal.)

'Although in my opinion it would be a good thing,' interposed Mr Takahashi, 'if correspondents were permitted officially to take part in trade deals and contracts for import-export. They are more experienced than some of the businessmen who come here with approved Occupation licences. Not,' he added quickly, 'that I am criticizing Occupation policy.'

I was slowly catching on. I could hear the mocking laughter of Harry Lee in New York.

'I was careful,' Mr Takahashi continued, examining his finger-nails, 'to respect the secrecy of your correspondence. I did not think it was necessary to show it to Occupation personnel, who might have misunderstood your interest. Although, if you will excuse my mentioning it . . .'

'Yes, yes, please excuse,' interjected Buddha.

'. . . I think it would be wiser not to conduct correspondence on the subject by open cards or unsealed envelopes, which perhaps mischief-making people could read. So,' Mr Takahashi concluded rather rapidly, 'we have come to see if we can help you.'

Buddha took over. They were a good team. 'I am sure, Mr Hooje, that no-one in old Japanese government departments know that Supreme Commander is intending to change our barbarous Japanese form of hanging for democratic electrocution method. Mr Takahashi is also confident that no American officers have been informed. He is sure this information would have come to his ear. It seemed to us that it would be useful to you and Mr Lee if we could have information of number of electric chairs Supreme Commander thinks might be necessary, and we could then help you in fixing fair and reasonable prices. Perhaps you will be recommending purchase of many chairs, and we agree – in interests of Occupation policy for wide influence in Japan – that many chairs would be best for us all.

'You see, Mr Hooje, we hang people only in one or two Japanese prisons. There is only one prison gallows in Tokyo and another in Sendai. People from other prisons are carried by the steam locomotive to Tokyo or Sendai for their hanging. It is Japanese custom – ha, ha. We are sure it would be more efficient, more proper, more sincere, more respect to prisoner and more dignified for prison governor, if we have electric chair in every prison. I am sure that, if we talk this over discreetly concerning prices and costs and so forth and such like, it could be of help to you and Mr Lee and us chairmakers and Occupation policy. We would be glad to help you humbly in this matter.'

'We have contacts in the old Department of Justice and among prison governors, who will support recommendations for a large order of chairs,' Mr Takahashi amplified.

Apart from mumbling and coughing, I had made no worthwhile contribution to the discussion. My confusion, I fear, was misinterpreted.

'There has, I think, been some misunderstanding,' I attempted, laughing feebly. 'My friend, Mr Lee, is a great joker, you understand? He makes stupid jokes.'

My reference to 'misunderstanding' was sympathetically received. Neither reacted to the suggestion of a 'joke'.

'I mean,' I persisted, 'that Mr Lee was only joking when he said that I had written about electric chairs. You see, I had not written to him at all. I know nothing of General MacArthur's plans. It is all very difficult.' My voice trailed off. What the devil could I say?

My visitors leaped on to the simple words which made sense to them and just ignored the difficult words which confused them.

This is a trait which I have painfully observed in acquaintance with the Japanese.

'You have not *written* to him,' Mr Takahashi repeated with satisfaction. 'That is very sensible. That is very discreet. But that is why he must respect your discretion and must write to you under seal or send information through a messenger.'

'You are very correct in knowing nothing of the Supreme Commander's plans,' Buddha agreed. 'It is always better to know nothing. We learned of General MacArthur's interest only when we – ha, ha – read Mr Lee's written greetings to him. Mr Lee – excuse – he is man you can trust, even if indiscreet? He would not deal with others too?'

'No, no!' I cried in despair, and then swore in futility. 'This is all too difficult, gentlemen. Mr Lee is not sending electric chairs from New York. He is only joking! Joking! This is meant to be a funny joke.'

Buddha and Mr Takahashi exchanged glances. Buddha laughed uneasily, to show that he understood a joke as well as any Westerner. Mr Takahashi's face clouded. They spoke together.

'Mr Lee is joking about hanging?' Mr Takahashi demurred. 'Why is this a joke? Hanging is a very serious matter here.'

'Why does he say he will sell electric chairs if he will not? This is not businesslike,' Buddha protested.

Anyway you looked at it, it was an impasse. Mr Takahashi, after a pause, impolitely shot a sharp remark in Japanese at Buddha.

'You are perfectly correct to be so discreet, Mr Hooje,' he then acknowledged, rising. 'Please tell Mr Lee to be discreet also. We should, I realize, have brought credentials.' I was left with the impression that this had been an issue between them in which Mr Takahashi had been overridden. 'However,' he shook my hand warmly, 'we shall send someone else. Of great discretion.'

I protested weakly. They laughed reassuringly. Buddha closed the door behind them with the air of a conspirator who has been checked but not checkmated.

Sure enough, another emissary arrived two days later. He was an influential industrialist who made it clear that he had important Japanese and Occupation contacts. He was more direct and impatient with me as, now angry as well as amused, I insisted that the whole subject was farcical. Our discussion was further confused by his pronunciation – unlike Buddha and Mr Takahashi –

of 'l' as 'r', so that he kept calling Mr Lee 'Mr Ree', which made it sound as though the intending exporter of death-chairs was the then President of South Korea. He never said plainly that he or anyone else would be able to make money out of the negotiated sale of death-chairs, and that the commission on an enlarged transaction, which he could help ensure, would be shared with me and presumably President Syngman Rhee in New York. But no-one could have missed his meaning. He had got it into his head that General MacArthur had decided that convicted Japanese war criminals, then standing trial, would be electrocuted instead of hanged in order to dramatize the advent of democratic Western justice. He pointed out that the Occupation had numbered the nameless streets of Tokyo 'in New York fashion'. He alleged that extreme US pressure was being applied to the Japanese authorities to change lefthand driving to righthand, to facilitate the import and use of US cars.

In our long, fretting interview, he interpreted my explanations first as a curious and frivolous Western bargaining stand, and then as tedious and needless discretion. He became wary only when I at last offered to go to General MacArthur's avuncular aide, Colonel Bunker, and in his presence solemnly disavow all knowledge of the projected electric chair transaction. This offer persuaded him that I had either prudently withdrawn from the deal or had appointed a front man with an authorized licence. I never saw him or Buddha again, but I once encountered Mr Takahashi accidentally in the Club; he turned his back. And a year or so later, a friend in MacArthur's intelligence section asked me casually how electric chairs were selling. I let it pass.

If I had been a bold, crusading reporter, I suppose I could have led them on and discovered what graft they were offering and how they were manipulating exchange grants, and then written a powerful exposé of Occupation naïvety and Japanese corruption. But I could never take the matter seriously. The best I could do was to try to embarrass Harry Lee in his New York office by forging a Buddhist abbot's signature on an open postcard of devout instructions to him which purported to answer his inquiries for guidance into the Zen sect.

Anyway, they're still hanging them in Japan today.

CHAPTER 10

Operation 'Honourable Greyhound'

As a personal memory, Operation 'Honourable Greyhound' is at once my saddest and bravest recollection of the dear, dead Occupation of Japan. As a Big Business deal, it could have been, I am still convinced, the most brilliant and unconventional trading transaction conducted between Japan and the outside world during MacArthur's autocracy.

The concept combined commerce, sport, culture, democracy, goodwill and high finance on a simple but noble basis of capitalist barter. But in operation, it was sabotaged by bureaucratic opposition and political inertia. Indeed, after two long decades, the tragic contradiction between soaring theory and deflated practice, as dramatized by Operation 'Honourable Greyhound', seems to me to symbolize the aspiration and frustration of the Occupation generally.

At the time, the story of the project was known only to a small but influential group in Tokyo, although widely publicized by certain Australian newspapers. I have the gloomy record in my files: yellowing newspaper clips with banner headlines; scores of dog-eared photographs of champion racing greyhounds; more than one hundred long, frank and detailed applications for passage to, and residence in, Japan by honest breeders and trainers of greyhounds in Australia; the ruling prices of Japanese cultured pearl necklaces; austere pronouncements by high-powered advisers to the Supreme Commander of the Allied Powers; a heavily embossed declaration of Australian immigration policy from the Attorney General's Department in Canberra; and finally the melancholy but historic newspaper picture of Mr Keita Goto, distinguished Japanese industrialist and sportsman, firing the starting pistol at a bicycle race in Osaka instead of releasing the Australian greyhounds which were his original hope and choice.

I first met Mr Goto in the Tokyo Press Club in Shimbun Alley in the late spring of 1948. I had been interested in his endeavours to establish the democratic sport of greyhound racing in Japan. He had been hampered in his efforts by (a) lack of Occupation and parliamentary approval for the introduction of gambling facilities in combination with dog racing, and (b) lack of any suitable racing greyhounds in Japan.

Mr Goto was a solemn, civil, little brown man, wearing flashing spectacles, a white waistcoat, heavy gold watch-chain and an immaculate light grey suit. It was understood that he did not speak English sufficiently well for an interview. His one opening remark to me, after introduction by his nervous secretary, was an expressionless: 'I am very fond of the entire animal kingdom.' He drank double Scotches with relish and despatch.

Mr Goto, who was then sixty-one (he died in Tokyo in 1959), frankly filled in his personal, governmental and business background for me. He had, he admitted, been purged from public office by the Occupation because he had been a Minister of Transport during the war. He had a capital of 30 million *yen* (then US $450,000) to float a company to be known as the Honourable and Democratic Dog-Racing Association as soon as permission for betting had been granted by General MacArthur and the then Prime Minister, Mr Hitoshi Ashida (on the eve of arrest on charges, later found unproven, of having confused personal gifts and political subscriptions from a big electrical undertaking).

Mr Goto still retained transport and sporting connections. He was the proprietor, as well as the president, of the Tokyo High-Speed Tramway Company. He owned a string of racehorses. He had already experimented with racing dogs in an enclosed area, but betting was not yet allowed under the feudalistic Japanese laws, and in the absence of greyhounds, the local dogs which he had tested had been of German shepherd and Hokkaido husky descent. They had preferred to savage one another at the barrier rather than show their paces.

'These disappointments have not discouraged Goto-*san*,' said his secretary in Cambridge English. 'He has a great and consuming attachment to sport, gambling and animals. He is a sincere Japanese Corinthian.'

Mr Goto identified the word 'animals'. 'I am,' he repeated impassively, 'very fond of the entire animal kingdom.'

Then, over several double Scotches and with some nudging on

my part, Mr Goto advanced and developed his unique offer of lustrous Japanese pearl necklaces in exchange for Australian pedigree greyhounds. I knew nothing of the value of greyhounds, but we both recognized that, as the *yen* was not convertible and trade was on a barter basis, he would need to exchange goods for dogs. It seemed to me that pearls, available in abundance in Japan, would be acceptable tender in the Commonwealth richly blessed with greyhounds.

So, after voluble discussion and sketchy pencilled calculations on the tablecloth, Operation 'Honourable Greyhound' was launched.

Mr Goto offered seventy-five flawless pearl necklaces, valued at 7,500,000 *yen* (approximately £A10,000 or US $30,000, at the current blackmarket rate in 1948) for twenty pedigree Australian racing greyhounds. He impressed me with his contempt for sordid detail in his brisk calculations.

Inspired by his enthusiasm and not unmindful of the possible news value of the proposal, I reminded him that he should have a dog trainer or breeder or some other professional expert to accompany the faithful animals and attend them in the manner to which they had become accustomed. He thereupon made an additional offer of a luxurious home in Japan, substantial living expenses and a yearly *yen* salary equivalent to £A1,000 for an Australian greyhound authority competent to organize and direct dog racing on a gambling basis in Japan.

Operation 'Honourable Greyhound' hit the headlines in Australia. My evening news editor in Sydney cabled me: 'Dog story wildfiring fullstop office flooded with applications and blockaded by greyhounds fullstop gosford (heart of New South Wales greyhound country) fears mass migration fullstop pearl market lowest fullstop keep sending fullest.'

Unhappily an error in my original telegraphic transmission had mutilated Mr Goto's name as 'Gota', and I never got around to correcting the error or explaining it plausibly to Mr Goto's naturally suspicious secretary. In my newspaper reports and in the minds of all Australian greyhound breeders, he remained – and perchance still dimly remains – Mr Gota. The use of the customary Japanese honorific '*san*', which I unwisely added to Mr Goto–Gota's name in later messages, to suggest that I had some Japanese scholarship, also helped to confuse the greyhound boys in Australia. Cables from remote and nostalgic post-office addresses in wayback Australia reached me, asking me to assure 'Mr Gota' or 'Mr Gotasan' that the clinching irresistible response to his offer was in the mail.

Then the Australian greyhound airmail began to pour in – registered, thick and bulging with photographs of dogs, which all looked the same to me but which were embellished with the most frank and explicit individual claims of potency and sex-drive as well as racing speed and ferocity. Some of these letters went through the Japanese mail, where they were opened and censored, to Mr Goto (alias Gota and Gotasan) direct. 'What is your purpose in changing Mr Goto's name?' his secretary kept demanding. Despite the wrong name, Mr Goto received them all because they invariably carried his haunting, non-racing address, 'Tokyo High-Speed Tramway Company.' But many letters came to him indirectly through me at the Press Club, thereby evading censorship and convincing the Japanese postmen, bowing to me respectfully, that I was engaged in some normal and rewarding blackmarket transaction.

Next – and most disturbing – development in Operation 'Honourable Greyhound' was the arrival of a tough, bullet-headed Japanese called (let us say) Mr Kenichi Kaneda, wearing a navy-blue, turtle-neck sweater, and accompanied by two grim and obvious bodyguards. Mr Kaneda introduced himself as managing director of the Tokyo-Yokohama Dog Racing Club. He said, with cold eyes, that he had had ten years' experience of greyhound racing in Shanghai before the war. He claimed to be the best and only licensed dog trainer and dog racer in Japan. He showed me a stack of letters in Japanese writing which I pretended meekly to read with ejaculations of respect and admiration. He denounced the credentials of Mr Goto. He drank neat tumblers of *saké* and, for some unexplained reason, inserted his right index finger firmly in his right ear as he downed each lip-smacking draught.

He warned me that Mr Goto – 'a shameless militarist and reactionary, rightly purged by the great General MacArthur' – had no legal right to own or race greyhounds, with or without tote or bookmakers. The only company properly and democratically authorized to do so was his, Kaneda-*san*'s, club, which, he insisted had the support of both Governor Yasui of Tokyo and a democratized capitalist (say, Mr Ono), who had formerly held a high post with the South Manchurian Railway and who commanded capital totalling fifty million *yen*.

'Goto is a swindler and a rogue,' said Kaneda-*san*, inserting his finger in his ear and tilting back his head. 'Fifteen hundred dollars is an absurdly extravagant price for a greyhound. We can buy dogs of sturdy mettle and sincere fertility in Florida for one-third that impost. And,' he lowered his voice, 'we will not need to squander Japan's pearls. With the Americans, there are other ways.' He winked.

He then raised a question that mystified me. 'What about the rabbit-car?' he inquired.

'Rabbit-car? *Rabbit-car?*' I replied.

They looked at me incredulously. 'Rabbit-car,' repeated Kaneda-*san*. 'That little, mechanically operated object which deceives the dogs, which they chase, fondly believing it to be their animal quarry, alive, furry and fleeing. You do not know, no?'

(I should perhaps have explained that our interpreter was a sensitive young university language student, acting as part-time glass-washer at the Club; I suspect that he favoured me with a flowery translation of Kaneda's stable talk.)

Embarrassed, I explained that in Australia we called the 'rabbit-car' a 'tin hare'. This provoked some confusion and resentment because it was thought at first that I was jesting about the absence of hair on Kaneda's shaven skull. When we got this sorted out, Kaneda-*san* explained that his club was the sole Japanese organization which was planning a correct, sincere, democratic, circular course with a mechanical tin hare for the greyhounds to chase, and that Goto's opposition clique was planning only a straight coursing track without a 'rabbit-car'.

Next day, Mr Goto, supremely unconcerned, almost indulgent, dismissed all the charges by Mr Kaneda. He explained that the Occupation purge did not affect his competence to organize greyhound racing but only to hold government office. He himself was a close personal friend of Governor Yasui, who would ensure that I was not pestered any more by visits from Mr Kaneda. (I was not.) And Mr Ono, the former official of the South Manchurian Railway, was, he knew, slated for arrest by the police next week. (He was.)

'I shall use the rabbit-car whenever it is desired by the democratic sporting public,' Mr Goto emphasized. 'And I have already selected the Japanese pearl necklaces for the Australian grey-hounds.' He flashed a magnificent necklace, rubbed two of the pearls thoughtfully against his back teeth, swallowed a double Scotch and, in English, without a flicker, reassured me of his unswerving devotion to the animal kingdom.

But then, alas, Operation 'Honourable Greyhound' faltered. The hopeful airmail from the Australian dog trainers continued to arrive. But the Japanese Diet was sluggish. Prime Minister Ashida and several of his ministers were in the pokey. General MacArthur was preoccupied with the operations of the prim, implacable little banker, Joseph M. Dodge, who was introducing notable reforms in the MacArthurian plans for the Japanese economy. The Australian embassy in Tokyo told me severely that any travel order for an Australian dog trainer to come to Japan, with or without dogs, to assist Mr Goto, would need to be personally approved by the then Attorney General, the Right Honourable Dr Herbert Evatt. 'There will probably be formid-able difficulties in the way of such a clearance,' I was warned. 'It is hardly possible that such an assignment would come under the heading of either "cultural" or "developmental" influence, according to the Act.'

A humanitarian US officer (a two-star general) in MacArthur's Economic and Scientific Section raised a new objection. 'It would be an outrage,' he protested, 'if racing dogs were fed meat while the people went hungry.'

Mr Goto, who was never flurried, responded affably: 'The small amount of meat which racing dogs will eat would neither help nor harm the health of the public. In any event, that loss will be offset by the simple, recreational exhilaration of watching the grey-hounds chase the rabbit-car in the sparkling open air. Besides the Japanese people prefer to eat rice, fish and noodles instead of dog's meat.'

So time rolled on. The Diet and the Occupation and the Australian embassy let it roll. The patience of Mr Goto's fellow shareholders rubbed away. Each of the 112 dog trainer applicants received a formal apologetic explanation from Goto-*san*'s secre-tary, urging them not to abandon hope; but – one suspects – that after six months they also became discouraged.

Finally, Mr Goto, discerning a new, democratic sporting trend in resurgent and rampant Japan, turned to bicycle racing, which the Diet and the Occupation jointly blessed (with gambling facilities, of course) on the ground that it would encourage the development of the local bicycle industry. I heard that Mr Goto gave the pearl necklaces away as prizes for winning cyclists. Operation 'Honourable Greyhound' died, silently, sadly, secretly, in the doghouse.

I can still spare a sigh for its bitter-sweet memories, so evocative of the Occupation in its early days of high hope and soaring imagination.

CHAPTER 11

The Crime Against Mamoru Shigemitsu

Mamoru Shigemitsu, Foreign Minister, who – ironically – signed Japan's surrender to General MacArthur after the lost war which he himself had vainly opposed, was victim of the grossest miscarriage of justice at the Tokyo trial of Japan's 'major war criminals'.

The circumstantial evidence is pretty strong that the victors also hanged the wrong man for the horrendous Rape of Nanking – General Iwane Matsui. And few would agree today that ex-Prime Minister Koki Hirota should have been hanged. True, there is room for argument over the fate of Matsui and Hirota. But the Shigemitsu sentence was indefensible and unforgivable. After twenty years, the forgotten case merits recall, re-examination and record, especially at a time when there is agonizing debate over the responsibility of superior officers for alleged US atrocities in South Vietnam. The case remains, also, a haunting study of the Occupation in confused and contradictory operation.

Mamoru Shigemitsu sat in the back row of seats in the crowded dock at the marathon Tokyo trial. He was always the last to be seated. He had lost his leg to a Korean assassin's bomb in Shanghai in 1932. Dragging painfully forward at the rear of the long procession of prisoners, he would slip into his seat, bow his thanks to the stolid military policeman who helped him, tuck his crutches out of sight, and settle back, immobile, to await resumption of the seemingly unending spate of evidence, argument and counter-argument which poured tediously through the lofty auditorium for nearly three years.

Two seats in front of Shigemitsu was General Hideki Tojo, with whom he had quarrelled bitterly. Over to his right was Hirota, the aged political chameleon, who had tried to be all things to all Japanese. To Shigemitsu's left was his old political rival and predecessor and successor as Foreign Minister, Shinegori

Togo, who was sentenced to twenty years and died in prison. The most evil-looking prisoner was Kingoro Hashimoto, one of the leaders of the Black Dragon Society, who should have been hanged if anyone was, but who escaped with imprisonment. Shrivelled little Doihara, the mastermind behind the Japanese intrigue, bribery and subversion in Manchuria, looked like a trapped monkey. Matsui, with the goatbeard, sat silent throughout.

They were a motley, unimpressive, largely dejected and essentially broken assembly, some in worn uniform, some in prison issue of civilian clothing. As Russell Brines, AP chief and pre-war Tokyo resident correspondent, wrote: 'For a fleeting instant, Japan was even ashamed of the appearance of her war criminals.'

Originally twenty-eight leaders were arraigned. Prince Konoye escaped trial and certain hanging by taking poison at home the night before his arrest. Former Foreign Minister Matsuoka and Admiral Nagano, naval chief of staff who approved the Pearl Harbour attack, also beat hanging by dying. Shumei Okawa, another Black Dragon boss, enlivened the proceedings at an early stage by rising, giggling, and slapping the bullet head of Tojo in the row below him; he was declared to be insane. So twenty-five prisoners lasted the distance, confronting the long, black-robed line of eleven judges, across the body of the court.

Set-up and performance were alike artificial and theatrical: indeed, the auditorium had been a theatre for War Ministry lectures, which had miraculously escaped the fire-bombings of Tokyo, and which was re-christened Pershing Heights during the Occupation. The world press filled the stalls, and officers' wives, distinguished visitors and diplomats reclined on what had been the stage. The dress circle, above and behind the press, was packed with goggle-eyed Japanese onlookers, for whose enlightenment and instruction the futile show had been staged.

Sir William Webb, an Australian of forceful character, vigorous speech and deceptive percipience, was chairman of the tribunal, and handed down the judgments – good and bad – with a wry and wise personal postscript that never got the publicity it deserved. The implacable judge was the Soviet army witch-hunter, who was resolved that no prisoner should escape, and who forced compromises when he could not get his way outright. Of course he represented Soviet policy at the trial. Russia had come in at the kill, breaking technically the same kind of expedient, Stalinist 'non-aggression pact' which had cynically given the green light for Hitler's attack on Poland, and manifesting in Tokyo the same blind retribution that kept the ancient lunatic Hess in solitary confinement in Berlin.

The show – a stale and anticlimactic encore of Nuremberg – soon began to pall. It never achieved its aim of impressing the Japanese people with the evil of its defeated leaders and the wisdom and justice of its conquerors; they were fed up with the performance after six months. They got the point – and got bored. 'We lost the war' – how often we heard this summation – 'and these *bakayara* (bloody fools) were to blame as our leaders. All right, so you won. Shoot or hang them.'

The trial would have lasted another year without the drive and impatience of Sir William Webb, who was without doubt the leading man in the cast. His fleshy nose, black eyebrows, silver hair, heavy jowls and rasping voice dominated the rest of the performers, as he called prosecuting and defence counsel alike to heel ... 'Sit down! ... You are not helping the court ... I have warned you before ... Objection overruled ... Sit *down*!' His harsh Australian accent whistled and cracked about the wretched heads of lawyers and witnesses like a tireless stockwhip.

It was difficult at first to follow the procedure of the tribunal, because each question, each answer, and each blistering interjection by Sir William had to be translated, sentence by sentence, into Japanese and Chinese. (If you wanted Russian or French, you had to slip on earphones and tune in to those translations.) A red light flashed in front of the witness, counsel or judge if his rhetoric strained the amperage of the desperate translators. ... Prosecutor Keenan asks a witness whether he saw Japanese soldiers slaughter one thousand Chinese civilians at Tientsin. Then he pauses, one hand on hip, inspecting the fingernails of the other hand, and the microphones splutter the same question in Japanese. There is another pause, and the microphones repeat the question in more sonorous mandarin. The witness replies in English that he doesn't understand the question. A red light flashes in front of him, and the Japanese and Chinese translations of 'don't understand' echo through the court. The question is repeated. The witness begins laboriously to answer. A Japanese counsel challenges the translation. The shorthand transcript is read aloud by a blonde secretary, whose crossed thighs – in those pre-mini days – distract the court's attention. Sir William explodes into the discussion, his jowls quivering like those of a furious bloodhound. He warns the defence counsel: 'I will not tolerate this deliberate flouting of the tribunal.' The ferocity of his rebuke is emphasized by the physical effort of pausing with swollen veins after each sentence for the double translation. . . .

So it dragged on for two and a half years. And then they finally hanged seven, sentenced sixteen to life, Togo to twenty years – and Shigemitsu to seven years. The death sentences – over which there was disagreement in plenty – naturally grabbed the headlines. In more objective mood, justice would have been served by the execution only of Tojo and Doihara – although, on their records, Hashimoto was more vicious than either Doihara or Tojo. At the trial, the crowded court was for once profoundly shocked – and few witnesses will forget the crumpled old figure swaying with closed eyes – when Koki Hirota was sentenced to hang.

Lord Hankey scored a damning legal point (*Politics, Trials and Errors*): 'The death sentences were imposed by vote of six to five in some cases, of seven to four in others, but in no case by vote of more than seven judges . . . The law of most of the civilized world requires unanimity for imposing a sentence of death, and usually for conviction of a crime.'

Sir William Webb, betraying the velvet hand inside his iron glove, added a personal rider that 'it might prove revolting to hang or shoot such old men as several of the accused. If the court must by law impose capital punishment, the prerogative of mercy would probably be exercised in order to save the life of the condemned.' And he hinted that perhaps the death sentences could be reduced to exile on a Japanese island – a classic Japanese punishment for errant ministers of state or advisers to the emperor.

Matsui, to repeat, took the blame for the Rape of Nanking. He steadfastly refused to offer any defence or to give evidence, although his frustrated us defence attorney could have proved that he was nowhere near the scene when the sack began, and rushed gendarmes to the city with orders to shoot down all rioting Japanese soldiers as soon as reports reached him. The plausible inside story – never properly researched – was that Matsui accepted the role of scapegoat to shield someone still higher in command. In the event, Matsui retired to Tokyo before the end of the war, declared that 'the Imperial Army had suffered indelible shame', and duly and conventionally entered a monastery, where he was arrested for trial, sentenced and hanged.

Then, at last, we come to the scandal of Shigemitsu's sentence – none the less shameful because it was the lowest sentence. Shigemitsu was demonstrably, factually and legally innocent. But that Soviet judge was after him – only when the Russian arrived in Tokyo was Shigemitsu arrested – and he withdrew support for other compromise decisions until he wangled, in exchange, a majority decision to brand and imprison Shigemitsu. Most legal observers did not believe that Shigemitsu should have appeared before the court. The Chief Prosecutor, Joseph B. Keenan, declared publicly that Shigemitsu should never have been put on trial, let alone convicted.

Shigemitsu's personal anti-war record was clear and outstanding. He had been a distinguished career diplomat, who became so friendly with British and US ambassadors in every world capital in which he served that they all, without exception, rallied, though vainly, to his defence after he was sentenced. In 1940, as ambassador to London, he had had conversations with Lord Lloyd and Lord Hankey (with the authority of Halifax and the knowledge of Churchill) to try to find a way to keep Japan out of the war. He had proposed first that a British mission be sent to Tokyo, and, in a final despairing move, he met Matsuoka in Geneva in March 1941 and tried to persuade him to return home via London and Washington. Shigemitsu was acquitted by the tribunal of charges of participation in 'the general conspiracy' with General Tojo and the others 'to wage war', and of 'ordering, authorizing and permitting the commission of conventional war crimes'. But, with three dissenting judges, he was found guilty of having:

Waged wars of aggression against China, the United States, the British Commonwealth, the Netherlands and France.
Deliberately and recklessly disregarded his legal duty to take adequate steps to ensure the observance and prevent breaches of the laws of war.

On the first question of complicity in aggression, the comments of the majority judgement of the tribunal, convicting him, were at once instructive and mystifying:

Shigemitsu was not one of the conspirators. Indeed, he repeatedly gave advice to the Japanese Foreign Office which was opposed to the policies of the conspirators.

By the year 1943, when Shigemitsu became Foreign Minister, the policy of the conspirators to wage certain wars of aggression had been settled and was in course of execution. Thereafter there was no further formulation or development of that policy. . . .

Shigemitsu was fully aware that the Pacific war was a war of aggression, for he knew of the policies of the conspirators which had caused the war and had indeed often advised that they should not be put into effect. Nevertheless, he now played a principal part in waging the war until he resigned in April, 1945. . . .

In mitigation of sentence, we take into account that Shigemitsu was in no way involved in the formulation of conspiracy; that he waged no war of aggression until he became Foreign Minister in April 1943, by which time his country was deeply involved in a war which would virtually affect its future.

As George Furness, Shigemitsu's able Boston counsel, warned in his petition to MacArthur after sentence, and as Mr Justice Roling (Netherlands judge) also emphasized in his vigorous dissenting judgment, this ruling, with all its precedents and implications, makes it a crime for an advocate of peace to join a cabinet during a war in order, openly or covertly, to hasten the end of the war which he had failed, or been unable, to prevent.

A great mass of evidence, supported by voluntary testimony from British and United States leaders, was presented to the tribunal to establish that Shigemitsu unceasingly opposed the military plotting that led to Pearl Harbour, and that his influence as a member of the cabinet – which he joined at a time when it was apparent to every intelligent and informed Japanese that the war was lost – was devoted to ending the war. The prosecution made no attempt to contest this evidence, which the tribunal, as indicated above, in large measure accepted.

On the second, and major, issue of Shigemitsu's guilt for the mistreatment of war prisoners, the majority verdict of the tribunal is again quoted:

During the period from April 1943 to April 1945, when Shigemitsu was foreign Minister, the Protecting Powers transmitted to the

Japanese Foreign Office protest after protest which they had received from the Allies.

The matters of protest were (1) inhumane treatment of prisoners, (2) refusal to permit the Protecting Powers to inspect all save a few prisoners' camps, (3) refusal to permit the Protecting Powers to interview the prisoners without the presence of a Japanese witness, and (4) failure to provide information as to the names and locations of prisoners. . . .

Protest after protest went unanswered or was answered only after months of unexplained delay. Reminder after reminder by the Protecting Powers went unnoticed. Those protests which were answered were met without exception by a denial that there was anything to complain of.

Shigemitsu took no adequate steps to have the matters investigated although he, as a member of the government, bore overhead responsibility for the welfare of the prisoners. He should have pressed the matter if necessary to the point of resigning, in order to quit himself of a responsibility which he suspected was not being discharged.

In mitigation, we take into account that the military completely controlled Japan while he was Foreign Minister, so that it would have required great resolution for any Japanese to condemn them.

To this, the defence reply was that the Japanese Foreign Minister had no control over, or legal responsibility for, the treatment of prisoners of war. He lacked even 'the authority and faculty to probe and investigate', which powers, it was submitted, were essential for the assumption of the 'legal duty' that he was adjudged guilty of having 'deliberately and recklessly disregarded'. All responsibility for the treatment of war prisoners was, specifically and jealously, vested in the War and Navy ministries at top level, and in the local commanders, responsible only to their service chiefs, at field levels. There was no dispute that, on this point, there was admittedly deliberate – and, it might be said, reckless – disregard for strange Western parliamentarian notions of collective cabinet responsibility.

Further, with awesome inconsistency, the tribunal acquitted on an identical charge the prisoner, Shigenori Togo, who twice occupied the same position of Foreign Minister – at the beginning and end of the war.

During Togo's first term of office, many grievous complaints, including the historic charges on the Bataan death march, were lodged in Tokyo. These Togo duly transmitted while he was in office – in the same fashion as Shigemitsu – to the War Ministry, receiving that sole authority's official replies and transmitting them, without comment, as officially required, to the Protecting Powers.

The tribunal briefly recorded this procedure in finding Togo innocent of the 'deliberate and reckless disregard of duty', of which it so sternly adjudged Shigemitsu guilty on similar evidence.

In terms of Shigemitsu's conviction, Togo could really be said to have been morally twice as guilty as Shigemitsu, because he resumed the post of Foreign Minister after Shigemitsu eventually stepped down. Togo himself, who was sentenced to twenty years on other major charges, shrugged at his clearance on this charge. 'Either Shigemitsu and I were both guilty,' he said, 'or we were both innocent. At least, that is according to Eastern justice.'

(It is an open secret that, despite the bad blood between them, the reason why Shigemitsu refused to go into the witness box to defend himself was because he would thereby have incriminated Togo – and other defendants.)

The inconsistency of the tribunal's verdicts on this count was further stressed by the rejection of a similar charge against four other military prisoners – the service chiefs Akira Muto, Kenryo Sato, Takasumi Oka and Shigetaro Shimada, 'who,' Shigemitsu's counsel pointed out in his petition, 'had primary duties with regard to prisoners of war, who had knowledge, the means of knowledge and the duty to gain such knowledge, who had power, control and command, and yet who are found not guilty (of that charge), whereas the defendant, Shigemitsu, who had no such knowledge, nor means of knowledge, nor power to command or control, was found guilty.'

Actually, the evidence was on the record that Shigemitsu did go outside the official limits of his power as Foreign Minister: he privately but fruitlessly pressed his doubts about the treatment of prisoners of war, and his personal dissatisfaction with the War Ministry's replies, to General Tojo (then Prime Minister and Minister of War), to the Supreme Command for the Direction of the War, and finally to Marquis Kido (the Emperor's adviser).

Shigemitsu came out of Sugamo prison with no bitterness over conviction or sentence. His first request was to be driven to the

'Double Entrance' of the Imperial Palace, where he alighted and bowed deeply in reverence to the Emperor – hardly a prudent act in view of jealous military surveillance over his parole.

He had no home to go to. The day after the announcement of his impending release, his family villa, with most of his personal belongings, was burned to the ground in an anonymous gesture of Oriental warning and spite; the police never discovered whether the terrorist hands that destroyed his home belonged to old Japanese militarist foes or new Japanese communist foes.

He at once accepted the leadership of the then Japanese Progressive Party, a conservative party which was practically indistinguishable from the existing Liberal and Democratic Party. Unprecedentedly, therefore, a 'major war criminal' – 'purged forever' from public life – returned, serene and philosophic, to political power and party leadership in time for Japan's first independent election, and to the accompaniment of general applause from the Western nations which had so recently sat in implacable and unjust judgment on him. This was an astonishing *volte face*, even against the strange and shifting background of the Occupation, when deadly enemies mysteriously became devoted friends overnight; when Western policy was steered in a masterful if unavoidable full circle; and when General MacArthur ended up by scuttling the 'no-war' preamble to his own original Constitution and by directing the Japanese, in the Korean crisis, to by-pass his 'no-army-ever-again' decree by adopting a simple new title, 'the self-defence forces'.

I met Shigemitsu often after his release. He knew, of course, that I had been one of the several Western pressmen who had denounced his conviction and tried to hasten his release. He did not have the *gaucherie* to thank us directly – no true Japanese or Chinese would ever do that – but his welcome, his advice and his help were warm and unfailing. Nor did any of us ever hear him utter a word of criticism of the tribunal or its verdict.

Looking back on old notes, I discover that he was on the mark with most of his policies, opinions and forecasts. He thought that Japan's worst domestic troubles would come from the extreme left, rather than from a resurgent right: perhaps this becomes more debatable today. He insisted that Japan must re-arm: 'But we must have rice with guns. We need balanced self-defence, which means food and education and international co-operation as well as an army.'

Trade with China? Of course, 'but the question will not be whether Japan wants to trade, or should trade, with China, but whether China will want to trade with Japan – and on what terms and conditions. Japan and China, tragically, have never been able to understand each other.'

He predicted Japanese co-operation with Russia in the development of Siberia – a long shot in those days, but dead on the mark today.

And he believed that Japan's Occupation education system had been made 'too elaborate and over-Americanized; there is too much emphasis on university development, which will serve only a minority, and too little on basic education, essential for all.'

'But Japan has been very fortunate,' he summed up. 'In defeat we have found victory.'

Once, accompanying him as he painfully limped along on his old-fashioned wooden leg, I presumed to suggest that he could now buy a more comfortable artificial limb. He was shocked. 'I wouldn't dream of it,' he protested. 'The Emperor himself gave me this leg.'

But he put me gently in my place when I once hinted surprise at worship by intelligent Japanese of a 'divine' Emperor. 'The Emperor *divine*?' he repeated with a smile. 'What nonsense. He is our supreme ruler. I thought – forgive me – that only British *gaijin* like Colonel Piggott (former military *aide* at the pre-war British embassy) believed the Emperor to be the Son of Heaven.'

'BROKEN FRED' POSTSCRIPT

I later lunched with General Francis Piggott (as he had then become) and Lord Hankey in London. Both of them had, of course, championed Shigemitsu and sought vainly to secure his release. They were both sincere if ill-assorted defenders of Shigemitsu; Hankey, the old fashioned professional diplomat, with bulging forehead and the secrets of cabinets in his heart, and Piggott, the old fashioned professional soldier, with bristling moustache and (may he forgive me) memories of tea parties with the Emperor in his diary; but each animated alike by the same loyal indignation at the shameful spectacle of injustice being done to a friend, and having been seen to have been done.

Both were anxious for firsthand personal news of their old friend's welfare. I don't think they ever saw him again after his release, although they corresponded. I remember wondering whether, and how, I could craftily but politely introduce into the conversation Shigemitsu's good-humoured reference to Piggott's belief in the Emperor's divinity. But the General himself raised the matter. He told me he had written his reminiscences of his service in Tokyo, his close association with the Imperial family, his grief at the breach between 'two old allies and two royal families'. The title of his book?

'*Broken Fred,*' he replied, I foolishly thought.

'*Fred?*' I repeated, surprised, but with quickened respect and sympathy. 'But, excuse me, I thought your name was Frank. *Broken Frank?*'

'*Broken Thread!*' he corrected me menacingly, as Milord Hankey avoided my eye. 'T-H-R-E-A-D,' and added gruffly, 'No British army officer or diplomat would ever use his name – his Christian name – in the title of a book, frivolously or otherwise; any more' – he groped for another impossibility as analogy – 'any more than a Japanese army officer or diplomat would doubt the divinity of the Emperor.'

With rare restraint, I refrained from repeating this story to Shigemitsu when I saw him again, carrying greetings from Hankey and Piggott. Maybe Hankey told Shigemitsu in a letter. I hope he did: the anecdote would only have deepened Shigemitsu's affection for Piggott.

CHAPTER 12

The Mystery of the Flying Elephants

On 1 November 1944 the Imperial Japanese Army issued the strangest and most mysterious directive of the war to secret army headquarters in Chiba, Ibaraki and Fukushima prefectures (all on the east coast of Japan): 'At five o'clock tomorrow morning, you will launch the authorized attack, "Operation Flying Elephant", against North America.'

The directive was issued jointly by General Kimura, of the Imperial Army Armaments Division HQ, and General Shinoda, of the 9th Army Technical Research Institute. Simultaneously, a staff officer was sent first to the Imperial Palace to inform the Emperor, and then to the Ise Shrine to offer prayers for the success of the operation – the most curious project of the Pacific War, and one about which nothing has been officially written or admitted by either Japan or the United States.

Operation 'Flying Elephant', which many foreign correspondents tried vainly to investigate during the Occupation, is now virtually forgotten, but, as will be seen, it was a desperate effort by Japan to carry the war physically to the west coast of America. At the end of the war, all Japanese documents and records of the operation were destroyed, and the directors – shaven-head and egg-head – withdrew modestly into anonymity. Nor did the Occupation authorities – for some reason, or probably lack of reason – order a post mortem into the exercise, or aid any foreign pressman who initiated futile and frustrated inquiries in Tokyo.

Militarily, 'Operation Flying Elephant' was a white elephant – a bizarre and useless exercise in warfare by giant unmanned balloons, but one which involved intensive scientific effort, requisitioned every ounce of dry ice in Tokyo for six months and the entire season's crop of *konnyaku* (devil's-tongue root, which is an essential ingredient in *sukiyaki*), and mobilized all the rice-paper manufacturers in Japan, and literally several million high-school girls for the most prodigious glue-pasting enterprise in history. The operation – which the Americans imitated with plastic balloons in the USA in 1952 and 1953 and in Japan in 1956 – surely merited some sort of an official and authoritative review of aims and achievements.

The operation 'remained active' for six months (November 1944 – April 1945), during which period Japan launched more than 9,000 huge hydrogen balloons, carrying incendiary bombs, hopefully against the forest-mountain regions of the north-western USA, although any that did get across the Pacific could have landed anywhere on the North American continent, from Alaska to Mexico.

The originator of the Jules Verne-like project, it is now known, was Dr Sakuhei Fujiwara, eminent director of the Japanese Central Meteorological Observatory, who had rejected the contemporary theory that the jet stream was a seasonal wind over the Pacific, and was convinced that it was 'a current of air, with directional stability, whirling at high velocity around the globe during the winter months'.

At least, 'Operation Flying Elephant' – despite the complete and abiding blackout of its results – confirmed that Fujiwara theory. However, the good doctor, it is now claimed, was ashamed of the prostitution of his scientific research to belligerent and destructive ends; it is, indeed, alleged that he refused to participate in the exercise unless the windborne Japanese tokens of illwill to the United States were restricted to incendiary bombs, designed to cause only forest fires. The army generally – so it plausibly appears – wished first to despatch bacterial and germ weapons, and then delayed-action high explosives. (For the record, Dr Fujiwara's non-military assistants in the project were Dr Hidestugu Yagi, Dean of the Tokyo Institute of Technology, Dr Tatsuji Sakai and Dr Nasaichi Majima, of the Tokyo Imperial University Aeronautical Research Institute.)

At surrender, all these scientists, like the generals concerned, agreed that they had seen and heard nothing of any 'flying elephants'. It is a singular fact that, during the Occupation, they themselves certainly offered no information, and were evidently not asked – officially and openly – to give information. Nor did they, for their part, glean any facts about the results of their enterprise.

It had been conservatively estimated that, of the projected 10,000 balloon-bombs planned for the six month jet stream period, at least 3,000 would make a fiery landing, centring (it was expected) along the fortieth parallel and covering a front of approximately a thousand kilometres (north to south). The Japanese planners never discovered officially whether a single balloon hit the widespread target or caused any damage. They must have been the most frustrated – as well as the most silent – scientists in history.

If they were informed later – when the Americans conducted their similar experiments – no-one else was. Obviously the Californian papers would have carried stories of any strikes, but these reports never reached Japan at the time. Of course, no-one cared much about the matter after Potsdam, Hiroshima, Nagasaki and surrender. One allegedly factual news-story appeared in 'a Chinese newspaper', which I have never been able to trace, but which the Japanese collector of this information did transcribe: 'Informed sources' – that last refuge of a scoundrelly newspaperman – 'say that a large number of balloon-bombs descended on Montana in north-western USA, causing forest fires and killing or injuring several hundred people. . . .' It seems absurd, of course, that this report didn't filter outside the US except to China – American pressmen deride it today – but it also seems improbable that all the rather pathetic home-made balloons could have been completely right in theory, but completely off-target in practice.

Shortly after the first balloons were released, US short-wave radio reports of weather conditions over the Pacific abruptly ceased.

Here, now, is the only connected story I have seen of this remote, baffling, baffled and macabre project. The facts were patiently gathered by Mitsutoshi Kondo, a tough, amiable economist-newsman, with a pilot's licence, who left the *Asahi*, Japan's leading newspaper, to work for the Japanese automobile genius, Honda. Kondo-*san* undertook the investigation in 1964 and 1965 for Torao Saito, then editor-in-chief of *This Is Japan*, and I had the honour of knocking his thorough and objective documentation into 2,000-word English shape for the now-defunct annual. The story is not mine; I wish it were; it is

Kondo-*san*'s; it is still full of queries and gaps; but it is the only attempt at a detailed record of this strange, silent campaign – so characteristic of makeshift but formidable Japanese ingenuity in any emergency.

Early in the war, despite his proclaimed scientific bias, Dr Fujiwara revealed his interest in winds and balloon flights – and also his Japanese chauvinism – in the introduction which he wrote for a Japanese edition of Professor Piccard's *Into The Stratosphere*:

In order to avoid falling behind the European bloc and the Americans at this time of war in Greater East Asia, we Japanese, as leaders of the various Asian peoples, must find ways and means of extending our frontiers into the stratosphere, to the North and South Poles, to the bottom of the sea, and possibly the very centre of the earth itself. Professor Piccard's account of his balloon ascent should make us painfully ashamed of our complacency up to this point. If we do fall behind, we shall no longer be able to lay the blame at the feet of our capitalists. The responsibility will lie with the government and people alike, with administrators and technicians.

Research on the balloon project, after Dr Fujiwara's sensitivities had been placated by a diversion from high explosive to arson, was undoubtedly influenced by Piccard's account of his ascents to the stratosphere in a sealed gondola in the thirties. Each 'Flying Elephant' balloon, with contents, weighed 182 kilograms: balloon and chassis, 52; flight apparatus, 25; sand ballast, 70; incendiary bomb, 35. So the total load to be carried across the Pacific by 10,000 balloons weighed 1,800 tons.

The balloons were caught in the jet stream at 10,000 metres, and then were projected eastward at 200 kilometres an hour, drifting slightly to the north, with the expectation of reaching, and setting fire to, the United States in approximately two days and two nights. Because the temperature fell to around 55° below zero at 10,000 metres, intense metal-testing was needed: hence the disappearance of all dry ice in Tokyo during the hot summer.

The balloons were inflated with 300 cubic metres of hydrogen – more than half their total capacity. Lifting power at sea level was 300 kilograms. The balloons swelled to total capacity at 4,500 metres, and floated to the 10,000-metre level in forty minutes. The timing mechanisms on the bomb-releases were set at three or four days, according to weather conditions, and began ticking a few minutes before zero hour for each launching.

The Americans used plush plastic balloons for their similar experiment from Japan a decade later, but the Japanese, typically, found that they could use their own ricepaper and even adapt vegetables for manufacture of their balloons. The devil's-tongue root (*konnyaku*) – tourists munch it doubtfully, or avoid it, in the beef and vegetables of *sukiyaki* – is endowed with a variety of cellulose, which, it is entertaining if fanciful to suggest, Dr Fujiwara, pensively chewing one night, suddenly reckoned would make excellent glue. It did at that – under the proper name of *mannan*.

This edible glue was proven to be far superior to other oils or fats, or synthetic rubber, or rubberized cloth in pasting together the long strips of stout ricepaper – six hundred to each balloon. Six million strips of ricepaper were needed for the 10,000 balloons, and a single worker could seal, at the most, four or five strips together in a day. Hence the recruitment of the hordes of high school girls.

Kondo-*san* interviewed some of the technicians who launched the balloons. At the outset, the launchings took place at early dawn. It was, appropriately, a near-noiseless operation, in which the harsh crinkling of the ricepaper under inflation could be heard, and then the huge balloons, in eerie procession, arose slowly and silently and soared away into the morning mists. Later there were launchings after sunset under floodlights.

'It didn't seem real,' one technician recalled. 'We were all silent as we worked, and then stepped back and watched. There was no cheering, no demonstrations. You had the feeling that it was a dream, or that you were watching the opening of a festival, and wondered why the balloons weren't gaily coloured and trailing pennants, and why the fireworks weren't being exploded, and why there wasn't a cheering crowd.'

In all, 9,300 'Flying Elephants' were unleashed: November (1944), 700; December, 1,200; January (1945), 2,000; February, 2,500; March, 2,500; April, 400.

To repeat: to this day, no one in Japan knows what percentage of the balloons completed the crossing; where, if at all, they came down in America; or the extent of any damage they may have caused.

(It is known that, of the twenty large plastic balloons of the same type which the US Navy launched from Oppama base in Japan, sixteen, radar-tracked, stayed in the air for eighty hours, covering an average distance of 11,263 kilometres at a speed of 160 kilometres an hour. Half-a-dozen crossed not only the Pacific but also the United States and the Atlantic and came to roost in Spain. One or two attained speeds of 450 kilometres an hour.)

Reflectively, if the Japanese had at that time managed to develop a 'Fat Boy', they could not of course have been sure of delivering it on target by plane, but they could have put it in one of the 'Flying Elephant' baskets – and let the jet wind carry it where it listed.

Today balloons belong to Jules Verne. ICBM's are dead on target. If Japan hasn't got *those* in five years' time, I, for one, will drink a tankard of that Japanese glue.

PART III

Moscow-Siberian Interlude

CHAPTER 13

The Finding of Burgess and Maclean

Ian Fleming, who was my immediate boss as Foreign Manager of *The Sunday Times*, decided that we should mount a hit-and-run sally into Russia at the end of 1955. The Twentieth Congress was set for the New Year, and 'insiders' were tipping – correctly enough – that Khrushchev would at last openly begin to cut Stalin down to size. The new Soviet variety show of Bulganin and Khrushchev had just shyly opened its road tours, and, after happy appearances to cheering audiences in India and Burma, expected packed houses in England. Fleming reckoned that K was ripe for his first exclusive press interview and this, he naturally assumed, would be the right and prerogative of *The Sunday Times*.

I happened to be in London, winding up my biennial leave before returning to the Far East, with new headquarters in Hong Kong and a first visit to Peking in the offing. So I was lucky enough to land the Moscow assignment – which failed miserably in its primary objective of netting Khrushchev, but fortuitously flushed out the two missing diplomats, Burgess and Maclean, in literally the last twenty-four hours of play.

Of course *The Sunday Times* didn't have the idea on its own. A mob of 'specials' were hammering at Moscow's embassy doors, besieging the press section of the Soviet Foreign Ministry, trying to scratch an aside or two from party brass at the usual dull cocktail parties. There was, as always, a tough, able, efficient, resigned and frustrated world press corps resident in Moscow, tolerating and helping the intrusive invasion for the Twentieth Congress. Each agency and bureau chief, like each 'special', was also chasing after interviews with the top comrades. But, for a variety of obscure reasons, which favour a visiting 'special' and which the resident correspondent everywhere learns to accept with a shrug, it is seldom the local expert who gets the break. He tends perforce to work in expedient union with his rival counterparts for the mass press interview. The 'special', usually smug, arrogant and spoiled, demands an 'exclusive' wherever he goes.

Theoretically, the Moscow news stage in December 1955 favoured English newspapers because of the preoccupation of B and K with their projected English visit, and, one would imagine, their attempts to improve public relations and encourage favourable press notices and posters before their variety show hit the rolling English road. In retrospect, it is quite apparent that they and their advisers had completely and stupidly neglected this elementary preparation.

I had never been to Moscow. I had never been so cold. No-one can really begin to understand the incredible Russians until he has reeled, blue and numbed, before the icicled blasts from Siberia. (Remember Churchill's remark in 1942, when, driving through a heavy snowfall in the Red Square, he glimpsed through the sealed windows of his heated limousine a long black line of wrapped and muffled Muscovites, erect and patient outside a general store. 'It is the ice cream ration,' he was told. 'God help the poor nazis,' whispered Churchill with frozen tears on his lashes.)

The Soviet customs reception – then conducted during a stopover at a Leningrad airfield – was warm enough, although enigmatic at the outset.

'Mr Hoojis, do you have any of the fruits in your luggage?' the tall, handsome Soviet official asked me.

'Fruit?' I repeated, puzzled.

'Yes, the fruits.' He became more explicit. 'Perhaps the apple, the banana, the pomegranate, the grape, the coconut? No?'

'No, no,' I was relieved. 'No fruit at all. But,' I produced my luggage keys, 'I have six large bottles of Scotch whisky in this smaller suitcase.'

'It is possible,' he responded.

I hastened to assure him that it was a fact. I was not to be betrayed into any trouble with the communist customs authorities on arrival. Had I not left all books, diaries and personal papers behind in London? Was not my transparently honest valise stuffed with good, sound, instructive official literature from the Soviet bookstore in London? 'Six bottles. Large bottles,' I repeated doggedly.

'I mean, Mr Hoojis, that it is possible for you to carry the

Scotch whisky into the Soviet Union,' the official explained with
a polite bow. 'There is not the duty charge on the foreign whisky
or the Western alcoholic beverages. Please not to worry about
opening the luggage. There is no necessity.' He made the usual
mysterious chalk markings on my trunk, suitcase, valise and
typewriter. 'Please to understand that there will now be no delay
on arrival in Moscow, where we hope you will have most
enjoyable stay of residence. *Spasebo* (thank you), Mr Hoojis.'

A smooth and cunning devil, I thought. Obviously they had
ratted my luggage, using skeleton keys, before it was brought
into the inspection hall.

An elderly, hunchbacked dwarf, with a crabapple face and the
shoulders of a giant, emerged to carry off my bags. He swung up
the case which sustained my reserves of prophylactic whisky. One
hasp of the slender handle parted under the weight. He averted
catastrophe and negotiated a forced landing for the maimed case
on the bench. I tried vainly to force the hasp into place with
anxious fingers. The small man waved me aside, stooped, applied
his stainless-steel teeth skilfully to the fracture and literally bit
the parted halves back into place.

The customs official escorted me – the only foreigner in the
Helsinki–Moscow plane – to the dining-room.

'You like to drink the Scotch whisky; no, Mr Hoojis?' he
inquired as we walked down a panelled hall on which hung the
fourth portrait of Stalin I had seen in a quarter of an hour at the
airport. It seemed a safe admission to make. I said yes, explaining
hastily that my import store was no indication of extreme
intemperance but merely prudent precaution against an understood shortage of Scotch in the Soviet Union.

'Yes, Mr Hoojis. Here in Soviet, as perhaps you have heard, we
like to drink the vodka. This we make ourselves – not have to
buy from other countries, you understand. It is, we find, an
encouraging and comforting drink. I hope you will learn to like
it after you finish the whisky – maybe next week. It contributes to
friendship.'

He stole a sidelong glance at me. He appeared to have something on his mind. He decided to speak in low, earnest, almost
conspiratorial tones: 'Mr Hoojis. I must make the explanation
about the luggage. Perhaps you did not understand. It is necessary
for Soviet Union to take the precautions.'

Ha, I thought, here it comes: a brazen confession that my luggage was searched surreptitiously. But why tell me? I was on my guard – although nonchalant and at ease.

'It is about the fruits, Mr Hoojis,' he continued, still speaking as one imparting a party secret. 'We cannot allow the fruits and the vegetables and other agricultural products to enter Soviet Union without what we call the quarantine inspection. Sometimes the disease may be spread – the fungi, the worms, the blight, the rash, the rust, the plant sickness and so forth. You understand? Comrade Lysenko, our great scientist, has explained all this in most informative books. We must ask everyone the question, therefore, about the fruits.

'And Mr Hoojis. Also, as you will quickly understand, we must be most careful about the reindeer horns. But this question I did not need to inquire of you. I can now tell at first glance' – he was assured but not boastful – 'the man who may have the reindeer horns hidden in the luggage. Not you, Mr Hoojis.'

It was, after all, a compliment. Relaxed if a little mystified, I devoured heartily a huge serving of excellent bortsch, a reasonable steak with salad and black bread and a raspberry jelly. When it was discovered that I had no roubles but only travellers' cheques and so could not finance alcoholic lubrication, the customs official pressed upon me a hospitable carafe of vodka – a normal pour of three liqueur glasses. He smiled approval when I disposed of each glass in one gulp.

'*Do adno*, we Russians say, Mr Hoojis,' he explained. 'It is same as your Western "up bottoms".'

We had flown from Helsinki over a sub-arctic wilderness in which it was difficult to distinguish iced sea from snowy shore. The sun was livid. There was no sign or evidence of Leningrad itself on the horizon of lonely landscape. Three or four narrow roads, flanked by tilted telegraph poles, ran, straight and empty, to nowhere.

Our plane was a Soviet version of the DC3. There were no frills, no decadent safety-belts, no hostesses. But the plane left Helsinki on time, arrived in Leningrad on the dot, left on time and arrived in Moscow on the dot. I gained a grudging impression of hard routine efficiency.

There were half-a-dozen other passengers – three men and three young women, who, the customs official told me with a primly apologetic air, were 'entertainers' returning to Moscow after a series of shows in Finland. They were gay and gregarious – although one sensitive woman suffered all the symptoms of heart seizure or apoplexy each time the plane took off or landed. I had eyed them with some trepidation as I boarded the plane at Helsinki, preoccupied as I was with KGB tails, *agents provocateurs* and secret police. Even in suspicion, however, I was driven to the conclusion that the KGB was employing a different kind of agent than the ones I had been warned about in London.

One of the men – a sturdy, amiable fellow, who wore his hat turned up in front like a press photographer – began to play a lively tune on a flute, apparently in a well-considered attempt to soothe the unhappy airsick girl when we took off from Leningrad. Standing in the aisle, he bent solicitously over her and tried to induce her to synchronize her flailing arms, as she distractedly beat the air, with the dancing flute tune. It was an animated scene. She did, indeed, appear to have a quicker recovery and, when the plane had levelled off at 8,000 feet, she embraced and kissed him with a grateful vigour that brought cheers from the other two couples, who then proceeded to dance in the aisle to the lilting flute.

I felt – as I was so often to feel during my three months in Moscow – constrained, inhibited, awkward, slightly pompous. I affected to whistle. One of the men approached me and offered me a cigarette. When I had made it clear that I spoke no Russian and he had made it clear that he spoke no English, he inquired: 'Deutsch?'

The question, as always, annoyed me. Because of a stockiness in build and a certain lack of cultural asceticism in appearance, I seem doomed to go through life in foreign countries being mistaken for a German. I was moved to an emphatic denial. 'Deutsch? *Nyet, nyet*!' I replied angrily, drawing my hand across my throat. 'I am Australian.'

The Russian, a large man with hot eyes and granite features, was delighted. He shook hands with me warmly and retailed the dialogue to his companions, mimicking my gesture with theatrical enthusiasm. Everyone beamed at me. The flautist removed his hat, bowed, put his hat on back to front, and said: 'I speak little English. Welcome to Russia.' He made a spirited attempt to play the opening bars of *God Save The Queen*.

The third man produced a flask of vodka. One of the women handed me some Made-in-Finland imitations of familiar Japanese children's puzzles and trick gadgets, which I civilly pretended I could not solve or manipulate. The man with the turned-up hat played Russian folksongs.

Suddenly we were dipping and swinging over Moscow – scattered lights, spread widely but far dimmer than the coruscations of Paris or London or Los Angeles. My companions pressed their noses excitedly against the windows. I managed to transmit a basic-English question to the flautist. 'How long since we leave Moscow?' he repeated. 'Why – one, two, four – no, three weeks. It is,' he shook his head, 'too long.' He resumed the flute to compose the girl who, under the pressure of descent, was once more behaving like a diver attacked by the bends.

I had another 'Mr Hoojis' greeting from an Intourist official in the snow and icy cold of Moscow. The waiting room for foreign visitors boasted heavy leather divans and armchairs, velvet curtains, an ornate chandelier and a musty, mid-Victorian atmosphere. Another heroic painting of Stalin, surveying rolling agricultural lands and a hydro-electric installation, covered most of one wall. There were half-a-dozen other warmly muffled passengers waiting – all, significantly, Asian.

I was escorted to an impressive black limousine. My friends, the 'entertainers', were seated in an exterior and cheerless waiting-room. We all shook hands. The flautist, who had greeted my reappearance by sounding a tucket, played a marching tune as I walked out – to the lively interest of other waiting local travellers. The man with the granite face drew his hand reminiscently across his throat and nodded in grim approval. The girl with the trick gadgets gave me a small squeaking rubber doll as a parting gift. I had the feeling, as I waved goodbye, that the KGB had not yet caught up with me.

I was installed in the Hotel National, the oldest and still the best pub for visitors in Moscow, a rambling, Tsarist survival, from whose balcony Lenin harangued the populace. It stands on the corner of spacious Gorky Street and Hunters Row, facing the Kremlin, with its 65-foot crenellated red walls, its soaring towers, its floodlit turrets and domes, and its five one-ton, ruby-red stars floating against the clouds.

The entrance lobby was crowded into a corner and slap-up

against the lift doors by an expansionist newspaper kiosk, and was dominated by two huge plaster statues of naked youths, decorously protected by light robes in a providential wind. A well-proportioned raven beauty, wearing a tight sweater and speaking excellent English (except for the universal mispronunciation of my name), told me with a flashing smile that Room 123, the Persian Suite, was ready and waiting for me. 'Please let me know, Mr Hoojis,' she said, leaning forward almost invitingly, 'if there is anything you need.' I rolled my eyes nervously. At the head of the stairs and just outside the ancient lift, where a stout, blonde, bejewelled Tolstoyan concierge presided over the floor-keys, was the closed door of Room 101 – the one hotel room in the world which I shall never forget.

The Persian Suite was warm and comfortable, with chandelier, large windows overlooking Gorky Street, an executive-size glass-topped table, late Victorian lampshades, two tables, two divans, an imposing oil painting of what appeared to be the road to Siberia, and a curious six-foot cupboard with handsome tapestried representation of a non-party Persian maiden resting beside a well with a red flower pot on her head. The canopied double bed was in a curtained alcove. The plumbing in the bathroom, sealed off by a door stout enough to resist a cavalry charge, was impeccable. I could detect no signs of the secret wiring which, I had been assured, was a free-service feature of all foreigners' suites in the National.

'Steady the Buffs!' I cried in a clear voice, as a first enigmatic message for the wire recording, and proceeded to unload my six large bottles of Scotch into one side of the Persian tapestry cupboard.

Here I was to live for seventy-two days – first expectant, then anxious, finally desperate, until the showdown. Towards the end, waiting for the phone calls that never came, I was reluctant to leave the room for even an hour lest I miss an on the spot appointment. As it worked out, I was absent when the decisive Molotov call came, and I had to be phoned twice to attend the Burgess–Maclean meeting in Room 101 while I was packing to leave.

I had a minor but instructive personal adventure as I went to the dining room for my first meal in the National. On the dark landing, a man in overcoat and furred cap turned sharply and seized me by the arm as we passed each other. 'Hughes-*san*!' he cried happily. 'When on earth did you get to Moscow?'

I shared his delight. It was my old friend Slitzinski (shall we say?), a Russian correspondent whom I had known well in distant Tokyo during the more distant days of the Occupation. I told him I expected to be in Moscow for at least a month, maybe two. I asked eagerly after Yodanzsky and Egoroff and Kiseleff and Mihailovitch – all good drinking friends, human and generous correspondents, in the old Press Club in Tokyo. The recollection of their faces and happy memories made me suddenly feel at home. They were all in Moscow, he assured me. I besought him to tell them that I had arrived. How we had all sworn in Tokyo to drink together, if and when I ever followed them to Moscow! My room was 123. I expected them all. The sooner the better.

Slitzinski laughed in agreement. He excused himself from a drink at that moment. He had work to do. He shook my hand again with both of his. 'One two three. An easy number to remember,' he said. 'But we won't need the room number to find you.' He left me with a gay flourish and ran downstairs.

I don't doubt that Slitzinski was glad to see me. He had instinctively approached me, after all, as I passed him, unrecognizing. I don't doubt that personally he would have been glad to see me again. But, during my three months in Moscow, I never heard from him. Or from any of my old Soviet friends of Tokyo. I did see him twice from a distance at press conferences. He waved sheepishly but did not approach me. My Western press colleagues, amused by my naïvety, warned me against any further advances – to him or my other friends. Maybe I should have tried harder. But I guess not. A pity.

Otherwise I got off, superficially, to a flying start. Leonid Ilyichev, the Stalinist chief of the press section at the Foreign Office, a cold, grinning gnome, who had twelve – I counted them twice – telephones on a side-desk, received me within two days: 'unprecedented,' said Irv Levine of National Broadcasting. Ilyichev listened attentively to my confidence-man talk, and, while I waited, arranged by phone an interview with a Khrushchev secretarial sidekick in a private dining room at the plush Praga restaurant for the next evening. That meeting also passed off satisfactorily, and, under encouraging instructions, I submitted

next day a lengthy and laboriously polished outline of my projected interview with the great man.

Fleming had suggested a Bondian formula: when I had made a
satisfactory contact, I was to request him in a filial cable to 'assure
my mother that I was in *adjectival* health' – the adjective to reflect
in degree my realistic evaluation of the contact. With bowed head,
I recall that my message to my dear mother rated my health as
'buoyant'.

Because that was the end.

Six weeks of frustrating silence passed ponderously by. There
was plenty of routine reportage. The Twentieth Congress met in
the Kremlin in dutiful revolt against the past and with well
organized 'stormy applause' for the future. Khrushchev brandished his new broom with pledges of crusading reforms. It was
a 'Back-to-Lenin' movement. Bulganin beamed behind him.
Molotov and the other old Stalinists had been thrust into the rear
row on the dais. Word spread that the embalmed corpse of Stalin
would soon be dragged, like a condemned exhibit of rotting meat,
from the snug double bed which he shared with the late Lenin in
the Red Square mausoleum, both comfortably on their backs,
chastely tucked in together.

For the new boy with a new dateline, there are always stories,
well covered and re-covered by the resident correspondents of
course, but invested with a spurious freshness because the fly-by-
night 'special' byliner hasn't previously written them. There were
hospitable embassies who welcomed arrivals with grapevine
gossip. There was the excitement of actually living in Moscow.
There were always front seats at the Bolshoi for visitors; I saw
Swan Lake ten times.

But there was no move, no stir, no hint, no whisper, no rustle of
action on the main front. Comrade Ilyichev never answered calls on
any of his twelve phones, or acknowledged polite, plaintive, hand-
delivered *aides-mémoire*. K's sidekick could have been in a Siberian
saltmine. Fleming's cables began to carry undertones of urgency.

I fretted in my Persian Suite, on heat for the calls that never
came, freezing bottles of beer between the double window-panes,
forlornly surveying the snowy tumult of Gorky Street. I began to
recognize, and wait for, the faces of strangers as they plodded
daily up and down the iced pavements. There was, I still remember, the gay, brave war veteran without legs, squatting on a

wheeled trolley like Porgy and prodding himself forward on two short sticks, who manœuvred himself through the rushing lines of traffic every morning punctually at eight o'clock, to grab hold at last of the rear bumper of a packed trolley-bus; up the steep hill he would go in a flurry of snow and exhaust-smoke, clinging to the bus with one strong hand and brandishing the other triumphantly in the air. I made friends, at a distance, with the large, grinning cop on duty at the roaring intersection of Gorky Street and Hunters Row, who had noted my lonely vigil at the window; we would exchange waves; sometimes in the early morning I would lift a vodka bottle and pretend to pour it into a glass, and he would look at his watch and shake his head forbiddingly, and then I would substitute a teapot, and he would grin and give me a permissive wave-on.

My anxiety infected the raven beauty and the stout concierge: they watched with eager sympathy as I tore open messages when I hurried back expectantly from minor missions, and shook their heads and sighed to share my invariable disappointment.

Then Graham Stanford, brilliant roving 'special' for the *News of the World* and an old friend from 8th Army days, arrived on the same interview mission. He got Lenin's old sumptuous suite down the corridor, with two entrances and a grand piano. But he never got to see Ilyichev. Of course, I knew smugly that if *The Sunday Times* had difficulties, the *News of the World* wasn't in the race for a Khrushchev 'exclusive'. The commies might be slow and stupid, but they weren't crazy.

Irv Levine, Sydney Weiland of Reuters, Welles Hangen, Dick O'Malley, Henry Shapiro, Roy Essoyan and other resident correspondents had all agreed by this time that neither Bulganin nor Khrushchev would give an exclusive interview. But they did expect a mass press conference before the departure for London.

As always, correspondents' talk, whenever we gathered, reverted to Guy Burgess and Donald Maclean, the wretched British diplomats, who, warned by the arch-traitor Philby, had vanished from England on the night of 25 May 1951. The disappearance and fate of these renegades had haunted the British public for five years. When I first arrived in London at the end of my leave in November, the whole scandal had been revived by a White Paper, and by Prime Minister Macmillan's warm rebuttal of scurrilous suggestions that the still lilywhite Kim Philby had been 'the third

man' who tipped off Burgess and Maclean to take it on the lam,
pronto. I had become slightly weary of the jest in London while
I was waiting for my Moscow visa: 'Be sure to bring Burgess and
Maclean home with you.' Even Editor Harry Hodson of *The
Sunday Times* said to me wistfully: 'And of course the jackpot
would be sight or smell of Burgess and Maclean.' Milord Kemsley,
then proprietor of *The Sunday Times*, himself remarked: 'I don't
have to tell you that someone has got to see those two scoundrels
eventually.'

In Moscow, the residential press corps had become understandably fed up with the wild recurrent rumours about the
missing pair. There was a dreary cliché in response to the query
'Anything doing?' – 'No, nothing special; only two persistent
sons of bitches, called Burgess or Maclean or something, who
keep phoning me to take them to lunch.' In the month before I
arrived, an ambassadorial wife swore that she had seen them at the
Bolshoi in a discreetly curtained box. 'Intelligence' whispers had
located them in Warsaw and Prague, reported that they were
playing chess in Lubiyanka prison, or related eyewitness accounts
of their execution in Siberia. Real 'insiders' knew that Burgess was
in charge of all communist propaganda broadcasts from Eastern
Europe; the skilled sub-editorial hand and FO experience of
Maclean was plain to see in the improved and craftier style and
argument of international communiqués from the Kremlin. One
visiting London presswoman got front-page play for a brave
report that she had seen two blond boys in a Zis limousine 'who
might have been the sons of Maclean'.

(Maclean's redoubtable wife, Miranda, had managed to steal
across the Swiss border to Russia, bringing their two children
with her. She became the consort of Philby, who, fleeing to
Moscow in 1963 and, having no country there to betray, instinctively betrayed his last friend and stole his wife.)

Ian Fleming's cable on 24 January – reminiscent of an abrupt
recall by 'M' of a defeated Bond – wound up my lost mission:
'Your coverage appreciated but Chairman decides you should
unfailingly return after further two Sundays since primary object
your assignment appears unattainable. Perhaps this decision will
hasten results. Best luck.' I replied meekly and hurled another
memo at the silent Ilyichev – had I indeed been so warmly

welcomed by him only six weeks before? – whimpering that 'continued lack of response over the next twelve days must necessarily be interpreted as refusal'.

Graham Stanford, also suffering 'hope-you-understand' reproaches from his office, had finally aimed an emotional telegram at Khrushchev personally: 'From the bottom of my heart I believe sincerely that your message to Britain's largest newspaper circulation etcetera, etcetera.' Then he left philosophically for Leningrad at the weekend. We cursed Soviet bureaucracy at a farewell dinner in the Praga, where our mutual despondency was partly lightened by the spectacle of a drunken and offensive citizen being half-rolled by impassive waiters at the dining-room door, and then full-rolled down the curving stairway to the double glass doors, which an alert attendant, springing obligingly forward, flung open to usher him, somersaulting, into the snow and mud outside. Graham and I agreed that it was the most dramatic and best co-ordinated bouncing we had ever witnessed.

But the real action was just around the corner. Now the roof came off the National. Early on 25 January (the day after Fleming's recall instruction), Graham, hustled back from Leningrad by a Kremlin telegram and the midnight train, was beating on the door of the Persian Suite with both hands. 'My God, your grace,' he cried, 'I think I've got it!' He had. Khrushchev had decided to give his first-ever exclusive interview to the *News of the World*. It ran triumphantly on Sunday, the 29th.

I had two hopeless weeks of sackcloth and ashes left. Fleming mercifully forbore from comment on Graham's well-won victory. I cabled on Tuesday: 'As directed I will retreat from Moscow Sunday 12 February. Despondent regards.' On Thursday, I plodded to the bank at 2 pm to collect a last remittance; I returned to 123 at 3 pm; the Foreign Office had phoned: I called back: Foreign Minister Molotov, whom I had at no time sought to see, would be 'happy to grant my application and meet me at noon on Saturday, February 4'.

A Molotov might not be as wide as a Bulganin or as deep as a Khrushchev, but he would suffice. I cabled Fleming, who replied with congratulations. At least Molotov would be a Sunday front page lead. . . . Which started some rather obvious reflection. Could I use the Molotov interview for another go at Khrushchev? No; even if successful, that would be only a limping follow-up to

Graham Stanford's *coup*. Bulganin would be anti-climactic. But, wait: Burgess and Maclean? Why not? A hundred-to-one shot, of course. But it would do no harm, and the top-level attempt, even futile, would still make a story of sorts in London, perhaps as the lead to a wound-licking round-up of all the Moscow scuttlebutt about the pair.

So, in the upshot, I drafted the memorandum for Bulganin and Khrushchev, via Molotov, before I drafted questions for the Molotov interview. I recalled that, only two weeks earlier, Khrushchev, on two separate occasions, had blandly but firmly denied that he knew anything about either of the two missing diplomats. I decided, after the run-around I had suffered, that politeness was a decadent bourgeois weakness, and that the blunter my representations the greater my chance of a response. I had a cup of vodka and let my head go:

FOR PRESIDENT BULGANIN AND PRIME MINISTER KHRUSHCHEV – This memorandum is intended for your eyes because the points which it raises will virtually affect the success of your impending visit to England.

I would strongly urge you to abandon at once your protracted, futile and absurd policy of silence about the two British defectors, Donald Maclean and Guy Burgess.

In your meetings with the British press, you will constantly be subjected to questions about these two men. Reports are now circulating in Fleet Street that they are dead or in a Russian prison. You must recognize that the monstrous nonsense of this 'we do not know' formula will utterly discredit your mission, and raise doubts of the sincerity of all friendly overtures and speeches which you may make in the United Kingdom. You will not be amused by the manner in which London newspaper cartoonists will ridicule you.

Mr Khrushchev's continued line of foolish denial makes it clear that your so-called advisers are completely ignorant of the deep and abiding British public interest in the Maclean-Burgess mystery, into which the British Government is now conducting yet another Select Committee inquiry.

You would be wise to produce Burgess and Maclean with some sort of agreed explanation of their actions before you leave Moscow.

I do not see that there is any real problem in the fact that until now the Soviet Government has chosen to deny that it knows anything of the two men. It could be expected that a friendly government which gave sanctuary to aliens in difficulty would also respect their expressed wish at the outset that no statement be made of their presence and activities until and unless they so desired. In view of changed circumstances – apart from your own immediate and vital self-interest – that original attitude by Maclean and Burgess, which the Soviet has so scrupulously respected, might well have changed also.

'I confess cheerfully that I myself have the most selfish interest as a working British newspaperman in recommending release of this story while I am in Moscow. If you decide to accept my advice, I naturally expect you to give me the benefit of the story. This bargain is implicit in my recommendation. I leave Moscow on Sunday week, 12th. If you agree, Maclean and Burgess should make their appearance on Saturday, February 11, and the deadline that day for my newspaper, *The Sunday Times*, should be, say, 5 pm.'

Foreign Minister Molotov – then on the skids, as he well knew – was affable, relaxed and forthcoming at our noon meeting, which lasted for nearly an hour and a half, and which was the last press interview he ever gave. Only his interpreter was present when we sat down, facing each other, at a long side table in the lofty, panelled and mirrored office, under the inevitable gaze of a life-sized Stalin portrait behind Molotov's huge desk, stacked with files.

He opened with a few conversational remarks: 'I lead a very normal life, Mr Hughes. I get up at a normal hour. I do a normal day's work. I go to bed at a normal hour. We Soviet communists are really quite normal people.'

His news lead, tied of course to the coming B–and–K visit to London, was a call for more face-to-face conferences between heads of state, and for treaties of friendship between the Soviet and the United Kingdom, Britain and France. A few of his points – after fifteen long years – still make interesting reading today:

The Soviet Union, China and the people's democracies of Eastern Europe remain the firmest, most trusting and dependable allies and partners in any undertakings.

There are different kinds of Germans. The East Germans are trustworthy and peace-loving and militaristic elements have no substantial influence there. . . . (But) ex-nazis, revenge-seekers and militarists hold economic and political power in West Germany.

We must continue to work for the peaceful reunification of East and West Germany.

The effect of the sale of arms by Czechoslovakia to Egypt has been greatly exaggerated in an attempt to place responsibility for the troubled situation in the Middle East on the Soviet Union.

(Dryly satirical) We are moved by the solicitude of President Eisenhower and Sir Anthony Eden (the Washington Declaration) in the welfare of the Soviet people, but evidently they have not acquainted themselves with details of our sixth Five Year Plan, which provides for an increase in production by sixty-five percent, a twofold increase in major agricultural products, an increase in real wages for all workers by thirty percent, and in living standards of collective farm workers by forty percent. I have not read of any similar plan of improvement by either the United States or Britain. (The failure of this Five Year Plan helped to erode Khrushchev's position.)

Our peace negotiations with Japan have dragged on far too long. They will be concluded within a year. (They still haven't been settled.)

I managed to get a Molotov *'nyet'* to round off the interview ('Are you ever pessimistic, Mr Molotov?'); and then, as we rose, I handed him the Maclean–Burgess memorandum, asking him to read it before delivering it to Bulganin and Khrushchev. He showed no surprise but passed it to the interpreter. I did not mention its contents, but told him that I regarded it as urgent and important and hoped that he would agree with me. My last glimpse of Molotov, as I turned to close the door behind me, was a reflection in one of the mirrors. He was leaning against his desk, still standing and donning his spectacles, and the handsome young interpreter had begun to read the memorandum to him.

I went straight to the Gorky Street cable office, typed the interview and passed over eight takes in customary triplicate (one copy for transmission, one for the censor's file, one for return later to the sender, showing cuts if any).

End of mission, I thought with a shrug. Overall, a flop. Nothing more to be done. I never seriously expected any response. But even the faintest hope can lurk, if not spring. I stayed in 123 all the week, scratching out some dull feature stories, and groaning in self-pity over an appropriate *da-svee-dahn-ya* ('good-bye') gift in the shape of a sudden tooth abscess, which began to bloat my right cheek to the size of a cricket ball. This damned kiss-off, I decided, could wait until Stockholm on Sunday night, or London on Monday afternoon.

Saturday morning arrived without dawn, but with steady snow. The phone, of course, was silent. At 3 pm I knew it was all over. I began to finish off a last bottle of vodka. By 5 pm – that absurd deadline! – I was not completely sober. I started to pack. I would have a late dinner, a farewell drink with Irv Levine (returning from London that night) in his Room 103, then early to bed. I was booked on the Sunday afternoon plane for Stockholm.

At 7.30 the phone rang. 'Mr Hoojis, can you please come around to Room 101?' A farewell drink, I realized, with the manager, a civil fellow. There was a television set in Room 101 for hotel guests. Who wanted another drink there? I kept on packing sullenly. The phone rang again: 'Mr Hoojis' – a touch of impatience – 'please come now. Urgent.'

The door of Room 101 was closed. I entered to find the television set in a corner and five men sitting at a white-clothed table, surrounded by late Victorian bric-à-brac, a marble clock above the fireplace, and antimacassars. Drifting snow partly obscured the view of the lights in the Kremlin and Red Square.

A tall man in a blue suit and red bow tie stood up and extended his hand. 'I am Donald Maclean,' he said with a wooden smile.

'I am Guy Burgess,' said a shorter man in a blue suit and an Old Etonian tie, with a bubbling smile.

I became at once stone sober. I had a Baker Street reaction. 'Gentlemen,' I said, 'this is the end of a long trail.'

Maclean cracked a grin, Burgess laughed merrily and they sat down to face Sydney Weiland (Reuter correspondent), the Russian representatives of Tass and Pravda, and me. There was some cautious verbal sparring while Burgess, unmistakably the gratified spokesman for the pair, opened a capitalist leather valise and produced with a flourish four copies of a signed, typewritten, three-page, thousand word 'Statement by G. Burgess and D. Maclean.' He handed each of us a copy, the last to me with a swift wink, a slightly stressed 'And this one for *The Sunday Times*', and a genial reference to my swollen cheek: 'Who hit you?'

A few harmless questions were vaguely answered. Maclean sat silent, smoking a long Russian cigarette. Where were they working? 'You won't find me sitting outside the Foreign Office,' said Burgess. 'I don't want to have correspondents trying to follow me around. . . . We don't intend to add to our statement.'

Sydney Weiland tried a reproach: 'Hardly fair. Not giving us a chance to read the statement and ask questions before you leave.'

'Don't try to tell me that.' Laughing, Burgess stood up jauntily, followed by Maclean. 'I have given out too many statements to

of
colleagues either his views or the fact that he had been a
communist.

His attitude in these positions was completely incompatible
with the allegation that he was a Soviet agent.

This statement of Burgess' position is necessary to understand the situation which arose a week or so after his return
to London from Washington in 1951. He went to see Maclean as
Head of the American Dept. of the Foreign Office. They found
that these information and opinions about the political situation
and the danger of war were in agreement.

What now happened was determined by the following facts.
Burgess who some months previously had himself initiated arrangements to obtain a new job with a view to leaving the Foreign
Office was faced faced with the fact that the Foreign Office
had independently and subsequently decided that they would no
longer employ him. It is of course obvious that no agent would
take the initiative in arranging to leave the Foreign Office.

However when the break came, Burgess was doubtful whether
he wanted or could conscientiously do the new job he had been
arranging.

Therefore when Maclean told Burgess that he himself had decided that he could no longer work for the Foreign Office and
its policies and suggested that they should both go to the U.S.S.R.
Burgess had no difficulty in agreeing. There alone there appeared to both to be some chance of putting into practice in some
form the convictions they had always held.

As the result of living in the U.S.S.R. we both of us are
convinced that we were right in doing what we did.

We are handing this statement to the Press.

Donald Maclean.

Donald Maclean

Guy Burgess

Guy Burgess

This is the last signed page of the statement which Burgess and Maclean handed to
us. My copy of the three-page statement was borrowed by other Moscow pressmen
who were not at the apparition and the markings (in ink and pencil) were made by
them. I never got back the first two pages.

the world press in my time not to know what a story I am giving you fellows tonight.'

The interview had lasted five minutes. I was up and making for the door. It was getting on for eight. The Russian reporters seemed amused by Sydney's and my excitement. I rushed to 123, scraped up typewriter, paper and carbon, and ran back along the corridor. Room 101 was empty, the lights still burning. Downstairs, the manager was waiting in the lobby, sensing that something curious was afoot. 'Have those two gentlemen gone?' I asked. 'Yes, Mr Hoojis; they just left in a limousine. Very nice gentlemen. I do not remember having seen them before. Are they friends of yours?' 'They certainly are now,' I replied, diving through the door. I had come out without coat or galoshes. I took two heavy, full-length tosses on icy Gorky Street. (Russians don't laugh but help you up when you fall, however ludicrously.) There were three placid girl receptionists on duty at the press cable counter: someone in authority had known that there would be a rush of copy that night.

The story, of course, wrote itself – as all good stories do. I only skimmed the approved statement and didn't even file it, telling the office to 'uppick from Reuters'. In the curious news trade, what mattered was to have seen and talked with the legendary pair. (The statement naturally carried no surprises. Maclean and Burgess had never been secret agents, of course. They had merely discovered that their 'information and opinions about the political situation and the danger of war were in agreement in 1951'; so, as patriots of probity and integrity, the only honourable course of action open to them was to scuttle into Russia, 'where alone there appeared to both to be some chance of putting into practice in some form the convictions they had always held'.)

By 10 pm, *Pravda* was out with the statement in full – but only on page three. In London, the BBC had broadcast some extracts. The Gorky Street typewriter cubicles were crammed with the entire Moscow press corps. But only Sydney Weiland and I had seen Maclean and Burgess. Once again it was demonstrated that the best news stories are nearly always based on good luck, chance timing, and a fortuitous presence.

My expense account showed that the Moscow mission, which lasted seventy-two days and was justified only by the last-minute, five-minute encounter, cost £2,000, plus salary, transport and communication charges. Milord Kemsley slipped me a £1,000 personal cheque – drawn, I noted, on his personal account, not *The Sunday Times*. I had my fiftieth birthday in Paris, and returned to Tokyo to break camp and shift base to Hong Kong.

I did not suspect then that, seven years later, I would return to Moscow, via Yokohama and the Siberian railway, on the eve of Philby's delayed arrival in the capital, and just in time to see Maclean fleetingly again at the funeral of Burgess – who died the same day I arrived in Moscow.

CHAPTER 14

The Non-Finding of Philby

The natives, who pronounce Siberia as 'Sea-beer' (rolling the second syllable), all insist that there are no saltmines anywhere in the vast, table-flat subcontinent. They all love Siberia and have only sophisticated scorn for the city slickers in parochial Moscow.

'I was born in Siberia,' Yuri, the efficient Intourist chief at Khabarovsk, told me severely, when I inquired, 'and I have lived here all my life. I have never seen a saltmine. Maybe there were some in Tsarist days. It was a most inefficient way to get salt, Mr Hoojis.'

So you will not be able to see any saltmines if you take the trans-Siberian railway trek – either during stopovers at Nakhodka, Khabarovsk, Irkutsk or Lake Baikal, or from the rolling train during eight days and six nights of rail travel. Or any ice or snow, because the railway marathon is open to visitors only in the genial Siberian summer of July, August and September. At that time, Siberia – or that part of Siberia south of the barren tundras – is most un-Siberian. The soft sylvan landscape, as seen from the windows of a trans-Siberian train, flows and undulates un-hurriedly and endlessly past, unfolding its emerald and golden steppes dappled with acres of sunflowers, closing back into the interminable forests (*taiga*), gently rising to arcadian hills, dipping into huge, silver rivers, opening on lonely lakes, and when hills and trees recede, spreading verdantly to a blue and empty horizon.

You will miss more of traditional Siberia than the saltmines and the ice and snow. I didn't see a single wolf or bear or droshky. Or a serf being knouted. Of course, the bears and wolves still survive in the forests of larch, birch, pine, aspen and fir, and Yuri assured me – I looked at him sharply but he stuck to his story – that there are giant tigers in the hinterland between the Amur River and that Manchurian border. And a scientific expedition

was then on safari, looking for the goral – a supposedly extinct
link between goat and antelope, which had allegedly been sighted
in the Maly Khingan mountains, but which seems to have been
as elusive as the Abominable Snowman.

A hungry bear had wandered into the suburbs of Irkutsk that
winter and, to the rage of the sympathetic citizenry, was shot by a
nervous militiaman (cop) as it nuzzled children's lunch-boxes in a
kindergarten playground. But it was more than twelve years since
a pack of wolves had devoured an unwary wanderer near Lake
Baikal, and it seems that he was of doubtful political and ideological antecedents, so that the incident was scarcely of news
value.

The double steel track runs 5,800 miles from Nakhodka (the
Siberian port between off-limits Vladivostock and St Vladimir
Bay) to Moscow, through the most extensive area of flatness in
the world. Along the iron road are small square log-cabins with
white curtains and red flowers in the ornately framed windows
that are heavily shuttered in the long winter nights. Dirt roads
and narrow paths twist occasionally through the lofty aisles of
smooth, straight trees, winding apparently from nowhere to
nowhere.

In the far east there are garrison towns and outpost stations;
but, once the midway mark has been passed at Irkutsk, the ten-car
train slides, every three or four hours, across a narrow bridge over
a wide river, and jolts to a fifteen-minute halt at one of the old
and expanding, or new and expanding, settlements in this illimi-
table, green, silent land, which is destined to become an industrial
empire as large as western Europe.

The trans-Siberian trek is currently made from Japan to
Moscow in four stages: three days and two nights aboard a smart,
Danzig-built motorship from Yokohama to Nakhodka; one night
and the best part of the next day to Khabarovsk by double-headed
steam train (US-built o-10-o locomotives); three days and two
nights from Khabarovsk (where the diesel-electric service begins)
along the Mongol border, through Chita (the old fur centre) and
past Lake Baikal to Irkutsk; finally, an unbroken four days and
three nights from Irkutsk to Moscow. For some obscure reason,
when I made my 1963 approach to Moscow from Japan, visitors
were required to fly by TU-104 jet from Khabarovsk to Irkutsk –
three hours, with a hot roast chicken lunch (no liquor), served by

hostesses with high heels and lipstick. And, of course, all tourist travel was suspended when the Russians were heavily reinforcing garrisons along the border and inside Outer Mongolia after the 1968 'incidents' with China.

I decided in mid-1963 to combine the trans-Siberian vacation trek with another sporting hit-and-run crack at Khrushchev. I was warmly encouraged by contacts in the new Soviet embassy in Bangkok, who had clearly been told to develop friendships with foreign correspondents and the local press. I sent a humble and respectful message to Prime Minister Khrushchev, through the Soviet embassy, serving a two-month warning of my projected reappearance, and hopes for an interview. I made formal application from Hong Kong to the Soviet embassy in Tokyo for my visa and had immediate and courteous approval. All futile in the outcome, but amusing now in retrospect.

When my passport was stamped in the Soviet consulate in Tokyo, I went on impulse to the Soviet embassy and asked if I could see the information counsellor. I was suspiciously interrogated; the reception officer was openly hostile and summoned a superior officer: I wanted to thank the embassy, did I? What for? I handed over my press card, controlling myself with an effort. Suspicion deepened. The superior used the phone, examining me balefully as he spoke. My old 1956 Moscow wounds began to ache again. I was grudgingly admitted to a hard chair in the open corridor just inside the door. Passing clerks eyed me with curiosity. Here we go again, I thought.

Then magically the air cleared. An almost fawning bureaucrat bustled along and, bowing, ushered me into a spacious conference room with a shining table and golden chairs. He withdrew, the door opened again almost immediately, and, to my stupefaction, the ambassador himself entered. 'I must apologize for the confusion, Mr Hughes,' he said graciously, rereading my card. 'The information counsellor is absent today.' I mumbled protests that the apology should come from me for having disturbed him. I had wished only to thank the embassy for having arranged my visa so smoothly. The ambassador laughed: 'No wonder there was a misunderstanding. Do you know, no visitor has ever before thanked us for arranging a Moscow visa at long-distance. The staff were confused.' I guess there is a moral here somewhere. . . .

The majority of the passengers on the crowded Soviet ship from Yokohama were Japanese – chiefly businessmen. Japanese – not English – was the first foreign translation of announcements in Russian over the ship's loudspeakers. One news announcement sent me in gloomy shock to the ship's bar: Khrushchev, it was reported, had suddenly gone to Yugoslavia for a visit of indefinite length. Was there no limit, I brooded, to Khrushchev's resolution to avoid me?

Khabarovsk, where I stopped over for three days, was then a bright, bustling and expanding city of half a million. Life seemed free and easy and non-communist-like, and everyone was amiable and helpful. There are scores of bookshops, crowded, as always in Russia, with young people. Caviar, surprisingly, was on ration – except for visitors. The city has Russia's only big-top outdoor circus. The girls are a dashing, bold-eyed, challenging mixture of the Middle East and the Far East. Serge, my interpreter, a tall, powerful, eagle-faced son of Tashkent, swore that Tashkent was better than Khabarovsk, but conceded with a grin that he had married a Khabarovsk girl; he carried a picture of the smiling beauty in his wallet: Chairman Mao and the Chinese communists would not have approved, and would also have banned the nightly open-air dancing to jazz music beside the Amur.

Technically speaking, Siberia begins at Irkutsk, halfway between Vladivostock and Moscow. The huge area (four days and three nights travel by train), stretching east of Lake Baikal to the Pacific and the Okhotsk Sea, although traditionally Siberia, is officially designated as the Soviet Far East.

Irkutsk is a gracious, 300-year-old city of log cabins and ancient buildings, trees, parks and university spires. The population is half a million. There are three universities. The city is two hours' distance by road, and less than an hour by hydrofoil, from Lake Baikal, the deepest (5,315 feet), and in many ways the strangest and most beautiful, lake in the world – now, alas, being polluted by factories. More than three hundred rivers and streams flow into the lake, and only one, the Angara, flows out. They say that if all replenishment were turned off, it would take four hundred years for the fast-flowing Angara to empty the lake. Behind Baikal's narrow ochre beaches and russet cliffs, ridges of pine, birch, larch and cedars rise sharply to the Baikal mountains. The crystal waters freeze deeply in the winter: the Russians built a railway over the ice across the southern tip during the last winter of the Russo-Japanese war. The shores are regularly shaken by good-natured earthquakes. The first snow flurries begin in early November and the lake freezes in December. There are thousands of seals in Baikal, huge sturgeons and a curious transparent fish which is thirty-five per cent oil and which literally melts away if it is left in the sun.

I had a simple but memorable lunch of sprats, caviar and black bread, under a blue sky mirrored in the blue lake, with a debonair Intourist interpreter, who had improbably survived Stalingrad and then marched to Vienna. The fact that his name was Lenin lent an air of historical fantasy to our conversation – 'Now, Lenin, what would you say to this?' – as, with bread-crumbs, he refought Stalingrad on the tablecloth.

Lenin took me later to visit the beautiful Russian Orthodox Church still open for worship on a hill overlooking Irkutsk. The great onion-shaped domes were being gold-leafed and the magnificent icons refurbished – at State expense of course: the church's takings would never have been sufficient. A handsome, sad-eyed, bearded priest gave us a heartwarming welcome when we toiled up the stone steps past a row of ancient crones and grotesque cripples, dozing in the sun. A small comet's tail of curious children trailed us into the empty, candlelit church; but it was evident from their chatter and pointings that they were not regular worshippers.

I asked how many young people came to the church. 'As many as can be expected,' the priest replied in gentle equivocation. His eyes filled with tears when, as a Roman Catholic, I knelt on the stones to ask his blessing. Lenin, a reverent atheist, interpreted: 'The holy father says he blesses you in memory of the great Pope John, who brought the people of the world of all faiths, and of no faith at all, closer together in the family of man.'

I had noted the evening before that there was another Russian Orthodox Church in the central square, enclosed by the municipal offices, party headquarters and the familiar statue of Lenin, pointing apparently towards a row of new public toilets. But this church was a sealed and rotting tomb, onion domes piebald and peeling, doors barred and windows shuttered. There was some sort of communal laundry in the basement and a smell of greasy cooking. An old man in a beret and bell-bottomed trousers was crouched on the church steps in the twilight, nursing a bottle between his knees, rubbing his hands and mumbling to himself.

I was the only tourist aboard the train on the long final haul to Moscow, but if a foreigner is lonely on the trans-Siberian express it is his own fault. My knowledge of Russian is not extensive, but I had my dictionary and there was generally someone around who understood English or my execrable French and Japanese. Passengers drift from compartment to compartment, carrying their own refreshments, and word soon spreads that there is a stranger aboard.

The dining car was always a gregarious rendezvous. Among friendly eaters, there is ever a working and understandable esperanto of signs, grunts, gestures and grimaces. (Some of the travellers did not know where or what Australia was; Austria was the immediate deduction when I tried to explain where I came from; and when I drew excellent maps of Australia on the menu it was assumed that I was an eccentric narcissist sketching myself in profile, with Cape York peninsula as a plausible nose.)

The food was abundant, if homely: bortsch (a meal in itself), unfortunate if well-intentioned steaks, fried potatoes, cucumber and tomato salad, plenty of eggs, butter and Russian cheese, stacks and stacks of bread, but little or no fruit. I have never seen so much bread wasted as in Siberian railway dining cars. I was served at least four slices of black and four slices of white bread at each meal; of this, I – guiltily calorie-conscious – would eat at most two salted slices of the excellent coarse black bread; I noted that, in common with all other diners' leftover bread, my untouched slices were always thrown away.

The vodka in the dining car was, strangely, cut out the second day on from Irkutsk to Moscow. This may well have been a prudent precaution, because the first-night diners, inflamed and waving empty vodka decanters, got off to a good roaring Russian start. There was no violence, but I sensed some lively meals ahead. Warm, flattish *peever* (beer) and what the Russians amusingly call 'strong wines' – *bombo*, in Australia – remained on unrestricted call, however, and there were lashings of cheap sweet champagne in bottles fitted dangerously with formidable clamped stoppers which exploded like pocket mortar-shells and which, effectively aimed, could raise a bruise at a distance of two tables.

Champagne, incidentally, won me a fictitious name among fellow-travellers, involving me in my only unfortunate experience on the trip. I had fallen into pleasant sign-doggerel at table with two young Russian technicians and an East German. (You could easily pick the East Germans on the train: they never shaved.) My chance companions were exhilarated and generous. I blenched when, in the wake of my offering, each also called in turn for another bottle of champagne. I blenched even more when one of the Russians laughingly pointed his unopened bottle at the bullet-head of the severe, one-eyed colonel, who, with a silent massive wife, shared my soft-seat sleeping compartment, and who was then seated a table away to starboard with his broad back incautiously turned towards us.

In alarm, I disturbed my companion's trajectory by jiggling the champagne muzzle at the last moment, so that the heavy stopper smacked against the ceiling of the swaying dining car and splashed harmlessly into the colonel's bortsch. As an old artilleryman, the colonel was admirably unruffled, but the technician may have been nettled with me as a spoilsport, and I suspect that a friendly waitress, who had been keeping the best steaks for me, imagined that I had been angered rather than concerned.

I still do not know what transpired in the diner after I bade the table goodnight and repaired with quiet dignity to my compartment, where the one-eyed colonel and his lady were already relaxing before retiring. The colonel, as was his custom after each meal, had removed his glass eye and was substituting another, which he fastidiously selected from a collection of spares in his wife's reticule; his wife, although glazed from the table, had fallen to heavily on a considerable mixture of muffins and rock candy, which she always carried in a small basket.

Suddenly the technician lurched in from the corridor, resentful and truculent. He whipped a notebook from his pocket, sketched a hasty diagram of his face (he must have been a factory draughtsman), scored it out with bold, black, angry strokes, and pointed a fierce finger at me. His accusation was clear: I had somehow made him lose face. Perhaps the waitress – and maybe other diners – had denounced him, after I left, for troubling a stranger. I earnestly asked him in pidgin Russian to clarify his indictment, peering for words in my pocket dictionary. I was at once placatory, apologetic, transparently mystified.

There was something of a commotion. Interested passengers from adjoining compartments, preparing for slumber and wearing identical mass-produced striped pyjamas, long underpants and sky-blue singlets, crowded our doorway, volubly explaining to others massed behind what was going on. Sympathy was wholly with me, partly because the technician was abusive and drunk, but largely because I was a visitor. The colonel, still fumbling with his spare eye, explained to me carefully in halting English that the technician was drunk. His wife, who had inadvertently bolted a large piece of candy while remonstrating with the intruder, was seized with a paroxysm of uncontrollable coughing, which made her bend and choke as though on the verge of a fit.

The unhappy but dogged technician – I still feel he had a legitimate grievance – leaned over me and began to pluck and strain at my lapels. At last I lost patience and cried, above the hubbub and roar of a passing train, 'Knock it off!' For some strange Russian reason, this remonstrance delighted the jostling passengers in the corridor. 'Knockitoff! Knockitoff!' they shouted, beating one another on the back. The colonel, having at last settled the glass replacement in his eye-socket, arose, pointed to the door and, in a Red Square parade voice, roared: 'Knockitoff!' The poor technician, ignoring my hand, retreated to the accompaniment of a mocking Volga-boat-song chorus of 'Knockitoff!'

I never saw him again, and for me the incident still has inexplicable undertones. But for the rest of the trip I was 'Mr Knockitoff', or, more formally, '*Gospodin* Knockitoff' (an honorific). My friend, the waitress, who had been calling me 'Mister Hoojis', adopted the new name eagerly and even with a certain pride; I am sure that she never knew exactly what had happened and perhaps decided that I had undergone a baptismal naturalization or modestly revealed an unsuspected and remote Tsarist ancestry.

Between Irkutsk and the Siberian–Russian frontier, we passed through four growing citadels of Soviet industrial power, rising suddenly and uglily above the flat green panorama: Krasnoyursk on the Yenisei River; Novosibirsk on the Ob; Petropavolsk on the Ishin; and Sverdlovsk in the foothills of the Urals. They all looked much the same to me – no factory expert, alas – with mile-long stretches of workshops, convoys of trucks, giant cranes, grain elevators, steel power pylons, radar towers, and gross yellow and brown, barrack-like, huddles of workers' apartments.

Gone were the brawling Mongol troops who had greeted the train in the garrison towns hundreds of miles east of Irkutsk; here were crowds of technicians with their families, on transfer or holiday, waiting to board the train, while other travellers, clutching bulging bundles and shiny brand-new suitcases – there had obviously been a recent nationwide release of mass-produced Soviet luggage – marched off, to be picked up by long lines of buses.

Tomsk is on a branch line; so is Magnitogorsk, the iron and steel bastion of Siberia, more than a thousand miles west of the Kuznetsk Basin, the coal heart of Siberia, south of Novosibirsk and Krasnoyursk. Here, backboned by the Siberian railway, is the bourgeoning Soviet equivalent of Pittsburgh and Detroit and Chicago; here, aboard the crowded Siberian trains and the crowded airliners between Moscow and Khabarovsk, are the new revolutionaries, the technicians who are developing and expanding the new Soviet industrial frontier.

The traffic on the Siberian railway is extraordinarily heavy. On the day we passed Omsk, I kept a desultory count of the trains passing us to the east: one every ten minutes between 7 and 11 am; then one every half-hour until 3 pm; finally, one again every ten minutes until 7 pm, when I signed off and went to dinner. All night the traffic rolls ceaselessly past. The trains, mainly freight, ranged from forty-five trucks for a single diesel to eighty-six for a double-header. Most of the trucks were oil wagons: Russia's need for a pipeline across Siberia requires no labouring.

When we rumbled into the great railway junction and industrial centre of Sverdlovsk, the passengers lining the corridor windows of our carriage burst into excited shouts of: 'Europe! Europe!' Sverdlovsk, still one night and one and a half days from Moscow, is the last large centre inside Siberia. Seven railway lines converge here, and northward – one presumes – stretch the Urals, which are only piddling, bald hillocks as seen from the train. (At Sverdlovsk, formerly Yekaterinburg, Tsar Nicholas and his family were massacred, and Francis Garry Powers was shot down in his U-2. There is a skyscraping radar tower here, easily the tallest on the whole route.)

Party members or not, young or old, all the Russians I met and talked with on the ship and the train and in Irkutsk and Khabarovsk were, not surprisingly, sturdy patriots. What did surprise me, after a seven-year absence from Russia, was the candour and freedom of their remarks. There was no hesitation in exchanges on political views and opinions – even when a casual interpreter, obviously unknown to the speaker, sat in. They did not of course promote heresy, but many – especially the young – were critical of short supply, poor quality goods and low wages. Voices were never lowered or heads turned furtively for possible eavesdroppers, as in Peking.

I even heard two anecdotes good-humouredly critical of Khrushchev – one a four-year-old joke which I first heard in Hong Kong; the other a brand new local product. Their appositeness – incidentally and significantly – has since been sharpened.

The first story: Comrade Premier Gomulka – a very appropriate selection, in view of recent changes – leads the Polish delegation to, say, the Twenty-sixth Congress in Moscow. In the night, his secretary is appalled to overhear him delivering loudly in his sleep virulent diatribes against Khrushchev as 'enemy of the people, assassin of communist principles, betrayer of Marxist-Leninism'. The secretary rushes from bed to arouse the voluble, sleeping Gomulka. 'Comrade Premier, do you know what you are saying?' 'Of course I do,' says Gomulka, awakening with a yawn; 'a good communist knows what he is saying, whether he is awake or asleep.' The incredulous secretary presses: 'But you were saying this-and-that.' 'I know, I know,' insists Gomulka placidly. 'But you know you are in the Kremlin?' 'Yes, yes, of course.' 'And attending the Twenty-sixth Congress?' 'My God!' cries Gomulka, sitting up, 'I thought it was the Twenty-eighth Congress.'

The second – and hoary – story dealt with Khrushchev's alarm on hearing that Eisenhower was bringing with him to Moscow the us doctor who, he had boasted to Khrushchev at Camp David, could revive the dead by opening the chest and massaging the heart. Mikoyan asks: 'So what? Why are you upset?' 'Because,' groans Khrushchev, 'I told Eisenhower, as a counter, that we had a Siberian athlete who could run the mile in a minute.' 'Don't worry, *tovarich*,' says Mikoyan soothingly; 'just have the doctor massage Stalin's heart and, if he can do what Eisenhower claims, you will run the mile in a minute.'

So at long last, at 10.40 pm, on time to the minute, twelve days and 7,000 miles from Yokohama, we drew into crowded Moscow station. A little girl with flaxen pigtails in the next compartment gave me shyly a children's picture book as a farewell gift – under no prompting, so far as I could see, from her beaming parents. Her brother gave me a green apple. The girl conductor and the waitress shook hands with me – no tipping until you are in Moscow.

'*Da-svee-dahn-ya* (goodbye), Knockitoff!' my friends called.

To my disappointment, Intourist put me this time in the Metropole Hotel, down the road past the Bolshoi, comfortable enough, but lacking the character – and memories – of the National. Such was the lingering influence of the train's unending smooth motion that, when I looked out of the bedroom window in the morning, my first impression was that eastern flowing traffic on the road was frozen into a curious frieze and that the hotel room was rolling along, still westward-bound.

I made phone appointments, went first to the British embassy and met wise, gruff Sir Humphrey Trevelyan, then up the steep stairs to the administrative office of the us ambassador and met wise, ironic Foy Kohler. Here I first learned of the macabre Burgess coincidence. 'Well, well,' said Kohler, leaning back at his desk. 'So you couldn't keep away from your friend's funeral? Well timed, indeed. Perhaps it would have been too well timed had you arrived the day before yesterday; you might have been suspected of having a hand in the death.' I gaped. 'What, you don't know? Why, Guy Burgess died suddenly yesterday, and will be cremated the day after tomorrow.'

I ricochetted from the first major shock to the second minor one: 'How did you know of my personal interest?' 'Oh, we are not without our records,' Kohler replied pleasantly.

Burgess, I discovered, had frittered away the past seven years in a Moscow suburban apartment, reading, drinking hard, misbehaving often, talking of the past, reading English newspapers. The Russians allowed him to keep a boy friend – a guitar-playing electrician – and an Alsatian dog. He gave both the same name – Tolya. The puritanical Chinese comrades would never have tolerated that. Unlike Maclean and Philby, he never attempted written apologia or memoirs – although he could certainly have set fire, in mischief or animosity, to some prim and respectable shirt-tails back home.

So, unexpectedly, two days later, I saw Maclean again at 'Gay Boy' Burgess' funeral in exile. Maclean looked tired and much older. He moved more slowly and was a little stooped. His wife had the dowdy, coarsening look of a once-fashionable woman fallen on hard times and merging, greyly and mutely, with a drab background. She was still Maclean's wife; Philby was still off-stage, defected from Beirut, unreported in the Soviet. Maclean uttered a brief and hollow eulogy beside the red-draped casket with the orchid tribute – sadly, obviously, and appropriately, artificial. A conscripted handful of bored Party 'mourners' slumped and fidgeted, yawned and whispered. It had been agreed that the press would not approach Maclean. I felt unashamedly relieved. Room 101 had not been that 'end of the long trail'. This was nearer to it – but still not quite the end.

I thought – naturally enough – of Philby as I left the service. Khrushchev had just returned from Yugoslavia and was unlikely to be available for press interviews during my fleeting passage. The press section of the Foreign Office was offensive over the phone, and scornfully silent to a written request and a telegram. A Philby interview – he had still not surfaced – was highly improbable. But, again, no harm trying. The effort, devious, was futile. But the attempt landed me an entertaining and instructive interview with Alexei Adzhubei, son-in-law of Khrushchev, member of the Central Committee, editor-in-chief of *Izvestia*, well-travelled, offstage fixer, probably the next Foreign Minister had Khrushchev not fallen downstairs next year.

A friendly and influential Soviet diplomat, enlisted through my Bangkok embassy contacts, first suggested, and then helped me wangle, the interview; he was partly motivated – he admitted frankly – by his own desire to meet Adzhubei personally. He thought that I intended only to raise the question of a Khrushchev interview; I did not mention Philby to him.

My friend, A, and I met Adzhubei, by appointment, in his editorial office at 10 am on an inauspicious Friday the 13th (September). He was a florid, stockily built, engaging, formidable man, with an

infectious laugh and quick Rabelaisian wit. He was accompanied
by his foreign editor and chief political writer. He said depre-
catingly that he understood 'a little English', but preferred the aid
of an interpreter – a role which A, my fixer, admirably filled.

He invited me to have some Russian tea, cakes or candy, spread
out on a long office table. 'What do you mean – candy makes you
fat?' he rallied me. 'This is excellent Russian candy, specially
prepared for workers, clears the stomach, makes you thin and
handsome like me. It's far better than the chocolate that your Lord
Cadbury makes – isn't he the English lord who destroys English
newspapers for profit? (A sharp reference to the tragic death of
the *News Chronicle*.) How you must all love him in Fleet
Street.'

'There's only hot tea. Western pressmen drink too much. Far
more than Russians. We Russians are very temperate. I myself
prefer Scotch to vodka. When I was in the United Nations, most
of the US pressmen were half-drunk all the time. They got me
half-drunk too before lunch; I gave away all our Kremlin secrets;
why do they have to work at such tension?'

I tried vainly to draw him out on China. He made a facetious
reply to my inquiry whether Russia would allow the Western
press to cover the coming Sino-Russian war along the Manchurian
and Sinkiang borders. 'Why, I believe so,' he said solemnly. 'We
don't particularly welcome representatives of the lying capitalist
press to our workers' paradise, but in the interests of world
information I think we should let you in for the war.' Then,
seriously: 'One thing you can be sure of: the Chinese wouldn't let
you in.'

At last I broached the matter of my requested interview with
Khrushchev. I pointed out that I had been vainly waiting two
weeks for a response from the press section of the Foreign Office.
I had made written application and I had spoken to an official,
who had been gratuitously offensive. Could he help me in the
matter?

Adzhubei said bluntly: 'You would have to wait at least another
two or three weeks. After all, he has been away in Yugoslavia.
It wasn't very smart of you to come and see him when he was
away.' I agreed, but I had not known that he would be away.

'I'll give you a straight reply,' Adzhubei said. 'You won't have
a hope of seeing him for an exclusive interview for at least two

and probably three weeks. I doubt if he will be back in Moscow from the country for two weeks. If things were normal, I would fix it easily. Mr Khrushchev never dodges the press. Pick your time better in the future and I'll make sure that you see him. But just now I have a list of vital matters as long as my arm' – he measured his wrist to his elbow – 'that I want to bring up with him myself. But I wouldn't dare approach him for a couple of weeks. And even if I loved you like a brother, I tell you straightly that your request would go right down below mine.'

'All right,' I said. 'It just can't be helped. I have already waited here too long. I work out of South-East Asia and China, not Moscow. I should be back there now, reporting about South Vietnam.' 'Yes, you should be,' he agreed. 'That's an ugly story that is going to get uglier. But don't blame us Russians for it.'

Now I sprang Philby's name. 'I am bitterly disappointed,' I said, 'but I accept your *nyet*. Now, as a press reporter, I ask you, as an editor, to give me a consolation prize. Let me see the British defector, Philby.'

My friend A looked at me and asked 'Who?' I repeated: 'Philby.' Adzhubei leaned back, looking puzzled, turned to his foreign editor and obviously inquired: 'Who is Philby?' His man gave him a quick fill-in. Adzhubei went through some miming and ejaculations while listening, and A hastily interpreted: 'He asked who Philby was. Then he said, "Oh no! Not another one of them! Yes, I remember now. Why can't we reach some arrangement with the Americans and British to get rid of these clowns. Sometimes I think their only use is to sell newspapers." '

(Now this, of course, could have been shadow-play. But, suspicious though I was, it didn't look as though he was putting on an act. I cannot see any advantage to him in trying to mislead me. And, frankly, I don't think any editor likes to admit any time that he knows nothing of any subject.)

Anyway, Adzhubei then ran on after the briefing: 'Yes, yes, I remember the matter now. But the less I ever know of these things, the happier I am. It's none of my business, and I am not interested anyway. What do you want me to do – presuming I can do anything?'

'Just tidy it up,' I said. 'Let me see and speak to him. I have a reasonable excuse for the approach because I work for a paper he was working for – *The Economist*. I think that if he is able to see people – I have heard of his personal difficulties (meaning that he was a known alcoholic when he ran out) – he would be glad to speak to a British correspondent.'

Adzhubei reflected for a minute or two. He did not speak to the others at the table. Nor did they offer a suggestion. At last he said: 'All right. What you say makes sense to me. I cannot raise the matter as editor of *Izvestia*, but I can do so as a member of the Central Committee. I shall recommend that you be given an opportunity to see Philby – if he consents. I do not know where he is or how he is. Nor do I care. If he won't consent, or if there are difficulties which my foreign editor has suggested to me, I still think that it would be wise to issue a statement. I shall recommend, in that event, that we give you the statement.'

It was then agreed that I would seek a third extension of my visa, which was due to expire on Monday afternoon, 16th, three days later. This would be a tentative extension. I was prepared to wait another week if, by Monday, there was reasonable prospect of seeing Philby or securing an official statement. I said: 'But please don't fool me –' Adzhubei broke in jovially in English: 'You mean, as an Australian, don't *bugger* me around?' I agreed. 'Then I am not a bad linguist,' he observed.

I must record his parting crack. I had said piously, on rising to depart: 'I hope there is no need to repeat my assurance that this interview and your statements remain off the record at this time.' Adzhubei laughed and made a brisk reply which made the other laugh also. My friend interpreted: 'Mr Adzhubei said that he believes you are a man of integrity; that is why he received you. However, he is a man of maturity; so he is never surprised when a man of integrity breaks his word. But if you did break your word – which he thinks unlikely – and embarrassed him by now publishing or attributing to him anything said here, he would at once say that he was not here, that he (indicating the foreign editor) was not here, that he (indicating the political writer) was not here, that I (pointing to himself) was not here, that you (indicating me) were alone in a deep dream of peace.'

That deep dream of peace, alas, was not broken. I am convinced that Adzhubei did his best. But the Party ruling – transmitted apologetically to me by a disappointed A – was that 'no official Party statement can be made, and that Philby would not make a

personal comment.' A told me privately that he had learned that
Philby had been 'a great nuisance', that he had 'made trouble',
that it was not believed that there had been 'any real reason for
him to run away at that time'.

PART IV

Hidden China:
Peking Dateline – Hong Kong Keyhole

CHAPTER 15

'What Sort of People do they think we are?'

It remains arguable whether the better balanced and better informed news reports and commentary on hidden China come out of the country itself, or from a properly organized observation and communications base with direct contacts like Hong Kong. In the curious newspaper trade, a poor story with a Peking dateline will almost always beat a good story with a Hong Kong dateline. This is fair enough: A solid Peking presence should be more reliable and respectable than the most assiduous keyhole-squinting from Hong Kong. But, as most pressmen who have worked in both Peking and Hong Kong will agree, the squinter, over the distance, sees more of the game. If you are at the keyhole, you can often see and hear what you are not supposed to know about, and you can tiptoe away, write what you like, and live to peep and eavesdrop another day. If you wish to stand firm on the Peking dateline, you must recognize that the dateline means the party line.

Of course, all the keyhole boys in Hong Kong would run barefoot across the frontier, day or night, to get the essential colour, detail, taste and feel of the country inside China. There is always news in the streets, in people's faces, in casual scenes, in the temper of the police, in the deportment of the wretched desk clerks, in shop windows, in the quality, quantity and prices of food and clothing. News stories from Peking are at least not censored on the spot, although they are all filed, studied and used in evidence against the transient or resident reporter.

On arrival the Western pressman is invited by the Foreign Ministry to state whom he wants to interview and where he wants to go. With notable exceptions, his requests can be granted – after a fashion. Unless he is a fool, he will not expect that he will get sensational secrets or blinding disclosures or anything other than the party line at official interviews; and he will soon find that he is treading a well-worn trail in requested interviews – whether they be political prisoners (not now available) or private citizens and factory and commune workers (always on call and briefed for 'sincere' responses).

Sometimes at government interviews, he is tossed to his delighted astonishment a rare new fact or a rarer bald statistic to gnaw on, and even a humble but calculated admission of failure, perplexity or disappointment; but generally he will sit and fidget over an endless cavalcade of teacups, frustrated by the pious clichés, repetitive jargon and smooth evasions of this or that 'spokesman'.

He must attend all the diplomatic cocktail parties and receptions to which he is invited, because an official statement or ruling may have been made unexpectedly to a foreign representative, or gossip and rumour may be picked up – most of it idle and unfounded, or planted and expedient – or a ministerial aside or calculated comment may be dropped blandly into his prehensile ear. There are never any ebullient drunken outbursts in the old Khrushchev cocktail manner, but Premier Chou En-lai sometimes unobtrusively makes an opportunity, with ping-pong deftness, to pass on a considered observation to a Western correspondent at a reception.

Otherwise the resident dateliner will lead an inhibited social life in Peking. He will be denied the consolation and instruction of converse with local newspapermen – which is at least possible in darkest Moscow. The food is still excellent – from the hottest Szechuan to the smoothest Cantonese cuisine, from Peking duck to 'instant boiled mutton' – but the restaurant lights go out at 10 pm and there is of course no night life, except sedate dancing at the desolate International Club on Saturday nights. Even there, the Western bachelor had better not depend on local girls as dance partners. Indeed, there is an aching absence of the capitalist temptations and distractions that swell the expense accounts of the most austere correspondents in Tokyo, Manila, Hong Kong, Bangkok, Saigon, Seoul, Djakarta or even Rangoon.

The doughty monocled Jacques Marcuse, who has been *Agence France-Presse* dateliner in Peking before and after 'liberation', has summed up life inside communist China with gallic force and lucidity: 'It is like living in a huge sanatorium with millions of inmates. The main rules, as in any such establishment, are: One, have implicit faith in your doctors; two, do as you are told;

three, don't ask yourself, or anybody else, questions; four, leave the thinking to those whose business it is to think for you.'

Robert Guillain, who has spent a lifetime in the Far East for *Le Monde*, wrote of one tour: 'A subtle veil was always kept skilfully and firmly drawn between China and myself . . . There are millions of Chinese, but if ever I was left alone to speak with one of them without a witness, it was a put-up job. It was a sheer waste of time to ask to stay for a few days in a village, or even to spend twenty-four hours there. I was never able, if I felt inclined, to visit with my guide at random a house in some district of my choice. I could never stop and make inquiries in a factory, a farm, an institution, or some other place unless the visit had been planned in advance.'

But always the new resident or visitor will tend to be disarmed by the politeness and hospitality of his reception. Hence the inevitable, open-mouthed tributes by so many innocent arrivals to Chinese warmth and friendliness – indirectly but intrinsically, an insult to the natural and spontaneous charm, kindness and generosity of the Chinese race, when undistracted or uninfluenced by either party or palace eunuchs.

And, anyway, there he is – *there*. He is on the spot – if in a double sense. He is seeing for himself – if dimly, darkly, fugitively. He has at least been allowed to put his hand in the wound in China's side – no matter how superficial the examination.

Back in Hong Kong are the foiled keyhole squinters, whose frustrations from outside are still balanced by compensations, because they are outside. They can study Chinese newspapers and party reports which are banned to resident dateliners in Peking. They have access to all monitored radio announcements inside China. They can interview the continual influx of escapers from the mainland, who bear firsthand news from villages and factories which the dateliner can never visit. They have direct, unbroken, uncensored access to all news of world events, magazines and books. They have exchanges with business travellers and Hong Kong Chinese who visit China, and who can talk to them while never daring to talk with dateliners. Most of them have contacts in Peking's international world, who keep them posted with gossip and tips through the diplomatic bag. They see the personal letters mailed or smuggled to Chinese residents in Hong Kong from friends and relatives in China. They hear in Hong Kong all important and hard news-breaks as quickly as do the dateliners – through Radio Peking's broadcasts of all official pronouncements and releases by the New China News Agency; and, with keyhole communication advantages, they can beat the dateliners' cables to Western capitals.

(Once, I remember, an Indian correspondent in Peking – righteously indignant, as always – complained at a Peking press conference that the Soviet *Tass* Agency was receiving priority in the handing out of news. He insisted that all correspondents were entitled to the benefit of the same time release. At three o'clock next morning all correspondents then in the Press Club (no longer functioning) were aroused from their beds and directed to dress and attend a Foreign Office press conference immediately. Half awake and half dressed, we drove in fear and trembling through the dark streets, recalling misdemeanours or imagining a war declaration or a Politburo *coup*. On arrival, after a half hour wait over the inevitable tea, we listened to an impassive senior official read aloud an utterly unimportant four-line announcement of the building of a new railway branch line. The official pointed out, with a delicate hint of apology for previous dereliction, that at least this story had been released 'simultaneously with issue to *Tass*'. One hour after we had returned to our beds, another Foreign Office press official knocked politely on our doors, placed a printed version of the oral story on each bed-table and withdrew with a gentle 'Goodnight'.)

And yet, and yet. . . . Whatever the drawbacks and the frustrations and the language barrier and the involuntary restraint in writing to try to preserve a dateline, no-one – however informed, intuitive or divinely inspired – can report properly about a country which he has never entered, even in solitary confinement, or a people whom he has not seen at home, even from solitary confinement.

Arthur David Schloss, *alias* Waley, gave the world incomparable translations of ancient Chinese and Japanese masterpieces, although he never once visited China or Japan; still, how much better would Waley's genius have been expressed had he himself ascended the marble steps of the Temple of Heaven, or from the pavilion on Coal Hill had personally surveyed the shimmering yellow roofs of the Imperial and Forbidden Cities and the rolling

green forest of courtyard trees in spring or summer, when
a Peking Burnam Wood does indeed come to Mao's high
Dunsinane.

To close on a final note of hope and encouragement for those
keyhole reporters who seek access to a dateline in hidden China.

The Peking mind will be hard and pragmatic in selection, and,
while it remains absurdly sensitive to criticism and, above all,
satire, it is not fooled by sycophants or duped by trucklers. At a
farewell lunch in the celebrated old Three Tables Restaurant, then
down the alley from the Foreign Office, an urbane official threw
me a copy of a 'confidential' visa application from a distinguished
contemporary keyhole specialist and an acquaintance of mine. I
read it with surprise that became embarrassment. It was a
nauseating 'assurance' that all his datelined despatches would be
written with dedication to 'improved understanding and goodwill
between our two nations', and would be dutifully and unfailingly
submitted for official criticism, correction and approval before
transmission. The additional pledge was given that, as the appli-
cant hoped to establish a permanent bureau in Peking, there need
be no misgivings that any of his subsequent reports after the
expiration of the visa would bring a frown or a blush to the most
sensitive cheek in the Politburo.

'It is mischievous of you to show me this,' I said righteously.
'Did you expect me to disclose the facts and name?'

'You can do what you like with it,' he replied. I tossed it back
to him. He crumpled it into his pocket. His aside was a multi-
word expletive: 'What sort of people do they think we are!'

CHAPTER 16

Datelines without Deadlines

These are random anecdotes from my 'Inside China' notebook of 1957, at the time of the party's intellectual witchhunt known as 'The Hundred Flowers' campaign. They are not news stories. They have no deadline and they would never merit a headline. They prove nothing. Perhaps they mean nothing. But I believe they could happen only in China – under the party or under an emperor. So skim or skip.

LANDLORD-BEGGAR

Hankow: There was a deplorable scene of unique violence when I landed at Hankow from the Yang-tze. The double-tiered, Russian-built bridge was only half finished, so we crossed the flooded river in a large, packed ferry. On the other side, I was approached by a venerable figure whom I presumed from his dignified bearing and outstretched hand to be the Mayor of Hankow. I at once extended my hand in grateful fellowship, but my companion, a burly representative of the China Travel Service, swept forward with an oath and sent His Worship sprawling in the roadway.

'There are still some beggars left,' he explained gloomily. 'Obviously he is a rich landlord.'

'A SIMPLE LITTLE CHINESE STORY'

The Summer Palace: I asked my shy little guide and interpreter, Miss Teng, to read me an elegant prose poem on a hanging tapestry in the Palace That Towers Into The Clouds. She studied it and made careful report:

'It is a simple little story of a man who met another man at the pond. They became friends that day but separated and did not meet again for ten years. "What have you done since I saw you ten years ago?" the second man asks. "Nothing," replies the first man. "Ah, you are a happy man," says the first. And so they smile and go fishing for another day and then part again. A very simple little Chinese story.'

Simple? I would have liked to ask her why the authorities tolerated this enigmatic record of happy ten-year idleness from the past in the new society of five-year plans for mass production in the future. But a question would have spoiled the mood.

Little Miss Teng gently gave me another moment of embarrassment – and also self-imposed humiliation – when we arrived at the Pagoda of Many Treasures, looted by Western troops in 1906. 'Here,' she recalled, 'we once collected many art treasures, necklaces, jade ornaments and precious stones. However, the invading forces took them away, and I am deeply sorry that we cannot therefore show them to you today.'

I glanced at her furtively. But she seemed innocently serious. A simple little Chinese apology.

PERCHANCE TO DREAM

Peking: Young Comrade S, university student graduate, now engineer and strong defender of 'thought reform', was chatting cheerfully to me about his early study-group experiences.

'It used to be very difficult for us old hands in the dormitories when the new arrivals came in,' he recalled with a chuckle. 'Some of them kept us awake, talking aloud to themselves in their sleep after their first experiences of questioning under "self-criticism".'

'Did you also talk in your sleep at first?' I asked.

He was surprised. 'I have no idea. No-one told me. We did not tell them. They grew out of the habit. Anyway, it is not important what you say when you are asleep, only what you say when you are awake.'

But then, I thought, he suddenly began to reflect.

A 'SECRET FACTORY'

Shanghai: ' "Secret factories" are generally doing useful work,' Vice-Premier Chen Yun had told me in Peking. 'They can do things which big plants cannot do, or are too busy to do. Some use up waste material which big plants reject. Of course, we can't officially allow them to operate, only secretly. But if any engage in harmful operations of the old sort, we can always intervene.'

So I drove with an interpreter through the maze of crowded cobbled streets in changed and unchanging Shanghai to 'the secret factory' of Mr Shin Chun-yung at No 2-345 in Shing-chan Road, not far from the Temple of the Jade Buddha. The Shin 'secret factory' was not heavily disguised. On one of the stone pillars at the gateway, a cardboard sign – on which someone had scrawled a naughty drawing – read simply but plainly: 'The Shin Factory (Unregistered) For Strongly Made Pens. Forward The Capitalistic Revolution In Aid Of Socialism!'

Indoors, we passed some children playing pingpong in the hall, stumbled under a shadowed staircase draped with drying towels and shirts, and entered a dark kitchen where half a dozen people were producing the Strongly Made Shin Ballpen.

I am no artisan, but it seemed to me that the Shin manufacturing technique – secret or registered – was primitive. An asthmatic man in overalls and a cap operated a wheel with pedals; two boys were compressing tiny cylinders between rolling pins; a couple of housewives with violet-stained fingers were apparently battering the ends off the completed product with hammers. 'Strongly Made' was right.

No-one had the slightest hesitation in answering my questions about this secret and illegal industrial complex. Mr Shin himself was absent – visiting, it was said, his sick old aunt in Soochow. (This alibi apparently was not meant to be taken seriously, as the most beautiful girls in China reputedly come from Soochow.) But the housewives reported that they produced 900 dozen pens a month at a fluctuating market price of approximately 7.20 yuan (say £1·05) a dozen or 8½p each. The Shin employees aggregated thirteen (mostly employed on a family basis), worked eight or nine hours a day, averaged from £5·25 to £9 a month. The pens were sold throughout China but mainly in Harbin. Raw materials were supplied and distribution and marketing arranged by properly registered and legal State organs.

One – and only one – awkward silence blanketed the interview. I asked what taxation was payable on the capitalist profits of the secret Shin Strongly Made Pen Company. It was made clear that only Mr Shin himself, presumably then presenting chrysanthemums to his ailing aunt in Soochow, could disclose that secret.

THE LOYAL OPPOSITION

Peking: Mr Sa Kung-liao was a lively and articulate politician, a leader of the loyal non-communist party opposition in China's parliament, and the only Chinese I interviewed who wore a Western-style tie.

He received me in the handsome quarters of the China Democratic League, a block or two from the Pavilion of Purple Light, to explain the Chinese mystery of the survival of a multi-party system and an avowed and official parliamentary opposition in a communist state. I inquired about the strength of the opposition parties in the National People's Congress. There were, it seems, 668 party deputies, 274 members of the Democratic League, and 284 non-party deputies. But these figures were constantly shifting in a strange Oriental fashion.

'Some of our members have joined the Communist Party,' Mr Sa explained expansively. 'Some communist members have joined the Democratic League. We work together, you understand. As an opposition bloc, we are not opposed to the Communist Party. All parties are working for the Government – the Government, you understand, *not* the Communist Party. This is surely the essence of loyal democracy?'

I suggested that the principle, although doubtless admirable, differed somewhat from the Western idea of parliamentary opposition. Mr Sa slapped his thigh in agreement: 'Exactly, exactly. You may find our ideas a little strange at first. East is East and West is West, as your philosophers say.'

How exactly did the opposition function? On what policy lines, in the opinion of the Democratic parties, was the Communist Party wrong, and how successful was the opposition in countering, amending or even correcting these Party errors?

Mr Sa considered his replies. 'First, you must understand that the basis of our operations as an opposition party is to consult with representatives of the Communist Party and non-party deputies – to *consult*, to discuss, to suggest, to consider, to agree. Our democratic aims in opposition are mutual supervision and long-term political co-existence. Second, on policy lines the

Communist Party is making no mistakes at all. *None*. Let us be clear on that.' He patted my knee. 'But on individual matters of detail there may be various *opinions*. You understand? It is our duty as opposition party to consider these opinions.

'Sometimes – let us be frank, Mr Hughes – our Democratic parties make mistakes. Sometimes I myself have been in error. I was a newspaper editor in Shanghai; Chiang Kai-shek suppressed two of my publications; he also placed me in a concentration camp in Chungking; therefore, I bore him no goodwill. At the outset of my parliamentary career, I confess I was opposed to the liberation of Taiwan by peaceful means and to the Communist Party policy of permitting, indeed inviting, Chiang Kai-shek to return eventually to China in a ministerial post to co-operate in the reconstruction of China as a Socialist State.

'But I have since recognized the errors into which my sentiments of subjective revenge had betrayed me and, in common with our opposition bloc, I am now in hearty accord with the wiser Communist Party policy on these points. And on all other policy, of course.'

But could he not give me a single specific instance of the opposition's successful influence in persuading or compelling a revision in intended Communist Party policy?

'There is so much detail,' he replied in amused toleration of my persistence. 'You should hear our suggestions when we consult, Mr Hughes, and you would understand. As for the future,' he continued solemnly, 'we are resolved as an opposition party to support the pleas of many professors who belong to the Democratic League that they be relieved of excessive social duties in attending cocktail parties and receptions and given more time, opportunity and facilities for research and study. This is vital, you understand.

'We shall also continue to consult with the Communist Party in the selection and preparation of parliamentary candidates, whether Communist Party or opposition, for submission to the electors. This preliminary preparation and agreement saves much money which might otherwise be wasted later on personal and party propaganda and which would allow undue influence to fall into the hands of rich men.

'There is, after all,' he discovered, 'little real difference in our parties. We of the opposition do not wish to change right things to wrong just because we belong to the Democratic League. Sometimes we may be running the risk of going too far to the left; sometimes the Communist Party may be running the risk of going too far to the right. In consultation, we are able to follow the correct road of Chairman Mao and to ensure, as I have said, long-term political co-existence. It is the wisest course of a truly loyal and democratic opposition.'

CAMEL DOCTOR STATUS

Urumchi: Hasim Sasimbayu was the wrinkled, middleaged Kazakh headman of the 'Marching Forward' commune, a cattle outpost of *yurts* and stockades in beautiful alpine country fifty miles west of the Sinkiang capital. The resident Communist Party cadre was an energetic, intelligent Chinese of about forty in peasant's dress, who spoke fluent Uighur and – I suspect – English (although he politely evaded my approaches).

I was talking with Hasim about the affairs of the commune, sitting in the sun on a green hillside. He was a teetotaller – although he had a roving eye and a practised slap for the buttocks of attractive Kazakh women – and I sipped again warm mare's milk, vinegary but stimulating, which I guess I can take or leave alone. Hasim paid tribute (through two interpreters) to improved breeding methods, pest control, the economic and production advantages of separating cows and horses from sheep, and other technical but prosaic matters. But I got no information from him on the financial side. 'Money,' he declaimed grandly, spitting with precision at a tree stump twelve feet away. 'Money! What is money? Only something to spend. But, look, we have the cattle. And the horses. And the sheep. And plenty to eat. And – look there! – ' And he whistled piercingly with his fingers between his teeth and waved at a pretty passing girl.

Then, as though on cue, the Chinese cadre gave me further striking evidence of the attraction of commune practices to the tribesmen. He chose that moment to ride down, between a caval-cade of camels and an aromatic pride of goats, dismounted with a hail, whispered some dramatic and welcome news in Hasim's ear, politely rejected an invitation to refreshments, and galloped away.

'The Chinese cadres are very honest,' Hasim mused. 'They

bring their own food, or pay us for what they get here. True, they prefer pork to mutton, and they do not care for mare's milk, and they don't dance after supper. But, after all,' he shrugged tolerantly, 'they are Han people.

'I do not know about this communism,' he went on. 'But the cadres have been good friends to us. They live with us, they know what we need, and they help us to get it. They have brought soldiers to hunt away the wolves in the forest. They have,' he repeated, 'been friends. And a Kazakh never forgets a friend.

'And now,' he declared proudly, 'the cadre tells me that my son Abdul is doing so well at the school which the communists built for us next to the mess-hall that he may expect a scholarship and perhaps go to Peking. Who knows?' – he turned to me, awestruck by the dazzling prospect of the final accolade of scholarship and distinction among the Kazakhs – 'thanks to the communists, Abdul may even become a camel doctor!'

FASHION NOTE

Peking: The saddest magazine cartoon I saw while I was inside China showed a pretty little Chinese girl buying herself a gay sweater, admiring herself shyly and guiltily in her bedroom mirror, and then hiding the sweater under her orthodox blue uniform coat before she ventured into the street.

In fairness, however, I must add the spontaneous and reasoned observations on approved feminine fashions by Mrs Chang Shiao-liu, attractive and intelligent wife of an eye specialist at the Tung-jen Hospital. She wore blue woollen trousers and a high-necked uniform jacket, but admitted that she personally preferred the old-style *cheong-sam*. Then she went on: 'You must remember, however, that at liberation the simple uniform of the communist woman had become a symbol of emancipation. It was the dress of a new way of life. Plain blue trousers and tunic, in a curious way, represented hope and trust and common sacrifice and unity – much more, I believe, than unthinking or frightened conformity. Unless you have lived through such a revolution, it is difficult to understand our confusion of emotions, our relief and gratitude. You are too sensible, I am sure' – her smile was Eve's, East or West – 'to imagine that Chinese women have left off being women because they live under socialism.'

SENTIMENTALISM

Peking: I asked Comrade Y, us-educated, converted Party member and office holder, how he could endure the prospect of his ten-year-old son submitting a report on his father's behaviour to a party commissar.

'Suppose your son said he approved of you,' I suggested. 'Surely that would be even more indecent than reporting to this abominable anonymous party functionary that he disapproved of you, and explaining why?'

Y shrugged: 'You are an incorrigible sentimentalist. You always use coloured words. I wish my son to form his own opinions and judgments on everything and everyone – including his parents. You, I note, cannot accept the idea of your son thinking for himself; he must, you clearly plan, be inhibited by your prejudices and ideas. Why otherwise should it matter to you to whom he writes, or what he writes, about you – or anyone else?'

STREET SCENE

Urumchi: It happened in 'The Street of the Grey-Eyed Men' during the tranquil noontime traffic 'rush'. The inexpert Chinese driver of a bus loudly tooted his horn and frightened a nervous, highstepping white mare, ridden by a tough Kazakh tribesman. The horse reared, neighing, and fell. The horseman skilfully sprang clear, raised and soothed the mare, handed the reins with a bow to the chairman of a council of dignified nomads seated in converse in the gutter, walked calmly over to the halted bus, and, with deliberation but no visible anger, fetched the apologetic driver a fearful backhand clout over the nose. He then remounted, saluted his quietly approving audience in the gutter, and rode off. The Chinese driver wiped his nose, bowed first to the seated gallery, arose, turned and bowed next to the amused but friendly passengers, and drove off, without tooting.

I reflected.

Had this happened in Peking, an excited crowd would have rushed to the scene as soon as the horse fell, vociferously taking sides, while two policemen – there are always *two* traffic police-men – reasoned patiently to effect a compromise between driver and horseman by which neither would lose face. This would perhaps be based, after a half-hour debate, on a tribute by the bus-driver to the equestrian ability of the horseman and on a complimentary reference by the horseman to the attractive colour scheme of the bus. Meanwhile, the horse would still be lying in the road, and traffic would have banked up as far as the Temple of Heaven. Eventually the flow would be restored by a squad of militiamen, chanting Chairman Mao's 'thoughts'.

In Tokyo, a group of gesticulating police would naturally have denounced the horseman because he was a peasant; and the horseman, after bowing respectfully to the bus-driver because he wore uniform, would have regained face by thrashing his horse.

In Singapore, a single policeman would have noted the number of the bus and waved it on, detained the horseman for inquiry into careless riding, arrested a watching pedestrian for spitting in the street, expertly mounted the horse himself, and cantered off to the nearest police station, with both detainees trotting meekly behind him.

In Manila, an artful mob would have assembled, pickpockets would have reaped a harvest, and by the time armed police had quelled a riot, it would be discovered that someone had stolen the horse.

CHAPTER 17

The Unpublished Thoughts of Chairman Mao

One of the windfalls of China's uproarious Great Proletarian Cultural Revolution was – and still is – the squall of party files, pamphlets, tabloids and speeches which blew across the border into Hong Kong and Taipei during the tempestuous 1966–69 period. They were undercover records of the cabalistic strife and intrigue inside convulsed China – printed and Roneoed documents; genuine and counterfeit; distorted or honest; official or unofficial, according to whichever side was prevailing in the different areas of discord.

Some of the claims, denunciations and unashamed propaganda were carried by refugees, visitors and officials from the mainland; some were smuggled by established arrangement from Peking 'insiders' to foreign diplomatic and intelligence contacts in Hong Kong; some flowed along the normal pipelines of espionage exchanges between China and Taipei; some – bogus or authentic – were peddled by agents in the colony: prices ran as high as £500 for the eager and unwary. At least two Chinese were officially detected in 1967 smuggling official files out of China; Radio Peking announced life imprisonment for one, the firing squad for the other.

Hardheaded experts in Hong Kong collected, sifted and appraised the windfall of offerings for submission to world capitals for further evaluation. The US State Department ultimately released some of the papers, with sagacious comment and observation by pundits on Chinese affairs. There were, of course, conflicting post-mortems and reactions, but there was an impressive if indirect tribute to Mao in the unanimous agreement that most phoney quotes or sentiments attributed personally to the old hero – whether designed to praise or bury, anoint or smear him – were immediately pinpointed.

Most of the serious content and useful instruction of that 'cultural' windfall has been published and examined. But I filed a dossier of trenchant comments by Mao, which we patiently garnered here in Hong Kong, which escaped proper note at the time, and which, in asides and blasts, now add human warts and wrinkles to the still impassive face of this formidable and dominant figure of our time. Neither the source nor the authenticity of these off-the-cuff quotes is in dispute. They were not released in the State Department selection of 'cultural' windfalls, and in particular exclude the published extracts from the Lu-shan conference of July–August 1959 (when Mao recalled his four-letter word exchanges with Peng Teh-huai and offered his celebrated advice to sluggish party bosses 'to move their bowels and break wind').

From Mao's address to the Central Works Committee, 25 October 1966:

One cannot reproach all erring comrades. Time is too short. Neither Comrade Shao-chi nor Comrade Hsiao-ping* can be blamed outright. They bear responsibility, true. But the Central Committee did not exercise sufficient supervision over them. So the Central Committee is also responsible. So am I. . . .

I think it is a good thing to give people shocks. I thought about this cultural revolution for many years, and I came up with the idea of shock, shock, shock.

From Mao's address to the Central Cultural Revolutionary Committee, 9 January 1967:

There are two thousand power-holders inside the Party who are following the capitalist road; if we do not prevail in the current cultural revolution, there will be twice as many next time.

Don't confuse achievements with burdens; once you are humble and desist from believing that you are experienced, you will be able to correct the mistakes you have made.

The Red Guards are politically immature. They are incompetent. They have not been properly tempered. We cannot trust them with affairs of major importance.

We want to use all sorts of people. We should have liaison with both the Left and the Right. I have never approved of a unit being cleared right out. However, the communes are perhaps a little soft in putting down anti-revolutionary elements. People have told me that when the

* The disgraced former President and Party Secretary-General. Mao, it will be noted, informally dropped their family names; it is as though Khrushchev referred to Stalin as 'Joe' or Beria as 'Laurie' at official party gatherings.

public security bureaux seize enemies, some people go out of the front door and in the back. . . .

I have ordered that a number of newspapers should be closed down, but they still appear. The problem is: who produces them?

We must also have a 'seizure of power' in the Central Propaganda Department. Although we are still feeding that mob, there are very many workers amongst them – and in the Ministry of Culture – who have become useless and worse.

When the fox seems friendly, put two locks on the chicken-coop.

Notes of exchanges between Mao and Premier Chou En-lai during the purge of the Public Security Bureau (February, 1967):

Mao: The Public Security Bureau has become an organ of dictatorship.

Chou: The 'power seizure' is being enforced. There are five categories: Members of 'the black gang with profound influence'; power-holders walking the capitalist road; those who obstinately support the bourgeois reactionary party; those who admit mistakes, but continue to make them; those who have made isolated common mistakes. The last category is in the majority.

Mao: Isolate the first two categories; divide them, and attack their minorities. Use discretion with the other elements. Do not be too severe with waverers. Some you may punish by suspending from office; others by dismissing while still keeping them employed; others by dismissal on 'reconsideration', while still paying them.

Chou: I agree. Let some sweep the streets in the daytime, but rest and sleep soundly and hopefully afterwards.

Extracts from Mao's address to the military mission from Mali, 31 August 1967:

We wanted to bring up some successors for Party leadership among the intellectuals, but now that seems to me to be an impossible task. As I see it, the intellectuals, including youths still receiving education at school, have a basically bourgeois world outlook, whether they are inside or outside the Party.

A thorough revolution can be accomplished only through workers, peasants and soldiers – the masters of our time – as our main force. This means workers and peasants, because soldiers in a revolution are only workers and peasants in uniform. . . . Intellectuals can always change quickly and have swift perception, but they have their natural limitations, lack the will for thorough revolution, and often show wavering character.

Bad men among the masses cannot be more than five percent, which would, however, total 35 million. If they were joined into an army and opposed to us in an organized manner, they would really be a problem. However, they are scattered everywhere and ineffective.

Some people say that the Chinese people deeply love peace. I do not believe that they do. I think the Chinese people are bellicose. . . .

The struggle between the two classes and the two lines cannot be settled in one, two, or four cultural revolutions. But the results of the current revolution must be consolidated for at least fifteen years. Two or three cultural revolutions should be carried out every century.'

THE PRIVATE THOUGHTS OF UNCLE MAO

Mao's favourite niece, Wang Hai-jung, preserved this Boswellian record of her uncle's philosophic, political and moralistic observations in a relaxed but lively conversation, published as a Party brochure by a Peking revolutionary cultural body in March 1967:

Wang: At the moment we are forbidden to read the classics. However there are some students and cadres in our class who read the classics when they are supposed to be learning English. Some of them are even reading *The Dream Of The Red Chamber* [a Chinese historical classic, which has been denounced by the Party].

Mao: Have you read *The Dream*?

Wang: Yes.

Mao: Which character did you like best?

Wang: I didn't like any of them.

Mao: You can read *The Dream Of The Red Chamber* because it is a good book. It is not merely a story. It is a great historical novel. Only by reading it can you realize what feudalism was like.

Mao then read aloud a poem, *Pei Cheng* by Tu Fu from *T'ang Shih Pei Tsai* – selected poetry from the T'ang dynasty.

Wang: Surely if you read that poem, you must have a precautionary injection beforehand; otherwise you will be influenced by it.

Mao: You are being purely metaphysical. Why should you need a precautionary injection? You can go deeply into any poem and then climb out. You don't have to learn the poem by heart; you just have to read and enjoy it. Does your school let you read the Bible and the Buddhist *Sutras*?

Wang: We don't read them. Why on earth would we want to read them?

Mao: It is useless to do translation without reading the Bible and the Buddhist *Sutras*. . . . How do you say 'intellectual' in English?

Wang: I don't know.

Mao: You are studying English and you are an intellectual yourself. And yet you can't even translate the word. Look it up in the dictionary.

Wang: Damn! It isn't in this dictionary. It has got 'knowledge' but not 'intellectual.'

Mao: This dictionary is no good. Many words aren't in it. You had better go back and ask your school to produce a proper Chinese-English dictionary with all the new political terms and examples of how they are used.

Wang: We have neither the time nor the people to do so.

Mao: Nonsense. You have so many teachers and students that you should be easily able to produce a new dictionary.

Wang: When you receive foreign guests and they speak English to you, can you understand them?

Mao: No, because they speak too fast.

Wang: Well, when you receive foreign guests, do you speak English?

Mao: No, I don't.

Wang: If you don't speak it and don't understand it, what's the use of learning English?

Mao: I study English in order to improve my knowledge and to compare the difference between English and Chinese. I want to study more English.

Other aphorisms by Uncle Mao were recorded by Miss Wang:

Whoever frequently seeks advice from others will never take the wrong road.

One should be broad-minded. One's demands on oneself should be strict. Treat people as equals and use reason to persuade others.

Adopt an attitude of possible defeat in dealing with others.

Those who blame others for not understanding them probably do not understand others basically. Those who blame the leadership of the organization for not believing them probably do not understand the organization leadership.

Give more to others and demand less from others. Believe in yourself less and in the masses more. When you look at other people's faults, you must look for their good points as well. When you look at your own good points, you must see your faults as well.

Don't wag your tail when you have achieved something, but do not lose heart when you have made a mistake.

Individualism is the root of all problems. The manifestations of individualism, such as money, pretty women, fame and position, should be destroyed by criticism and self-criticism.

One must have a feeling of revolutionary glory but not of individual glory. One must have a feeling of revolutionary responsibility but not of individualistic achievement.

If you want to put your views forward, don't follow in the wake of everyone else. When party policy changes, your head must be specially clear.

Give yourself room for manœuvre in discussion and argument. Do not flog a topic of conversation to death.

One should apply the energetic and serious approach appropriately. If one is too serious, one becomes wooden, lonely and deserted. If one is too energetic, one becomes superficial and wastes energy.

One can always make concessions on those questions which do not involve principles.

THE GRAFFITI THOUGHTS OF TSE-TUNG

Guinness' Book Of World Records does not mention it, but in December 1968, the Chinese army magazine, *Chieh Fang-chun*, proudly claimed that Chairman Mao was the writer of what must be the longest message ever inscribed on the walls of a public convenience anywhere in the world. This breathless graffiti ran to an alleged total of 4,000 characters, and was a spirited but scholarly attack on the principal of twenty-two-year-old Mao's old school in Changsha – a reactionary named Chang Kan.

'Chairman Mao personally wrote this "Expel Chang Kan!" message on the Gentlemen's Pavilion in the backyard of the school in June 1915,' the magazine claims. 'The hand-written proclamation exposed the crimes of the head teacher and severely criticized the entire feudalistic educational system and the dark old world.'

It is not disclosed whether Mao wrote his marathon pronouncement on the lavatory wall or walls in crayon, whitewash or paint. Nor is any estimate attempted of the time occupied on such a Herculean task, which presumably was undertaken at night to avoid the risk of arousing the curiosity of the school staff.

'Principal Chang trembled with fear when he read the inscription,' the magazine adds. 'One thousand progressive students at the school followed the lead of their heroic comrade Mao and shouted: "Chang Kan get out!", and so the all-powerful revisionist and reactionary was pulled down from his throne and thrown out of the school gate.'*

* Recent visitors to Changsha testify that the old school is maintained as an honoured memorial to Mao, but say that they were told nothing by party guides of the historic 4,000-character inscription on the walls of the 'Gents' Pavilion'. It would appear that this privy novella unhappily was erased over the ensuing years.

CHAPTER 18

'Brute Reason' and 'Brute Force'

'In reasoning,' Mao Tse-tung wrote a long time ago, 'we must begin by administering a shock and shouting at the patient, "You are ill!", so that he is frightened into a sweat, and then we tell him *gently* that he needs treatment.'

That is – or was – the theory for punishment or correction of heretical crime in China after the mass-accusation meetings, public trials and executions of 1951 had become bloodstained history. This is 'Brute Reason', which, as non-party member Oscar Wilde once protested, 'is far more unbearable than Brute Force, which only hits below the belt, while Brute Reason hits below the intellect'.

The Mao formula for 'Brute Reason' was primarily concerned with ideological offences and deviations. It was also the reformatory influence for many long-term political prisoners, who had been convicted as spies, Kuomintang 'terrorists' and counter-revolutionaries. I visited the Peking prison, in which 1,200 men and forty women were serving sentences of from three to ten years, with a few lifers. There were stone walls and a squad of armed sentries; but there were no locks on the cell doors, the prisoners did not wear uniforms and corporal punishment was forbidden: a difficult prisoner was – believe it or not – punished by not being allowed to work. More than one hundred former prisoners, who were free to return to their homes, preferred to remain and live in the prison, working amid their still-imprisoned comrades at the textile mill or the weaving plant.

'We aim to correct the prisoner, to reason with him, to reform him, to teach him to think correctly,' I was told by Comrade Gi Dong-han, a tall, intelligent and intense young Chinese, described as 'Secretary' of the prison. 'We re-educate him – patiently and thoroughly. He learns the truth and seriousness of his offences against the people. He works nine hours a day and studies two hours a day. There are regular group meetings of prisoners for self-examination, self-reflection and self-criticism, at which the older prisoners help the younger ones.'

Secretary Gi conceded that sometimes there were stubborn and rebellious prisoners. 'But they must never be beaten or scolded,' he insisted. 'Compulsion changes no man's mind. We persuade. We teach. There is no hurry. If a man is perverse or stubborn, we may decline to allow him the right to work at the spinning and weaving machines. He can idle in his cell, stroll around the grounds, sit by himself, take it easy – as you Westerners say. But he knows that he is being disobedient, non-co-operative. He suffers the silent disapproval of his comrades. Sooner or later, he will recognize his errors, and testify to them voluntarily and openly. There is sincerity and penitence in every offender's heart, if we seek reasonably and earnestly and patiently enough.'

As a lofty principle of reform, 'Brute Reason' is supposed to control ordinary crime also. There is still neither a criminal nor a civil legal code in China. Sentences, imposed openly by a people's court or privately by a national security commissar, are influenced by the personal and political background of the offender rather than by the nature and gravity of his offence. A robber or a rapist will escape lightly if he has a 'reliable' background, while a petty thief or minor transgressor can cop a long stretch if, say, he has been unwise enough to have a landlord for a father. In all communist and fascist states, crime and punishment tends to be a deep and dark, fascinating and terrifying mystery. In China, the mystery has darker depths and Oriental undertones of horror.

During the cultural revolution, confusion was worse confounded when, having flung thousands of officials into prison for 'revisionist' crimes, the proud new 'Revolutionary Committees' found that they could run neither party nor administration effectively without their services, and accordingly were constrained to 'forgive' and release the officials, and to ask them humbly to help get the Mao show on the road again.

Increased juvenile delinquency was a natural legacy of the approved and organized violence by the Red Guards, and 'Brute Force' of necessity replaced 'Brute Reason' in a bloody showdown of public trials and mass executions. This stormy period in 1970, with bland Oriental understatement, was called 'The New Trend' – hsin-ssu-ch'ao. On the hard evidence of provincial radio news, monitored in Hong Kong, the public trials were staged for more than six months in 1969–70, beginning in mid-December in Harbin, Shanghai and Sinkiang. There were also factual reports of similar trials in Kwangtung, Heilungkiang, Inner Mongolia, Fukien, Peking, Tientsin, Wuhan, Kwangsi and Honan. In the month of March, in Canton alone, according to the Kwangtung provincial radio, more than one hundred male civilians were found guilty at three mass trials, and were shot on the spot. In addition, some 300 to 350 were sentenced to long terms of imprisonment in 'corrective labour establishments'. The 'jury' at each of these public trials, by official count, averaged 10,000 – attendance compulsory.

The absence of regular news services from Yunnan and Szechuan probably conceals the similar staging of similar trials in those turbulent provinces. The conservative judgment in Hong Kong was that more than 5,000 'major criminals' were tried and at least 1,000 executed in the first six months of 1970.

Here are documented reports of two typical public trials, under 'Brute Force'.

Radio Peking (20 January, 1970): Six prisoners were found guilty this week at a People's Court of political crimes, counter-revolutionary plotting against the masses and the state, and conspiring with the arch-renegade, arch-revisionist, ugly scab and traitor Liu Shao-chi. They were found guilty of corruption, bribery and embezzlement. After a public hearing of evidence, all pleaded guilty and – amid shouts of 'Long Live Chairman Mao!' – they were executed on the spot.

Eyewitness Report (from neutral Asian diplomat): probably 20,000 members of the 'jury,' dominated by a huge billboard portrait of Chairman Mao, were assembled in the sportsground near Peking's West Gate when the six prisoners, with shaven heads, were dragged into the arena. All rose and shouted: 'Guilty! Death!'

It was 9 o'clock on a bitterly cold January morning in this Year of the Dog, with a pitiless wind cutting high over the Great Wall and the Western Hills from the Gobi Desert.

Three guards handled each prisoner; two grasped his arms, the other forced down his head. On each man's chest was a placard proclaiming his crimes. Five judges marched into the arena: two women, two men in uniform, and a senior in civilian clothes from the secret police. A band blared *The East Is Red*, and the execution squad, with submachine guns, stood at attention and then relaxed for the trial, bored, chatting, smoking.

Charges were read against each prisoner in turn. Witnesses were called and bawled their evidence through loudspeakers, brandishing the little red book of Chairman Mao's Thoughts. No defence was allowed or plea taken. Following a lead from the claque in the front seats of the bleachers, the whole 'jury' rose once more, shouting: 'Guilty! Death!'

The first prisoner was dragged before the firing squad, tied to a post in front of a high screen, and shot immediately and efficiently. The body was dragged to one side and turned over on its back. Justice had taken twenty minutes.

The same procedure was followed with the remaining five prisoners, except that proceedings were hastened, and only ten minutes were needed to try and shoot the last man. By 11.30, the 'jury' was marching out to the tune of *Sailing The Sea Depends Upon The Helmsman*. Some crossed the arena to file triumphantly past and spit, and even urinate, upon the six bodies. By noon, the crowd had been cleared by waiting trucks or had dispersed on foot to neighbouring factories. But the bodies lay there all day.

Radio Canton (28 May 1970): Six enemies of the people, who had been convicted at a Canton People's Court of having been supporters of Liu Shao-chi, of having started factional fighting during the cultural revolution, of having helped people to escape, of having listened to reactionary radio stations, and of having been employees of a foreign state, were publicly executed yesterday at Shumchun (on the Hong Kong border). All admitted their guilt before execution.

Eyewitness Report (from a Hong Kong resident who was in Shumchun after visiting relatives in Canton): 'The shooting started at 9 am, after villagers had come to the hillside outside the village. This execution centre cannot be surveyed by Hong Kong police from their lookout at Lowu (on the Hong Kong side of the border). The six men were dragged, in turn, to the execution spot and killed by a firing squad with submachine guns.

The first man kept shouting, 'I am innocent,' and was crying and wailing as the army men tied him to a pole. The other five offered no resistance. One was shot sitting on a box; three were shot standing up; the last man refused to stand up and was shot kneeling. There was an interval of ten minutes between executions. Soldiers photographed each execution.

During the executions, there were heavy showers of rain, but this did not delay the performance. Afterwards many of the audience, men, women and children, filed past the corpses, which had been kicked over on to their backs in a row by the armed men. The bodies lay there all day and night. I did not return. But I am told that they remained there until the next noon, and were frequently defiled by passing groups, organized by the army.

Another Eyewitness Report (from a child of Hong Kong parents, also returning home): My Number One uncle and aunty took me up on the roof to see the men shot. I did not like to see. One man was shouting out before he was shot dead. I started to cry and hid my eyes. My aunty was very angry with me and took me off the roof, while people laughed at us, saying she had lost face.

There are now three categories of prison camps, which are described as Corrective Labour Establishments, in China. First, there are the 'Labour Reform' camps, reserved customarily for long-sentence offenders, who are engaged in hard labour, heavy construction, basic agriculture, railway and road building, and the like. Secondly, there are 'Education Through Labour' camps, for lesser offenders serving shorter or indefinite sentences, and sometimes the victims of what is amusingly called 'administrative justice', which means simply that they have not been specifically charged in a people's court but have fallen foul of national security. Up to the mid-sixties, the maximum period of 'Brute Reason' in these No 2 category camps was supposed to be three years. But no-one has any definite notion what the rules are or who makes them. The third category constitutes 'Forced Labour' camps, where petty criminals, migrants and the unemployed are put to work. Many of the prisoners in these camps have not been charged with an offence, and indeed are generously classified as 'volunteers', who sign a 'labour employment certificate', testifying to their willingness, nay eagerness, to enter the camps.

All prison escapers with whom I have talked in Hong Kong, Macao and Taiwan accepted a cynical party line approach to crime and punishment. One party cadre in Canton was found guilty of corruption, involving commune funds, but escaped with a reprimand because his superior (who was known to have shared in the offence) testified to his devotion to the party and to 'the importance of his work for the state'. Conversely, an elderly professor in Chungking, who had been under fire during the 1957 'Hundred Flowers' campaign, was sentenced to eight years – in a Tsinghai prison camp, where he would have no friends – for 'spreading rumours of an anti-government nature and attacking government policy'. The evidence showed that he had casually asked someone how long he thought Chairman Mao would live. He died in the Tsinghai camp, but 'only from loneliness', my anti-party informant told me with frightening Chinese objectivity, and not from ill-treatment or heavy labour: 'He was a kind old man, and all the army guards in Tsinghai loved and helped him.'

In certain circumstances, however, the Party can be toughly 'reasonable' against even its hopeful new generation. One bright young Cantonese student, with a good party record and the 'reliable background' of a 'revolutionary peasant' father, was sentenced to two years, making chamber-pots in a No 2 labour camp, because he had contested the right of his commune production leader to transfer him from university studies to urgent river dike construction. Examples must be made.

Here are the ruling scales of punishment for crimes committed in Kwangtung province until the height of the cultural revolution; since then, new and unknown, but constantly shifting, adjustments have reflected changing political influences. The maximum applies to those who have 'unreliable' backgrounds; the minimum to those who, in a word, have friends among the party or army brass:

Theft and burglary	... one to eight years.
Sabotage of the national economy	... one to fifteen years (or life).
Vagrancy	... two to five years.
Rape	... Two to ten years.
Corruption	... three to five years.
'Living like a playboy and being obsessed with lascivious thoughts' (this includes adultery)	... five to ten years.
Carnal knowledge of minors	... ten to twelve years.

Murder, a rare crime, draws death without exception – unless, of course, it has been committed in the line of pro-Maoist duty, and is therefore an act of patriotism. A party member made a nice legal and moral point in a deadpan explanation to me of the relatively higher penalty for adultery over run-of-the-mill rape: 'Only two are involved in rape – one unwilling; but three are involved in adultery – two willing, and deceitful.'

Conditions inside the rough 'Labour Reform' camps varied,

one gathers, from area to area, but more especially from political crisis to crisis. But certain conditions, rewards and penalties have been constant. Food was carefully rationed according to the physical labour of the prisoners and the usefulness of their heavy construction work; yet mass hardship and deaths were accepted with a shrug among the incorrigible 'lifers' or long-term prisoners sent to mining camps and to 'glorious reproductive work' in the frontier 'virgin lands'. During the national food shortage in the early sixties, after the 'Great Leap' had become the 'Great Retreat', there were thousands of prison deaths from malnutrition and plain starvation. Tuberculosis, on the testimony of a former national security cadre, now living anonymously in Macao, is maintaining a death toll of around forty percent among old workers in most 'Labour Reform' camps in mining areas – a legacy of those hard days, which admittedly were hard for all Chinese.

Irrespective of the urgency of labour programmes, all prisoners attend self-criticism meetings of from two to three hours every night. A section-leader, himself a prisoner struggling for early parole, supervises a group unit of from twelve to twenty prisoners, each of whom in turn each night must stand up and denounce himself and other prisoners. Failure to co-operate 'sincerely' can mean harder work, a reduced food ration, or continuing deferment of technically overdue parole.

Bed spaces in dormitories are changed regularly to prevent friendships developing among prisoners. Right or wrong, most of the ex-prisoners with whom I have talked believed the camp legend that 'criticism' – i.e., betrayal – of a minimum of six other prisoners was a necessary condition for parole. The camp authorities might not always accept the 'criticism' officially, but they appreciated the 'sincerity' which prompted it. Normally, army and security guards, dedicated to Chairman Mao's homilies on 'Brute Reason', do not persistently maltreat prisoners. But they stand aside, look the other way or only murmur gentle remonstrance when bullyboy 'activists' seek to hasten remission of their own sentences by beating up non-co-operative or 'unreliable' fellow prisoners.

As a general rule, the régime has sought to appoint northern guards to prison camps in the south and southern guards to camps in the north. Prisoners in Kwantung province count themselves lucky if they are sent to a camp controlled by locally born guards. The historic enmity between northern and southern Chinese persists; it prevailed even before the cultural revolution, and its roaming Red Guard hoodlums, widened and deepened regional differences and animosities.

Parole, when won, is indefinite. The ex-prisoner, wherever he ends up, must visit the resident national security representatives at least once a week and provide evidence of his enduring reform, penitence and continuing self-criticism. His family and neighbours must assume personal responsibility for his rehabilitation, and are themselves harassed by spot-check interrogation by local cops on his progress and behaviour. Paroled prisoners, consequently, are seldom welcomed by neighbours or – after a lengthy absence – even by their families.

Attempts are made in hardship areas, where the prison camps naturally flourish, to 'persuade' released prisoners to remain on developmental work by bringing, sometimes unannounced and unexpected, their families to join them. Early releases are then offered on condition that the offenders remain in the area, technically 'free'. Wages are also offered, ranging up to sixty *yuan* (£9) a month, which is far above the average income in the commune to which the 'released' prisoner would return.

I was able to interview selected prisoners, serving 'Brute Reason' sentences in Peking, Sinkiang and Shanghai: they are not 'on show' today. I never got to see a prisoner in a 'Brute Force' labour camp: they have never been 'on show'.

It was an embarrassing experience to make a tour of the rambling, red-brick workhouses and dormitories of the Reformatory for Delinquent Young Women in an industrial suburb of Shanghai. More than 200 girls in blue dungarees, alert, docile and dignified, were working silently at long rows of buzzing sewing machines on trestles, with a huge portrait of Chairman Mao benignly surveying them. They arose humbly and bowed from the waist when addressed by Comrade Yang, the homely, venerable supervisor, then resumed their seats and sewing with downcast eyes.

Comrade Yang was astonished when I inquired about the circumstances of their arrest, trial and sentence. They were never 'arrested', she explained patiently. They had 'fallen into bad habits' and they had volunteered to enter the reformatory after neighbours and friends had reported their delinquency to the authorities, and first the local street committee, then their 'friends', family and relatives, and finally – if necessary – the police had plagued them – that wasn't the word Comrade Yang used – with tireless 'persuasion' and 'Brute Reason' to 'volunteer' for reformatory treatment. The average term of reformation was reckoned by Comrade Yang, as she blew her nostrils delicately without a handkerchief, to be about eighteen months.

Comrade Yang was most interested when I inquired whether she had studied the results of Empress Theodora's somewhat similar experiment in the redemption of 'fallen girls', and said that she would certainly consult the history books immediately. . . .

At Secretary Gi's 'show' prison in Peking, I was frankly terrified by the testimony of Chang (shall we say), a dignified, good-looking giant of a man, wearing a jaunty white sporting cap. He was serving a twelve-year sentence – cut to nine because of his frank self-criticism – for Chiang Kai-shek intrigue, sabotage and terrorism.

'I was the son of a Peking landlord,' he confessed, as one who admits the final abomination. 'I frittered away money in self-indulgence. I never cared for other people – '

'Your wife?' I interposed.

He hesitated. 'She is dead,' he said, and swiftly resumed his recital. 'I never helped the state. I engaged in terrorism of the people. I have always lived a selfish life. When I am released, I shall seek profitable work at weaving, which I have been taught here. If I am asked to remain in prison to help others, I shall do so.'

Chang said he had a son aged twelve, who then belonged to Chairman Mao's Young Pioneers (the precursors of the Red Guards). He never saw or heard from him, naturally. His son would rightly be ashamed of him. His landlord father had died in 1950, shortly after China's 'liberation'.

And here I was a coward. I forbore to ask him *how* his father died. I was afraid – really afraid – that he would reply, briskly and happily, that his father had been executed because he had been a landlord, and that he, his son, now reformed by Chairman Mao's 'Brute Reason', agreed that that execution had been amply justified.

CHAPTER 19

Party Masks for Chinese Opera

An emperor with his face painted white (denoting duplicity) stalks stiff-legged in imperial yellow robes across a stage while cymbals crash, turns to the audience and announces that he is evil and resolved to achieve his will. The appalling music swells, and a beautiful bejewelled concubine (her face painted green for passion) slinks in accompanied by two black banners at half-mast (signifying the arrival of sweet-scented night).

This is old-style Chinese opera.

An army officer with his face unpainted (denoting honesty), and wearing the uniform of the Long March, stalks with the same stiff-kneed stride across the stage, while the same cymbals crash, turns to the audience and announces that he is good and resolved to achieve Chairman Mao's will. The same appalling music swells, and a beautiful uniformed girl commune worker (her face unpainted) slinks in accompanied by two red banners rampant (signifying that she has helped surpass Chairman Mao's production norm).

This is new-style Chinese opera.

It is all very enigmatic and depressing – but inevitable. It is as though the Russian communists changed the title of *Swan Lake* to *Self-Criticism In A Commune*, transformed the swans into model workers and the noble prince into a slender Karl Marx.

Curious and heavy-handed influences have reshaped the uniquely Chinese traditions of classic Peking opera as part of the all-out drive to remould Chinese thought, labour and recreation to meet the needs of the State, the people, the Party and Chairman Mao. Because of its universal appeal in China, as the most highly developed national theatrical form, Peking opera obviously could not hope to escape.

'Reformation is essential because it is a product of the feudal era', to quote the Party's theoretical journal *Red Flag*. 'If Peking opera portrays only the ancients and not contemporary people, only monarchs, officials, scholars and beauties of the ruling class, or at best the masses of ancient times, but not the new era of workers, peasants and army men, it would be difficult for this art to serve effectively the socialist political economy.'

The party pundits admitted that it was easier to introduce Marxist themes and Maoist dogma into films, songs and television – all of which have undergone similar 'reform' – than to meddle with the stylized combination of grand opera, ballet, pantomime, gorgeous robes, towering personalities and other traditional forms of the classical theatre. The uneasy mood of doubt and confusion in which the opera purification crusade was launched was admirably reflected in a vigorous debate conducted by the Ministry of Culture on 'the wickedness of ghosts', of which there was an Hitchcockian multitude on the classical stage.

A 'moderate' Marxist school of thought sought to distinguish between 'ghosts' and 'spirits', arguing that there could surely be 'progressive spirits', and citing as an example a play (1959) which depicted the return to the modern world of an eminent ancient statesman to read the works of Mao. This argument gained force when its advocates pointed out that Chairman Mao himself quoted legends like the one about the peasant who could move mountains. It was therefore tentatively ruled in 1961 that there could still be a place for 'spirits' in the Peking party pantheon, but that 'wizards, fairies and ghosts' were definitely out because they were 'feudalistic, harmful and a throwback to the religio-capitalist concept of delayed justice and revenge in another world for evils suffered in this world'.

Compromise in communist doctrine, however, usually smells of revisionism, and slowly but steadily the party withdrew its endorsement of even party-member and party-line spirits. The final judgment was delivered against the ghost-deviationists in *Literature*, the old magazine for red eggheads, by Comrade Liang Pi-hui of the Ministry of Culture. Recalling that Mao had warned that 'old habits and old ideas inherited from history were the enemy inside the brain of the masses,' he closed the debate on a stern note: 'The enemy in the brain is not only the belief of the masses in ghosts and spirits. There is also the superstitious belief of the masses in ghosts and spirits. There is also the superstitious belief of writers and artists in an abstruse "human nature and humanism" and in' – grievous heresy! – '*jen-ching* (courtesy to all).'

For Westerners, a first night at Peking opera old-style – which had its origins in the lyrics and dances of the Shang dynasty, 1000 BC – can be a stupefying experience: brutal music, painted faces, absurd beards, piercing voices, stylized pantomime, blazing colours, legendary plots, and a casual intermingling of stagehands with players at dramatic moments. In Western musical theatre, the players sing, dance or act in alternate bursts – not, as in Chinese opera, all the time at the same time. Speech is set to music, as are all expressions of emotion from laughter to tears, rage, heroism or deceit.

I remember one pre-'reformation' opera in Peking, when a Chinese friend proudly pointed out how effectively the dying coughs of an abandoned concubine, accompanied by the cough-music of scraping fiddles and tiny bells, conformed to the Chinese *idea* of a cough.

'But it doesn't sound like real coughing,' I whispered. 'Of course it doesn't,' my friend snapped, impatient with the gross scrutability of the West, 'if it did, it would be bad opera.'

The only character who is supposed to sing, speak or laugh in a normal manner is the clown or comic (the *ch'ou*), whose behaviour naturally provokes the audience to paroxysms of laughter because it *is* normal. The conventions of Chinese opera are more often than not something unconventional and illogical, yet strict tradition imparts a kind of logic.

The audience can immediately identify a character's character by the paint on his face. In general, white represents deceit and cunning; red (fortunately) means loyalty and honour; green means passion and justice; black means cruelty. In case anyone is colour-blind, the actor also introduces himself and his intentions on his entrance in a high-pitched chant, accompanied by monotonous percussion and, at the end, a thunder of gongs.

If an emperor or general intends to mount his (invisible) horse, a stagehand in the Chinese equivalent of shirtsleeves strolls out and gives him a small horsewhip or tasselled stick. To show that he is 'riding', the actor prances forward with raised knees, extending the whip. When he lifts it above his head, he has halted; when he casts it on the floor, his 'horse' had been led away.

The heroine should be played by a man. All the great 'feminine' stars in Chinese opera have been men, except in Shanghai, where, by a perverse Oriental logic, the men's roles were played by women.

Though no actual eating or drinking is permitted by the actors, stagehands can sip tea in view of the audience, and in the provinces spectators also dine *en famille* in the theatre and even heat their aromatic Chinese food during the performance. One evening in Sian, while trying to concentrate on a performance of *The White Snake*, I was fascinated by members of the orchestra, their shaven heads level with the stage, noisily devouring noodles, pork, fish, rice and soup as they awaited their cues, while on stage the beautiful maiden 'rowed', by rhythmically swaying her arms in an invisible boat, to the Temple of the Golden Mountain in search of her lover.

The plots of old-style Chinese opera are based mainly on folk lore and legends, historical and imperial dramas, providing a spirited dialogue between good and evil and extolling the ancient Chinese virtues of filial piety, loyalty, justice, chastity and gratitude. By Western theatrical standards, it all vaguely resembles the old fashioned morality plays, as they might be presented by the Marx brothers in an extravagant mood of Oriental fantasy.

Chiang Ching (which means 'The river is green'), the shrewish fourth wife of Chairman Mao, quickly identified herself with 'the revolutionary realism and revolutionary romanticism' that reshaped Peking opera during the cultural revolution. She did not of course have the talent to undertake the re-writing and re-composing and re-styling herself, but she presided over the revolution and officially directed, sometimes revised and finally approved the new line.

She has always been ambitious, resourceful and unscrupulous. As Lan Ping ('green apple'), she was a B grade film actress from Shanghai, who attracted the Chairman's roving eye in the Caves of Yenan in 1939 (when she was twenty-nine), and then discarded her current actor husband, Tang Na, who, in proper show business style, accepted as compensation for his withdrawal a higher party-ranking post in the old City of the Mud Flats.

She has taken the byline credit for the first super-opera, *Red Lantern*, into the score of which the Western invention of the piano was sensationally introduced, outraging many party opera-buffs, but demonstrating that the revolution could graciously adopt and rewardingly adapt cultural ideas from the decadent West. Although she cannot play the piano, it is politely pretended that she composed 'the first piano concerto to portray people's war': *The Yellow River*. Eventually she slid down the opera pole, and a series of plays which she had proudly 'revised' were quietly but drastically revised again by the Central Cultural Revolution Team.

Chinese opera, communist-style, represents a convulsion of plot and a distortion of character, still designed to harmonize – however grotesquely at times – with the classical formula of the ancient art form. The new performers continue to ape stylized traditions and declaim in the same high-pitched voices to an accompaniment of the same explosive percussion. Yet now they invoke the wisdom of Mao and Marx instead of the wisdom of the celestial gods. Raw wine is being poured into old bottles.

No-one can doubt that, in undertaking to convert an ancient established tradition into a modern ideological weapon, the Chinese Politburo took on its toughest project since the disastrous 'Great Leap Forward'. It was like transforming a shining rapier into a blunt instrument. Apart from the manifest difficulties of replacing cherished entertainment with dull propaganda, the change initially aroused the instinctive resentment of actors, playwrights and audiences.

Professional and amateur opera troupes throughout China employ at least half a million actors and actresses. Most of the seasoned veterans had been nurtured in the old classical tradition. According to one angry Canton newspaper, some touring companies, at the outset of the change, made a practice of choosing second-string players for new-style opera and skimping on costumes and rehearsals. Worse still, when forced to take part, resentful actors occasionally lampooned the propagandist plots and took unworthy liberties with their honourable roles.

A member of one cast, for instance, playing the role of a model worker, 'appeared wearing a bizarre hair-style called "owl-wig" and a pair of tight trousers in the fashion worn by *ah fei* (juvenile delinquents)'. And, in a production of *Red Rock*, blessed by Chairman Mao himself, the leading actor 'cynically came on stage mincing, in an immaculately laundered white shirt, although he was supposed to have just been gruesomely tortured by a rich landlord'.

Early audiences also responded with something less than acclamation, and Dr Ma Yen-hsieng, a leading operatic musician who doubled as a dependable party henchman, admitted that there were not enough good playwrights to compose themes for new-style opera, with the result that old operas were still being staged, though less often and almost furtively.

Yet such is the power of the authoritarian state and such is the vulnerability of captive mass audiences that a great measure of success has now been achieved in imposing the new party-line opera on the people. The style is being slowly 'reformed', as the Politburo rewrites the stories and re-directs the choreography, and the characters are being adroitly inverted. The brave new world of robot peasants, workers and soldiers, students-turned-labourers, informers, lickspittle officials and neuter-sexed young men and women is replacing the corrupt old world of emperors, adventurers, drunken poets and lovely courtesans, peacocks and ghosts. The flaming coruscation of primary colours in the traditional opera is becoming a predominant red, which now ironically reflects an alien foreign ideology instead of ancient Chinese virtue.

What would Lenin have thought? The Russian comrades never found it necessary to meddle with the cherished Tsarist tradition of the Bolshoi, Stanislavsky or Leningrad ballet schools. In non-affluent Moscow, when unshaven chins and soiled shirts were the hallmark of party dedication and Soviet patriotism in the red plush boxes of the Bolshoi Theatre, the bitterest old Bolshevik never suggested that the choreography was decadent, the music class conscious, or the splendid costumes and feudal plots of the ballet an affront to the workers or an incitement to deviationism.

Among the new offerings of Peking opera that carry high official recommendations are works bearing such names as *Taking The Bandits' Stronghold*, *Red Sister*, *Sparks On A Reed Lake*, *Red Lamp* and *Heroic Sisters On The Grassland*. There was another which rejoiced in the proletarian title of *Delivering Manure*, and starred the renowned actress Tung Tan-ling. Its plot hinges on an argument between husband and wife over whether a bucket of manure should be given to their commune farm or withheld for their own family plot; happily, the commune wins out, because of the irresistible logic of Chairman Mao, cited by the husband. To quote one critic: 'Miss Tung's sprightly movement of the body, fluttering of the hands and rolling of the eyes eloquently illustrate that, although she is hard working, she is not free at the outset from bourgeois suspicion of the advantages of private ownership and city life.'

There is fervid inspiration also in the engrossing synopses of six prize-winning one-act plays by unknown writers which were published in *The People's Daily* for operatic adaption.

One of them was called *The Shop Counter* and it described the conversion of a young girl student who had failed her university examinations. Reduced to selling farm implements in her father's shop, she derides her cousin for deciding to marry a humble shop assistant. As the father vainly pleads with his angry daughter to forget her university career, a thunderclap from an approaching storm coincides providentially with the voice of Mao from the shop radio: 'In our country there are everywhere diligent salesmen respected by the people. But there are also a handful of people who despise work in a shop, particularly young people who have studied for a few years and believe that they have talents that are being wasted.'

Another thunderclap, the electric light fails, and the radio falls silent. In the dark, the young girl is admonished by her mother, who reminds her of father's hard life before the coming of Mao. The electric light is blindingly restored as her mother declaims: 'But now it is like creeping out of the dark into a bright new world.' The chastened girl begins to weep and swears to sell picks and shovels and to marry a shop assistant.

Another play, *First And Second Importance*, is set in an army barracks and has equally obvious possibilities for operatic adaption. The lieutenant and sergeant of a platoon differ on the relative importance of military drill and political training. The lieutenant wants to concentrate on drill, even during the brief spare time before and after meals. 'Three bayonet lunges before eating! That gives you an appetite!' he roars. 'Then three bullet-shots after eating! That makes you hungry again!'

But the sagacious sergeant respectfully presses for greater attention to party instructions. The value of his advice is demonstrated when the platoon registers only fifteen hits out of a nineteen-shot firing exercise. The record is sixteen. It is discovered that one soldier who missed his target had been worried about his old mother in a distant village. If only the lieutenant had taken the time to assure him that party care and aid would be forthcoming for her, he would have gained confidence and hit his target (drolly labelled 'Bald Head of Chiang Kai-shek'). As the crestfallen lieutenant strikes his forehead in despair, a soldier comes running in, carrying the target, to point out that in fact it had been grazed, and that a sixteen-hit record could be claimed. But the modest sergeant now advises the lieutenant to waive the claim to a record, in token of their resolve to combine party training with military drill in the future, and the platoon, responding with a humility that would shame a us marines shooting team, agrees.

Curtain.

CHAPTER 20

The Asian Intruders

Appropriately if confusingly, the most influential, insecure and explosive racial intruders in South-East Asia are Asians. These minority intruders are not *kwai-lo* ('foreign devils'), but they are aliens. They are Chinese – the 'overseas Chinese'. They are Asians trespassing in Asia. They call themselves *hua-chiao* – literally, 'sojourning Chinese'; poetically, 'flower' (meaning 'China'), and 'inn' or 'resting-place'. But they prefer money and influence to flowers; they don't sojourn; they seldom rest; and if they stay at an inn, they own it or run it.

Numerically, they total, at the most seventeen million*, or no more than six percent of the swarming Oriental congeries of races, creeds and cultures in South-East Asia; but economically they dominate the area; and politically their conscious or involuntary choice between continuing loyalty to China and the challenge of loyal nationalism in their foster-states must decisively shape the future of South-East Asia in the next decade. It will be a hard and bitter choice – for them and for their adopted governments.

For generations the *hua-chiao* have clung to their Chinese characteristics and traditions, united – whether impoverished or wealthy – in their blood loyalty to the great motherland and the Yellow Emperor, and complacently assured, in the face of persecution and segregation, of the transcendental superiority and inevitable resurgence of the Chinese race. Their way of life invites the discrimination of which they complain. Most of them in the past preferred stubbornly to retain the status of colonists, and this is one reason why many who may now prudently wish to become absorbed as legal citizens still find the doors of

* The four million Chinese in Hong Kong should not be classified as 'overseas Chinese'. Hong Kong may have a colonial administration, but it is geographically China and intrinsically Chinese, and if Peking moved into the colony tomorrow, the native population – however anti-communist or neutral now – would expediently shout a deafening if hollow Maoist welcome to the 'liberators'.

naturalization and assimilation closed against them. They chose to turn inward, and now they are usually forbidden to look outward.

The giant Chinese umbilical cord links them strongly to the motherland – young and old, industrialists and coolies, bankers and smugglers, communist terrorists and Rotarian merchants, millionaires and beggars. They may often be isolated among themselves by native dialects, but they are united by their common written language. The elderly, amid alien temples, remember and celebrate Chinese festivals. At the local Chinese-language schools – now being closed or restricted in many areas – the young proclaim their Chinese uniqueness: '*Wo shih Kuo jen! Wo chu tsai Nanyang! Wo ai Chung Kuo!*' ('I am Chinese! I live in the Southern Ocean! I love China!'). Yet the 'sojourners' do not want to go back home – except sometimes in old age to die or to be buried there. Nor do Peking or Taiwan want them to come home.

Most 'overseas Chinese' expect and hope that their renascent homeland will eventually extend its authority over the more indolent, less enterprising, and of course less intelligent, non-Chinese people of South-East Asia. This sentiment is strong and natural enough.

Their talents, their hardships, their industry, their success, their closely knit sense of family and history, their basic insecurity, their gusto, their inward-looking warmness have given them the title of 'the Jews of the Orient'. and, in a perverse world, the economic benefits which they have brought to, and shared with, the country of their adoption are denounced as 'alien exploitation'. Their racial unpopularity is a direct reflection and measure of their success. And their putative threat to their local alien rulers is too often nourished by those rulers' stubborn refusal to encourage assimilation – indeed, their blind discouragement of assimilation.

It is curious to note that the *hua-chiao* brought with them, nurtured, and still preserve, traditional aspects of Chinese life and philosophy which, ironically, no longer exist in their motherland. In fact, under a new Chinese régime, whose unifying energy appeals to most of them and whose pragmatic success impresses them all, these anachronistic survivals have become downright offences against the *mores* of the new China.

For example, they cherished their native instinct for gambling. They tolerated opium smoking until their foster rulers prohibited the practice. They retained their tongs or triads or secret societies. They developed to a fine art the Chinese talent for amoral adjustment to administrative corruption: they could, and can, flourish impeccably under a government which is honest, but they could, and can, also prevail when illicit methods are the rule and when commercial transactions must budget for a normal and accepted scale of bribery.

Many of the wealthy and successful have also upheld the sturdy principles of polygamy and concubinage, which were originally presented to Western colonial governments as integral canons of Chinese 'religion'. The basic Chinese family togetherness, which the communists are assailing at home, also persists passionately in alien cities and villages; the compulsion of this tradition is stronger in fact than it was in pre-communist China because foreign pressures, threats and persecution automatically demand and strengthen loyal and unquestioning family unity and obedience.

To a large extent, therefore the *hua-chiao* are devoted to an artificial and outdated image of China, which has been facelifted, transformed and disfigured since the forefathers of the present generation of 'overseas Chinese' left the motherland.

A scant ten percent of Thailand's population, the Chinese control ninety percent of the kingdom's retail business and the lion's share of the rice and export timber trade. They are less than two percent of the population of the Philippines, where they are at once courted and villified as money-lenders and brokers, and where they control two-thirds of the republic's export trade and half of its retail business. Because of governmental discrimination, they must often operate behind Philippine front-men and pay heavy 'protection' fees.

Philippine politicians always insist indignantly that the total number of Chinese residents is far higher than the official census shows, while the leaders of the Chinese community insist humbly that the count exaggerates their number. 'The dishonest Chinese are far stronger than they pretend to be, and as our corrupt officials misrepresent them to be,' say the honest politicians, pocketing their 'protection' fees from the Chinese businessmen. 'No, we are far fewer and poorer than we are said to be,' reply the Chinese, paying off their critics, who wish there were more Chinese to 'protect'.

In South Vietnam – a harried six percent – they are dominant middlemen traders and rice pedlars. Chinese own nearly half of Malaysia's tin resources (representing thirty percent of world production); they control, openly or through front-men, ninety percent of the world's rubber output; they earn approximately sixty percent of Malaysia's national income, and virtually monopolize trucking and transportation. Wealthy descendants of Fukien labourers are key operators of coastal shipping in Indonesia, Thailand and Malaysia.

The Chinese are the eternal middlemen of South-East Asia. They are the distributors of consumer goods, the brokers, the investors, the managers, the entertainment kings, the shop-keepers – and the workers. It has been well said that if all the Chinese in Malaya simply stayed home one day, not an ounce of rubber would move out of the country.

There is inevitably a concentration of Chinese capital and financial genius in Singapore, which has become the Switzerland of the Far East, the home of the 'Asian dollar', and the sanctuary for Zürich-style, numbered bank accounts. A powerful Chinese Establishment, backed by traditional mutual trust and clannish loyalty, can grant more attractive credit terms, can authorize binding deals by oral contract, and can mastermind, at a distance, correlated investment schemes and even recommend prudent policy shifts from individual holdings to public corporations which will smooth the ruffled fears of host governments.

On a different level, Indonesian pedicab boys work for Chinese; so do Bangkok pedicab boys. Native artisans in South-East Asian towns stop work at dusk; Chinese families who have been making furniture or selling goods all day are suddenly the smiling operators of small restaurants at night: Chinese cuisine is adapted to local taste with a genius for dietetic assimilation that is a challenge both to themselves and their alien rulers for realistic assimilation.

The trespassing 'sojourners' dedicate their loyalty to China – not to Chairman Mao, not to Chiang Kai-shek. It should be stressed that this racial mystique mostly transcends ideology. If the native governments, which sullenly isolate these self-sufficient communities, while benefiting communally from their industry and acumen, choose to regard them as agents for an alien – and enemy–

power, the fifth column influence should be labelled more correctly 'Chinese' rather than 'communist'.

They are an actual or potential vanguard for the superior civilization and dominant race which, they are confident, will once again extend its influence over the inferior peoples and cultures of the South Seas. Imperial Peking exacted tribute from the southern lands at the time of Christ, and the local rulers of the Indies, Burma and nearer Annamland acknowledged its suzerainty. The great mass of the 'overseas Chinese' cherish the same loyalty today for communist China as their 'sojourning' predecessors preserved over the centuries for the Ming and Ching dynasties and the weak, struggling republic of Sun Yat-sen.

This basic patriotism is one explanation for the strange contradiction by which a Chinese capitalist in, say, Malaya can accept – and even welcome – the achievements of the Chinese communists. Instinctive racial loyalty is often blind and irrational, and every Western traveller in the Far East, conversing with cultivated, sophisticated, wealthy Chinese, has had the shock of hearing his host suddenly pay tribute to the Maoist-Marxists in the Forbidden Palace for setting up a strong central government over a unified China and restoring the motherland to the counsels of the world's great powers.

Other Oriental factors are also involved – acceptance of the inevitable; fatalism; expedience; rationalization, and wishful self-persuasion that an expansionist China, despite its ideology, will still find room for free-wheeling and freebooting methods in the outer peripheries.

Then there is the paramount factor of security. Chinese communities in Burma and South Vietnam, and Singapore families, whose arrogant sons in other days returned crestfallen from China, may have no illusions about conditions in the communalized motherland, but they believe they now have a strong protector.

The widespread anti-Chinese rioting in Java in 1963, so soon after the obsequious welcome to Liu Shao-chi, and the mass slaughter of tens of thousands of Chinese, communist or not, in the aftermath of the abortive 1965 *coup*, served to underscore the precarious status of the *hua-chiao* in Indonesia in particular and South-East Asia in general. Here, revived, was the ever-present smouldering resentment of native sons against prosperous aliens and successful trespassers, flourishing, it is complained, at the expense of the country which they craftily choose to live in and exploit. Here, renewed, was the explanation why the *hua-chiao*, in turn, still look to their motherland and, in their own proud insecurity, revel in mother China's growing strength and prestige.

Theoretically, the Chinese Nationalist claim to represent all 'free' Chinese living outside the prison tyranny of the Peking Politburo is the only valid justification of Kuomintang survival and for continued American support. Yet, in practice, the South-East Asian anxiety over the chauvinism and political potential of Chinese minorities is based on the rejection of this Nationalist claim and on fears of communist subversion.

Accordingly, the *hua-chiao* are bedevilled by the persecution of local governments which would like to liquidate them, and by the infiltration of subversive Chinese communism, which would lead them to their own destruction. In their countries of 'sojourn', they are often barred from specific trades and professions, ordered to change nationality and names, and to discard their language. Unless they have 'connections', they cannot buy land. They are in constant fear of riots, maltreatment, pogroms, destruction of property, looting and confiscation. They are under rigid surveillance and subject to threats of mass eviction and deportation.

When local governments are anti-communist – as in South Vietnam, Indonesia or the Philippines – they still foolishly place too many obstacles in the way of assimilation, which remains the ideal, and indeed the only, alternative to communist takeover of the *hua-chiao* communities. Over the years, when circumstances were favourable, the Chinese have intermarried and merged happily with their local communities. In Thailand, Burma, the Philippines and Vietnam, it is difficult at times to make any useful racial blood counts. The Thai royal ancestry goes back to Imperial Chinese blood. Burma's strong man, General Ne Win, is partly of Chinese stock; Jose Rizal, Emilio Aguinaldo and Arsenio Lacson, proud Philippine patriots, were all part Chinese. (Arsenio Lacson, the late volatile mayor of Manila, was called 'Arsenic and Lace' by English-speaking friends, but he was equally proud of the correct derivation of his name, a corruption of English and Fukienese, meaning 'Sixth Son'.)

The great and continuing obstacle to assimilation – which means, in the last resort, intermarriage – is religion. Assimilation is still impossible in Malaysia and Indonesia because marriage between heathen Chinese and practising Moslems is out of the question. Yet these are the two most explosive areas in *Nanyang*, where the local Chinese 'sojourners', if indefinitely isolated, will remain a potent communist threat to national stability and a ready-made alien challenge to government authority.

Indonesia is enforcing a crude and self-defeating process of 'assimilation', which in effect is driving the three million *hua-chiao* into second class citizenship and fomenting cynical 'con-version' to Islam (350,000 'conversions' since 1965). Even when the Chinese bow to governmental decree and adopt an Indonesian name, hostile local officials frequently add their former Chinese name in parenthesis to ensure continued harassment for employment and other applications.

Singapore, of course, is a new shining exception – thanks to Premier Lee Kuan-yew, the Cambridge-educated Asian Chinese. Lee, in far more difficult circumstances, has followed the lead of Thailand, historically the wise and subtle Asian promulgator of assimilation of the Chinese trespassers. Lee has succeeded in founding and forging a Singapore identity for his multi-racial little island republic of two million Chinese, Malays and Indians – overwhelmingly Chinese by race, but increasingly, willingly and rewardingly Singaporean by choice, education and practice. Here, however, ideology – not inheritance – threatens Lee's persuasive strategy for local co-existence.

For the independent states of South-East Asia, the warning is stark and simple. If there is no assimilation of the 'overseas Chinese' where religion permits, and no intelligent accommoda-tion and co-operative effort for mutual benefit where inter-marriage is forbidden or delayed, China's dragon-seed, widely and thickly sown in *Nanyang* soil, must eventually become communist Cadmus teeth.

HON JEKYLL AND COMRADE HYDE

A Chinese consul-general in Saigon was confronted with the dilemma, as the wealthy landlord owner of the Nationalist consulate building, of insisting on heavily increased rental from himself, as the austere Taiwan diplomatic representative. The landlord prevailed over the diplomat; both, after all, were reasonable and patriotic Chinese in an alien country.

Ambivalent *hua-chiao* merchants in Cambodia, in the days of Prince Sihanouk, were gratified, as Chinese nationals, to know that Peking had opened a glue and plywood factory in Phnom Penh as economic aid, but simultaneously relieved, as middleman importers of rival Japanese products, to learn that the factory was being closed down – because of inefficient equipment, poor quality and high costs. They didn't know whether to laugh or frown at the Soviet diplomat's crack: 'Much more of this Chinese economic aid and Cambodia will be ruined.' . . .

A second generation Chinese restaurateur in Sumatra, whose Shantung cuisine attracted Chinese communist celebrants on 1 October (Mao's 'liberation') and Chinese Nationalists on 10 October (Sun Yat-sen's 'Double Ten'), patriotically displayed an impressive and flattering portrait of Chairman Mao in the private dining room on 1 October, but revised it to display patriotically an equally impressive and flattering portrait of Generalissimo Chiang Kai-shek, painted by the same artist, on October 10th.

Chinese officials of the Kuomintang minority group in Djakarta always placed their propaganda manifestos for translation with a venerable Chinese scholar and for publication with a Chinese-owned printery. The Indonesian Communist Party (PKI) chiefs used the same scholar and publishers for their Indonesian editions of Chairman Mao's *Selected Thoughts*. Some of President Sukarno's bureaucrats went to the Kuomintang officials and 'advised' them to transfer their translation and printing business to Indonesians. The Kuomintang officials discreetly passed the news on to their deadly communist enemies, who immediately and directly transmitted a protest to equivocal Foreign Minister Subandrio, who in turn warned the bureaucrats to lay off the Chinese Nationalists and allow the Chinese to keep the business in their racial family.

When the Saigon government in 1967 belatedly tried and publicly executed a wealthy Chinese businessman for war profiteering and bribery, other Chinese leaders of commerce suspended trading operations in protest; they were joined by impoverished Chinese pedlars in Cholon (Saigon's Chinatown), who also closed their small shops. So the Government quietly released half-a-dozen other Chinese under arrest for similar crimes; some of these lucky ones were gouging usurious interest on life-and-death loans to their humble supporters, who shared their blood if not their riches.

WHEN MAO KNOCKED OVER THE WINE CUPS

The late Anna Louise Strong, one of the few honest and dis-interested Western admirers of Mao-type communism, who derived no personal benefit from her long experience in China, where she chose to live and die, has recorded a fascinating if forgotten close-up of the younger Mao Tse-tung's first ex-pansionist dreams.

She and Mao were at table together in Yenan in 1946 – one year after Japan's surrender but three years before China's 'liberation'. Mao was in an expansive, as well as expansionist, mood. He set up tea cups and Chinese wine cups to demonstrate his original theory of 'an intermediate zone',* which would include curious temporary 'allies' against the United States government, which he branded then – as now – the supreme enemy.

'He set up a big tea cup at one end of the table,' Anna Louise Strong wrote, 'and said: "See, here are the American re-actionaries." Then he put up a ring of porcelain wine cups around the tea cup: "These are first the American people. Here is Soviet Russia" – a tea cup at the other end of the table – "and between the United States and Soviet Russia are all the other existing capitalist countries – Western Europe, England, Japan, South-East Asia, Canada, Australia." Mao marked these with a long zigzag line of cups of all sizes, supplemented with match-boxes and cigarettes.

' "The people oppressed by the United States reactionaries are not the Russians, but the people of the various capitalist lands and of the subjugated and exploited areas of Asia" – he gestured at the small teacups, matchboxes and cigarettes – "and in the coming years this intermediate zone of different peoples, including

* The Chinese communists have always had a calculated weakness for high-sounding 'zones'. In 1954 – 'a zone of peace in Asia'; in 1958 – 'an atom-free zone in Asia and the Pacific'; in 1959 – 'buffer-zones'; in 1964 – Mao's resurrection of his 1946 'intermediate zone'.

China, will revolt and develop rapidly against the aggressive policy of America." '

'And Mao swept the United States teacup and some of the winecups – the American people – from the table to the floor. "A few of the wine cups must also be broken," he said.'

Today, that old and odd theatrical flashback has a revived and reinforced impact. Instructively, in this initial declaration of abiding conflict with the 'United States reactionaries', Mao distinguished semantically between 'peoples' and 'governments', and excluded Soviet Russia, then the ally of the struggling Chinese communists, from his predicted 'intermediate zone' of popular revolution against United States occupation and aggression.

(Mao metaphorically put the wine cups of Africa and Latin America in 'a second section' of his 'intermediate zone' when he resurrected the vision in Peking in 1964.)

In his writings, Mao has specifically listed the following impressive line-up of 'Chinese territory and *dependent states* seized from us by imperialist powers':

Burma, Butan, Sikkim, Nepal and Hong Kong – by Britain.
Korea, Taiwan, the Pescadores and the Ryukyu Islands – by Japan.
Outer Mongolia – by Russia.
Indochina – by France.
Macao – by Portugal.

He said nothing then of the vast tracts of Soviet border territory – Kazakhstan, Kirghizia and Tajikistan, and Siberia – which were seized by Tsarist Russia under 'the unequal treaties' of Aigun (1858) and Ili (1881). Lenin had handsomely conceded in 1921 that all this territory rightfully belonged to China, but Moscow's contemporary tsars refuse to confirm this omniscient ruling by the Messiah as merely a comradely preliminary to discussions on vexed local frontier issues, with not, Premier Chou En-lai generously insisted, even the implication of possible formal Chinese claims for restoration of any of the raped territory.

All those areas, however, are faithfully incorporated now in official party maps of 'the sacred motherland of the Chinese People's Republic'. So is a huge expanse of the South China Sea – including the Paracels (correctly belonging to Vietnam) and the

Spratleys (claimed also by Britain, France and the Philippines) –
and extending as far south as the sea-coast of Borneo (with
implicit claims on a projection of the Brunei offshore oilfields,
now being drilled inside territorial waters).

No competent observers on the spot seriously suggest that Mao's
armies will begin physically to march south and break the tea
cups or the wine cups in the former 'dependent states' of South-
East Asia. Given those grand old Chinese virtues of patience and
deviousness, the symbolic crockery can be attended to by remote
control and by proxy. The theory of 'falling dominoes', under
which one forcibly displaced government knocks over its
neighbour, does not correctly describe the process of creeping
communism or guerrilla 'liberation', which is more like a spreading
stain that flows, meanders, isolates, finds its level, soaks and
coagulates. In each area, the minority of 'overseas Chinese'
represents both a magnet and a target.

All guerrilla tactics – from Burma and north-eastern Thailand
to the northern borders of Malaya and the jungles of Sarawak and
Sabah in Borneo – derive from the classic teachings of Mao. As
one bitter Indian diplomat said to me in Peking fourteen years
ago: 'Chinese policy has always been "*Dah, dah! Tahn, tahn! Dah,
dah!*" ' – (meaning, 'Fight for a while; talk for a while; fight
again!').

Here the point should be fairly made that, if Chiang Kai-shek
had prevailed over Mao, he would have been as equally resolved
to impose the authority of a unified China over Tibet, to restore
and reinforce China's old Imperial frontiers, to insist that Taiwan
was an integral part of mainland China, and, like the non-Marxist
emperors of China, to set up buffer states in other strategic zones.

Chiang denounced Hong Kong as a colonial affront to Chinese
nationalist pride more fiercely than Mao has yet done, and
Chiang's Nationalists, when in power in Canton, imposed a
boycott on made-in-Hong Kong goods. When the Chinese
communists inscrutably removed their guards for a month from
the Hong Kong frontier fence in 1962, thousands of refugees –
men, women and children – poured into the colony; had the
Chinese authorities refused to accept them when they were
rounded-up and returned, Hong Kong could not have stemmed
the unarmed civilian invasion. Chinese students everywhere,

whatever their differing ideological convictions and fantasies, united instinctively against both Japan and the United States – in Hong Kong and Taipei – over the proposed transfer of the pinpointed Senkaku islands to Japan. The Hong Kong and Taipei slogans echoed the denunciations of Peking.

The prospect from the mountain top varies, after all, according to the whim and stance, attention and intentions of the gazer. Nehru protested that the Tibet–Nepal highway gave China access for the first time to India. Chou En-lai replied blandly: 'On the contrary, it gives India access for the first time to China.'

That comment would be understood and approved by all *hua-chiao*, Kuomintang, Communist or just plain Chinese, bristling Cadmus-teeth or blunted Thai-assimilates, sipping from Taiwanese tea cups or *shaoshing* wine cups in whatever corner of a foreign land they have made forever China.

PART V

Mystery, Crime – and Baritsu

CHAPTER 21

The Blind Bonze of Luang Prabang

The Blind Bonze (monk) of Luang Prabang, royal capital of Laos, died, at the estimated age of eighty-seven, in early 1967.

He was venerated as the holiest man in Laos, a primitive and doomed land of holy men, simple peasants, tough opium growers, innocent but seductive women, Communist Pathet Lao terrorists, and 'one million elephants'. He lived in a remote *wat* (temple compound), unimportant and unpretentious, on a hilltop half an hour's drive from the little capital through tiger and elephant country. He had been stone blind for most of his life.

Tales of his prophecies, warnings, miracles and healings are legendary among the faithful, long accustomed to magic and the supernatural, but still moved by the special powers of the Blind Bonze.

I have two haunting memories of personal meetings with him.

In Luang Prabang on a brief first visit in 1959, I suddenly recalled the Blind Bonze and one of his more celebrated prophecies as I was jeeping down past a line of elephants, trudging and swaying, with bells on their heels, behind a troop of saffron-robed monks who were collecting their breakfast offerings from the market stalls.

This forecast had made world news in 1954, when the Communist North Vietminh, having defeated the French, were advancing confidently across Laos from fallen Dien Bien Phu towards Luang Prabang.

The Blind Bonze had then boldly prophesied to the ailing king that the invaders would never reach the capital, but would halt at a point so many kilometres east and south on the Plain of Jars, remain there two days and one night, and then retreat. This, precisely and inexplicably, they did. The world news cables carried the forecast in advance; you can read it in the files.

On the spur of the moment, I suggested to my driver-interpreter, an earnest Buddhist from Bangkok, that we drive up to see the Blind Bonze. I began to formulate some idle questions for him. I thought his replies might make an amusing story. Blind holy miracle man, indeed!

It was a hard rough drive to the hilltop *wat*. The temple was dilapidated. A group of shaven-headed novice bonzes and half-a-dozen flea-bitten Asian mongrels were sunning and scratching themselves. The dogs barked and the monks yawned at us.

The Blind Bonze's thatched hut was tilted on stilts. We dragged off our shoes and climbed a creaking ladder to the front door. My guide entered on hands and knees and was bumping his forehead on the matting when I reached the top rung.

The Blind Bonze, a wrinkled, hairless ancient, wrapped in a yellow blanket despite the heat, was squatting on the floor, chewing betel nut, with a spittoon beside him. He turned his staring, blue-white, cataract-hooded eyeballs in my direction, pointed and cried out aloud.

My guide was clearly surprised and even embarrassed. He looked at me, hesitating. Then light suddenly dawned on him. 'Mister Huggers,' he asked, 'is your wife dead?'

Taken aback in turn, I said, 'Yes.'

He was vastly relieved, even gratified. 'Oh, that is all right then. I thought The Master had made a mistake. He called out, "That man has brought his wife with him." I thought he meant there was a woman with us. Of course he saw the spirit. I mean,' he amended, 'he *sees* the spirit.'

The Blind Bonze himself had lost all interest in the subject and apparently in our arrival. His head was sunk on his chest, and he was mumbling prayers and rattling his wooden beads.

'Ask him some more,' I said, shaken.

The holy man raised those terrible, unseeing, milky eyeballs to the thatched roof and, with unconcealed impatience, crackled out a few sentences in reply to my guide's apologetic questions.

'Holy man says your wife is always with you,' the interpreter said, 'but she came here specially today because she wishes to tell you so.' (I had the feeling that the interpreter muffed that sentence.) 'Holy man says she died maybe ten years ago in some Asian city north of here; he thinks perhaps in Japan, but he has not been there and so does not recognize the landscape. She is a small, dark-haired woman, laughing, very gay. That is all.'

My wife did die in Tokyo on April Fool's Day in 1950. The Blind Bonze's description was precise. The exact and evocative word 'gay', surviving awkward and defective vocabulary and translation, seemed to haunt the hot shadows of the Asian hut.

I forgot my shrewd newspaper questions. The Blind Bonze, dismissing me with evident relief, withdrew again into himself and his prayers, chewing, spitting, mumbling, bead-rattling. It is impossible to exaggerate his supreme indifference to our presence, questions and reactions.

He had not known, of course, that I was coming. No-one had known. Not a soul in Luang Prabang – or Laos – knew anything about my private life. The driver, I discovered by discreet questions later, thought that I was 'an English writer', who had just arrived from London.

I can offer no explanation of this experience. I do not attempt one.

'Does he often say things like that?' I asked the guide as we drove away.

'He always does, but he does not talk often now. He is an old man' – a touch of reproach – 'and is very tired. Tired. He is preparing for his next incarnation. He should not be interrupted. He is very wise. And very holy. The next world is always there – clear behind the thin veil for the holy and the old to see. So, of course, he sees. It is difficult for you Christians to understand.'

I visited the Blind Bonze again about a year later. This second and last meeting seemed prosaic and anticlimactic at the time. But later?

He had moved to another hut. His reputation and influence were higher than ever. The US authorities, I discovered, always talked, or tried to talk, with him before he was received by the new king. Whenever he left his hut, he walked slowly but surely, hands clasped, head bowed, past kneeling rows of villagers. The king received him with reverence and sought his advice on all problems.

He had the knack, my friends told me, of walking as though he could see – 'not us and our surroundings, but somewhere else and something else.'

He looked frailer when we entered on our knees, but was still mumbling his prayers. He appeared to recollect me – or affected to do so. He was more brusque and even less interested in impressing me with clairvoyant insight than he had been on our first meeting. Rebuke as well as impatience emerged clearly enough from slow and clumsy translation. (I had another interpreter, who knew no more about me than the first man had known.)

The shrunken little yellow man, staring sightlessly towards us, got across the message that he was no idle fortune-teller, no gipsy palm reader, with the time or interest to ponder the personal inquiries of stray visitors.

I bowed to the inevitable, and asked his blessing. He gave it immediately, fumbling his red wooden beads. And then, perhaps, he relented – if that is the word I want. As I crawled out, he called a final, innocent-sounding remark. I accepted it as a farewell, but the interpreter looked at me curiously, and I asked, 'What did he say?'

He answered, 'The Master said to be sure to say goodbye to your friend.'

'Which friend?'

'He did not say. Just "your friend".'

Frank Corrigan, Irish-American Pacific and Korean war veteran turned US Information representative, in whose Luang Prabang home I always stayed, drove me to the airstrip an hour later in his jeep. He gave me a message to his wife, who, in common with all US dependents in Laos, had been ordered, with their baby son and adopted Laotian child, to Bangkok.

We chatted in the sun. I had forgotten the Blind Bonze's message. I told Frank that I would probably be returning in a month or so. He walked off briefly to talk to technicians discharging oil drums from a transport plane a couple of hundred yards away. Suddenly the crew called me aboard the waiting DC3 to take me back to Vientiane and Bangkok.

Inside, I waved perfunctorily from a window as Frank came hurrying back, peering through the dust. He waved while the plane revved up. But he did not really see my face at the window.

I did not say goodbye to him. I never saw him again. He was killed accidentally the next week, taking off in a small plane for a hill village.

Only in the shock of the news did I recall the Blind Bonze's farewell remark. A coincidence? I wouldn't think so much about it if it hadn't been for that first meeting. I revisited Luang Prabang several times while the Blind Bonze was still alive but I never had the courage to call on him again.

At the urging of Ian Fleming, with whom I was travelling later in Japan, I related these two anecdotes to Somerset Maugham, at lunch at the Imperial in Tokyo. Maugham was then making his *sayonara* tour of the Far East. He sat in silence after I had finished. I suggested that he detour to Luang Prabang from Bangkok and visit the Blind Bonze. 'Two hours by plane to Vientiane; one hour by plane to Luang Prabang,' I said. 'Back the next day. Two hours together: the wise old man from the West, the wise old blind man from the East.'

Maugham shrugged and replied: 'It is bad enough to know the past; it would be intolerable to know the future.'

CHAPTER 22

A Fakir's Curse on the State Department

The hard-headed US State Department is not normally responsive to supernatural or superstitious influences. The strange affair of the US consulate in Karachi accordingly merits passing note and a raised eyebrow. The imposing consulate was originally intended to be the embassy. There are Punjabis who attribute its down-grading to a *fakir*'s curse, and who reckon the Americans have got off lightly – so far. But the State Department – for the first and only time in history – did bow to local superstition, did adjust an architectural design to placate the supernatural, and did seek the ecumenical intervention of Muslim and Christian holy men to lift the holy beggar's curse from the haunted land on which the ill-omened building was built. At least, the long funeral procession of corpses, whose grotesque deaths were blamed for that curse, seems to have ground to a halt.

Today, the empty plot of land at the entrance to the consulate – carefully and reverently confined by the two four-storied wings of the building – looks like the elegant gap of a missing tooth in a handsome skull. Here, a hundred years ago, the doomed Rustomji family had built the beautiful residence known later as 'Sudden Death Lodge', and razed in 1925. The large block of land remained a damned, shunned and vacant lot in the expensive and fashionable area of Karachi's Victoria Road for thirty years, while hotels, apartments and a shopping centre arose around it. Only pilgrims ventured in to pray at the unmarked plot which the walls of the US consulate have meticulously embalmed and preserved.

It all started in the 1860s, when a wealthy Karachi Parsee named Sohrabji Rustomji decided to build his home on the estate. Slap in the centre of the estate was that fateful plot, reputedly the tomb of a *pir* or Muslim saint. A *fakir* appealed to Rustomji not to trespass upon the grave, of which he was the dedicated, self-appointed curator. The Parsee rejected his pleas. The workmen arrived. And the *fakir* solemnly pronounced his dread curse, invoking death and disaster on Rustomji and his family and on all who lived or served in the projected residence. For good measure, the *fakir* then had a fit and fell dead at the feet of the Parsee.

The curse became effective at once. Four workmen were killed in headline circumstances as the building took shape above the tomb. One died from a cobra bite; another broke his neck in a fall from the scaffolding; a third was burned to death in red-hot pitch; the fourth copped a dislodged brick on the head. Whatever his qualms, the dogged Rustomji moved his family into the completed residence.

One night, he saw his brother's son perched on the balustrade of the high stairway; he frightened the child by calling to him to get down, and then lumbered forward to catch him as he fell. They rolled together down the stairs: Rustomji broke his own neck, and, a heavy-set fellow, killed the boy underneath him. Rustomji's son and heir then contracted fatal blood-poisoning by scratching his hand on a rusty window nail; the despairing mother and widow fled to an accidental death in the north, where the curse still pursued her; and the grandson promptly committed suicide.

The ghost of the dead saint remained unappeased. English tenants named Reild moved in, and within a month the husband, previously a man of normal habit, became crazy and cut his wife's and his own throat. 'Sudden Death Lodge', according to official police records, became the popular Karachi name for the Oriental Charles Addams' house.

The continuing fatality list has been gruesomely but faithfully documented by a sober English educational official, resident in Karachi, Percival Christopher Wren, in *Dew and Mildew* (published in England), which profoundly affected the architect, Richard Neutra, when, half a century later, he drew up his protective design for the US embassy-turned-consulate.

Wren's factual roll-call of additional curse victims details the bizarre record of four young British army officers who derided the legend and shared quarters in 'Sudden Death Lodge'. One of them related, half-amused, a graphic dream about a holy beggar, squatting beside four empty graves and chanting: 'Earth and air;

fire and water!' He awoke with the words ringing in his ears like an alarm. His friends smiled with him; but then each in turn – either by contagion, imagination or the curse's influence – grudgingly admitted an encore of the dream.

The first officer was the first victim. In a Karachi morning mist, he fell and was buried alive in a pit being dug by workers at the army camp. The earth death? The second was killed in a plane crash. Air? The surviving pair, shaken at last, adopted serious precautions; but the third was duly burned to death in a kerosene lamp accident; and finally, the fourth, earnestly seeking to evade water risks by a no-swimming and sponge-instead-of-bath régime, met his death literally when a soda water bottle inexplicably burst in his face.

Other deaths were relatively prosaic but monotonously repetitive and cumulatively discouraging, and tenants eventually began to bypass 'Sudden Death Lodge', which, at last empty and deserted, fell to pieces and was demolished.

The US embassy decided to buy the deserted lot for the site of its Pakistan embassy at a bargain price in 1955. Pakistani authorities were agitated by the American imprudence, and their objections and warnings, dismissed by the original negotiators, found a more receptive audience in the architect, who hailed from Vienna. He imposed his final design, which embraced but did not obliterate the durable tomb, on the State Department. A former President of Pakistan, General Iskander Mirza, laid the foundation stone in September 1957, vastly reassured by the discreet compromise over the vengeful saint's grave, and also by the presence of a Muslim holy man and a Christian missionary, who offered prayers to the holy man and the holy beggar and blessed the grounds and the foundation stone.

But, while the putative embassy was still being built, the Pakistan government suddenly decided to transfer the capital from Karachi to Rawalpindi. And so – half-curse or not – the building was perforce reduced to a consulate, and a new embassy had to be set up in the new capital – severely sited, this time, on more expensive but unhaunted and uncursed ground.

The State Department has maintained a discreet silence on its architect's 1955 covenant with superstition, but its Karachi building remains a unique example of Western diplomatic compromise with Eastern powers of vengeance. No foot treads that sacred plot at the entrance to the humbled embassy; and – although the fearful faithful claim that weird laments and ghostly scufflings are heard at night down the empty, air-conditioned corridors – no consular corpse has borne involuntary witness yet to a deadly revival of the ancient curse.

CHAPTER 23

The Teikoku Bank Incident

The Teikoku bank robbery – with its awesome design for mass murder – was unique, and as near-perfect as any planned crime could be. It could have been committed only in Japan. It could not have been solved except in Japan. And only Japanese superstition could continue, after more than two decades, to postpone, illogically but legally, its logical and legal consummation.

The *Teigin Jiken* ('Teikoku Bank Incident) of 1948, as indexed in the homicide files of Tokyo metropolitan police headquarters, was the first and only venture into crime of a mild, fifty-seven-year-old Japanese artist. He conducted and survived two frustrated rehearsals, and then sprang his cool plan – unarmed and unaided – on the entire staff of a busy Tokyo suburban bank, left a visiting card and sixteen men and women, dying, dead or unconscious, behind him, and departed, unhurried and on foot, with as much money as he could grab – an anticlimactic haul of only 182,000 *yen* (say £200).

The super criminal had left different false visiting cards at each of the three banks which he boldly entered. He was finally traced through the first card (Dr Shigeru Matsui) – not the card presented at the Teikoku Bank (Dr Jiro Yamaguchi) – after a seven-month, nationwide police hunt, which cost an unprecedented six million *yen* and involved the interrogation of 8,796 suspects and witnesses.

Officially, there were two police heroes: Detective Tamigoro Igii and his chief, Inspector Shigeki Horizaki. But the credit really belonged to Igii, whose intuition and perseverance prevailed over all his superiors' doubts – and who was later an honoured member of the Baritsu Chapter of the Baker Street Irregulars (q.v.).

So what was the artist-'doctor's' deadly and inspired technique?

On that day in January 1948 he simply appeared at closing time (3.30 pm), told the manager that he was a doctor from the

Government Welfare Department, engaged in the disinfection of the premises against the recent outbreak of dysentery in the neighbourhood. His manner was assured and professional; he was wearing a white cotton jacket with an armband marked 'SANITATION' and carrying a medical kit.

Bank Manager Yoshida accepted his card, bowed and – Japanese custom – presented his own card. Dr Yamaguchi produced two large medical bottles containing a liquid which, he explained, was a preventive against dysentery and said that he would give a preliminary dose to the staff, who were all duly summoned. The doctor suggested casually that office teacups would serve admirably for the simple dose.

Traditional Japanese respect for authority ensured no challenge to a governmental instruction. The doctor syringed the prophylactic into the waiting cups, and was considerate enough to advise the staff to swallow quickly and so avoid undue contact of the medicine with the teeth.

The sixteen unsuspecting men and women dutifully drained their doses of potassium cyanide, which killed most of them in a matter of minutes. Dr Yamaguchi stepped over the writhing, gasping bodies, scooped up all the *yen* in sight, and quietly let himself out into the busy street, carefully closing the door behind him.

Ten of the sixteen died on the spot; two of the six who lingered, because they had vomited, died in hospital. Food poisoning – not uncommon in early Occupied Japan – was first suspected, and only after a lapse of three hours was cyanide diagnosed and the cold-blooded mass-murder and robbery discovered.

Japanese tradition and behaviour had set the stage for the impossible crime; now Japanese tradition and behaviour provided the clue for the improbable arrest. It was belatedly learned that the killer had similarly approached a first bank in mid-October, 1947, and a second bank a week before he went properly into action at the Teikoku bank. He had presented a 'Dr Shigeru Matsui' card at the first bank, and a 'Dr Jiro Yamaguchi' card at the other two. Because all the staff could not be assembled together at the first two banks, the government welfare representative postponed his preventive dosages and disinfection and left. The visit was not reported by either bank.

The Yamaguchi cards were soon traced to a dead-end – a job-printing shop off the Ginza, where the printer couldn't recollect the man who ordered the cards. But the first card belonged to a real doctor, who at once came forward and identified it and himself. It was one of an order of a hundred which he had had printed ten months before. He had only four left.

Exchange of name cards is mandatory in polite Japan, and most Japanese keep the cards of the people they meet for reference. Dr Matsui sat down, referred to reciprocal cards which he had kept, and, by a prodigious effort of memory, recalled the names and identities of most of those whose cards he did not have. Nowhere else in the world would such a roll-call have been possible. In the outcome, eighty-four of the ninety-six persons who had received the Matsui cards were patiently tracked down within four months by the large team of sleuths.

One of the first to be questioned was Sadamichi Hirasawa, an artist of some repute, with a respectable background, a happy family and a conventional retinue of two mistresses. He bore no resemblance to the confused description of the wanted man, and was a young-looking fifty-seven instead of the official estimated age of forty-five. (Cyanide delirium and paroxysms do not facilitate precise personal identification.)

Dr Matsui himself remembered clearly the gentle, modest artist, with whom he exchanged cards on the train ferry between Hokkaido and Honshu six months before the crime. Hirasawa-*san* had been carrying one of his paintings which the Crown Prince of Japan had graciously consented to accept.

The artist was quickly cleared as the detectives followed up likelier prospects and in fact detained several suspects, who however, proved alibis. But, with a thoroughness that Sherlock Holmes himself would have approved, a counter-check was ordered by a new team of detectives, and Hirasawa-*san* had the misfortune to be included in the list allotted to Detective Igii.

The detective was surprised to find that Hirasawa – unlike most Japanese – did not have (or said he did not have) a photograph of himself; and he noted that – like many guilty men – he was over-eager with a detailed alibi for 26 January before it was requested. He talked too much: he recalled chattily that Dr Matsui had written an address with a fountain-pen on the card which he had been given. Unfortunately a pickpocket had stolen his wallet, containing the card. Lawlessness was certainly increasing in occupied Japan, wasn't it? (Dr Matsui later told the painstaking Igii that he never carried a fountain-pen.) Igii politely took the artist to dinner for a friendly termination to his official interrogation. When he suggested the customary dinner-table photographs 'for remembrance', he noted with interest that the reluctant Hirasawa contorted his features and ducked his head for the two snaps taken of them both.

Igii's Tokyo superiors, however, were not receptive to his suspicions. They had cleared Hirasawa, and were looking elsewhere; but Inspector Horizaki at last grudgingly yielded to Igii's persistence and allowed him to follow his hunch and press his discreet inquiries for a few more days.

And so Igii broke the case. Hirasawa, he soon discovered, was in financial difficulties. His wife had cleared up old debts when he was suddenly and unexpectedly in funds immediately after the robbery. An alleged telegram from a friend, repaying an 'old debt', was traced, not to the friend, but to Hirasawa himself. Another alleged payment had been attributed to a man who, Igii found, was in fact dead. The alibi, under renewed examination, broke down. Then Hirasawa broke down also and confessed.

He had desperately needed money. He had sold investments to gamble. His mistresses were becoming restive. He had first planned the robbery as a theoretical plot for one of the crime stories which he was writing anonymously on the side to swell his dwindling income. He didn't have – and, anyway, couldn't use – a gun. But he had a store of potassium cyanide which he had bought for colour painting. He even got well-timed cloacal inspiration for the welfare operation from a personal attack of dysentery in the current Tokyo plague. If only he had left a 'Jiro Yamaguchi' card at his first rehearsal.

After twenty-three years, the Teigin case is still not closed. Hirasawa soon recanted, alleged that his confession had been extorted under police torture and hypnotism, and claimed that a rabies injection for dog bite in 1925 had affected his memory. But the Supreme Court sentenced him to death by hanging in 1955. An enterprising appeal was based on the ingenious argument that his hanging would be 'unconstitutional and undemocratic', because the exercise was 'self-strangulation' and not 'strangulation'. The condemned man, his lawyers argued, would be choked to death by his own weight, and this was clearly a violation of Article xxxI of the new Constitution which protects all Japanese against participating in self-destruction. The appeal intrigued lawyers and newspaper leader-writers, but the Court tossed it out.

And the long, unending wait began.

Successive Japanese ministers of justice, down the years, have evaded signing Hirasawa's execution warrant. The death sentence must be carried out within five days of authorization. Japanese ministers – of all parties – habitually shrink from this responsibility, not because they are opposed to capital punishment, but because they believe that the signing of a death warrant leads to personal misfortune.

One former Minister of Justice, Ryogoro Kato, inherited a stockpile of ninety execution warrants, deferred by his apprehensive predecessor, but finally had to get rid of them – 'one by one, in a solemn mood' – because all the solitary confinement cells were filled. Another Minister, Toshiki Karasawa, lighted a candle in his family Buddhist temple every time he had to sign a warrant. Yet another, Koshiro Ueki, who belonged to the Jodo-Shinshu Buddhist sect, wrapped a rosary around his left wrist and pronounced the words, 'Save us all, Merciful Buddha', in the presence of a bowed muster of his staff, whenever he signed.

Hirasawa, now eighty, is a relatively pampered inmate of the death-cell in Miyagi jail. His cell comprises two rooms – one for sleeping, and one for working. He suffers from haemorrhoids, rheumatism, anaemia and dyspepsia. He is allowed to wear traditional *kimono*, and can receive three visitors a day. He draws, paints and composes poems. A current project is a series of a hundred paintings of Mount Fuji *in tempera*.

Obviously he will never hang. He may indeed be released under an expected general amnesty when Okinawa is returned to Japanese sovereignty by the United States.

He has already written his last testament in verse:

DEATH OR LIFE?

It serves you right! Didn't I tell you so?
Sadamichi Hirasawa is dead.
He is really dead.
Nobody can see him any longer.
He has become ashes, for sure.

He was obviously a better murderer than a poet.

CHAPTER 24

The Colonel Vanishes

No-one knows what happened to Colonel Masanobu Tsuji, Japan's 'god of strategy' and staff planner of the fall of Singapore. He vanished into Laos from Saigon in April 1964. He was officially declared dead by a Tokyo court in 1969, five years after he was last seen by reliable witnesses. The date of his death was set with legal precision by the court at 20 July 1968, after inconclusive testimony and curious official reticence. But many who knew him best still doubt the finding.

Anyone can vanish easily enough in Laos without trying. But the colonel, who had had considerable practice as a jungle phantom, strangely and irrationally complicated his disappearance. He had in fact once vanished successfully, and returned triumphantly, nearly twenty years earlier; on that occasion he had a life-and-death incentive because the Americans were hunting him as an alleged war criminal. His baffling encore, as a distinguished Japanese member of parliament, had – and has – no official motive. He had obviously planned a secret assignation in Saigon for his vanishing act in Laos, and, on the scanty evidence available, had abandoned hope and was returning home when the summons finally came.

The Japanese government swore that it knew nothing of his purpose – if any – but sent intelligence agents to try to pick up his trail and track his contacts from Saigon to Laos and the Plain of Jars. He was, after all, an elected member of the Diet, one of Japan's most respected if controversial defence planners, and the solitary Japanese army officer who never technically 'surrendered' to the Americans.

The mystery thickened. Radio Peking suddenly claimed that the CIA had executed him. Six months later, Chinese contacts approached the Japanese consulate in Hong Kong with a first demand for a half-million *yen* ransom for his 'release'. The Japanese government has consistently maintained strict silence about the disappearance, implying that the fact of his death was not accepted.

What the devil had he been up to? How and why did he vanish? He would never have consented to act as a spy. And the Japanese government would never have dreamed of selecting him as a spy, had there been the slightest Tokyo interest in such a preposterous mission at that time and in those circumstances.

There is, I believe, only one explanation.

I got to know Colonel Tsuji tolerably well in Tokyo in 1955-59. Personally, he was an engaging man, with a shaven, gleaming skull, large ears, large nose, large spectacles and – occasionally and disarmingly – a large grin. His bald head and normal air of repose lent him a monk-like appearance. He was correct but never warm in his associations with American and British military officers, but he organized – Japanese custom? – a red-carpet reception for General Gordon-Bennett, when that Australian leader, who had fled from Singapore after surrender, visited Tokyo.

He was a proud, high-principled patriot, honest in his aims if devious in his methods. He despised General Tojo, revered General Yamshita and blamed the Japanese navy for the loss of the war. He hated communists generally but admired Ho Chi-minh personally, and believed the Japanese could come to terms with the Chinese. He distrusted the Russians utterly and disliked the Americans. His implacable post-war policy line – as maverick politician and dynamic militarist – was 'independent neutrality' for Japan, freed from the embarrassing physical presence of the stupid and harmful Americans, but armed openly with 'made-in-Japan' nuclear weapons – for 'self-defence' only, of course.

He was utterly absorbed in the theory and practice of irregular guerrilla warfare, which he angrily insisted – in those pre-Viet Cong days – the Americans had never experienced nor tried to understand. I believe today that in that obsession lies the explanation of his secret mission, mysterious disappearance, and probable hidden death.

He was born in Ishikawa and graduated brilliantly from the Imperial Army Academy in 1931, when he was only twenty-nine. He was top staff planner of the invasion of Malaya and the capture of Singapore. He personally directed the field and jungle training on Hainan Island of the numerically inferior but militarily superior Japanese force which outflanked and overran the British in Malaya. He also served in the field in Guadalcanal and Burma.

He was not openly boastful, but he relished tributes to his bravery and military successes. He proudly amplified a personal record of his combat injuries in the first of two articles which I helped him prepare for the *Asahi*'s annual *This Is Japan*: 'I was wounded seven times by the bullets of the Chinese, the bombs of the Americans, the shells of the British and even bullets from Japanese-made machine-guns supplied to the Burmese, who later fought against the Japanese. I was hit by more than thirty bullets and fragments of shell and bomb, and more than twenty pieces still remain in my body.'

I once asked him for his assessment, from his own experiences, of the fighting qualities of the soldiers of different nations. He ranked them quickly: 'The Chinese, Russians, Koreans, Gurkhas and Australians, in that order. Then the Americans, followed by the Filipinos, the British, the Thais and the French.'

'But the Japanese?' I asked, surprised. 'The Japanese?' He was also surprised. 'Why, of course, they were the best.' He added: 'You must realize, as the Americans never do, that the Asian soldier, normally, can endure bad conditions and poor rations better than Western soldiers can.'

When Japan surrendered, Colonel Tsuji was in Thailand and was on the 'wanted' list as a 'war criminal'. He then pulled his first vanishing trick, disappeared for an interval of meditation in a Buddhist temple, and, disguised in a *bonze*'s robes, later managed to make his way through Laos to Hanoi. Here he reported to Ho Chi-minh and General Giap, the victor of Dien Bien Phu. He accompanied Vietminh guerrillas as an 'observer' and claims that he rejected invitations to become a combatant not because he favoured the French or even because he disapproved of communists, but 'because I felt I could not serve in any other army than the Japanese without permission of the Emperor'.

However, by his own account, this scruple did not prevent him from acting as an 'adviser' to Chiang Kai-shek's forces, when he continued his firsthand studies of guerrilla operations – this time, the Maoist variety. He returned, still secretly, to Japan in 1949 after Chiang's defeat, remained underground, but finally emerged in independent Japan and ran successfully for the Diet in

1952. His outspoken criticism of us-dictated plans for Japanese defence, and corruption charges against Prime Minister Kishi, led to his expulsion from the governing Liberal-Democratic Party. He easily won immediate re-election to the Upper House as an independent. He was never given an official appointment with the Japan Self-Defence Forces, but his war record, prestige, strong convictions and personal contacts commanded wide influence behind the scenes.

He promulgated in parliamentary debate and written polemics those basic arguments which still divide Japanese public opinion. 'We must defend neutrality by our own hands. . . . Let us equip ourselves with the latest American missiles and spend our defence budget on reorganizing the Self-Defence Force into a nuclear-equipped military force. If this is to be done, the Government must obviously overcome the people's opposition to nuclear weapons. Laws must be enacted for the protection of military secrets. This is admittedly a difficult task, but a responsible politician should have the will-power and courage to accomplish it.'

Also and always, there was his second major argument, which reflected his own personal combat experience and overriding interest in mobile tactics. 'All the essential conditions to meet indirect aggression have been ignored (by the us-directed organization and arming of Japan's defence forces). The Japanese army, for example, has been given us heavy weapons. Transportation of Japanese troops is based, us-style, on motor vehicles, which is irrational and ill-advised for Japan, which has no oil supplies. Motor vehicles should be limited to transportation of heavy weapons, ammunition and supplies. Men and lighter weapons should be moved by bicycles. The part played by bicycles in the Japanese campaign against the Allied forces in Malaya should surely not be forgotten.'

At sixty-two, Colonel Tsuji was, therefore, an established if independent political figure in Japan, and a respected if unofficial military authority. But his prospects of gaining further direct military experience – on which his political career was based, and which always enjoyed priority over that career – were obviously fading. It was then that he suddenly departed on his vague 'mission of inspection' to Bangkok and Saigon, ostensibly of his own volition and with no known governmental or military sponsorship, official or unofficial.

For the following reconstruction I am indebted to old newspaper and military friends in Japan, to an exhaustive but little-known report by Mimoru Omori in the Tokyo paper *Bungei Shinju* (April 1967), and, above all, to documented notes from Mr H. V. Howe, of Sydney, who arranged for the translation and publication of Colonel Tsuji's book *Singapore* in Australia, who conducted long personal correspondence with him and is still in personal communication with the Tsuji family in Tokyo. (Only the facts here are, in large part, attributable to Mr Howe and my other sources; not my subsequent theorizing.)

On 20 April 1964, Colonel Tsuji, winding up his curious Bangkok–Saigon 'inspection', suddenly wrote from Saigon to his family, saying that he would be home on May 1. But, on 25 April, the manager of his hotel reported to the Japanese consulate that Tsuji had vanished with his luggage on the previous night, leaving no word of his plans. The consul at once notified the Japanese Foreign Office. A month later, a Government mission arrived from Tokyo, comprising a senior parliamentary secretary, several military intelligence officers and Tsuji's eldest son. They made searching but discreet inquiries, offered no information, and departed. In Tokyo, the Government declined all comment on the ground that it might jeopardize Tsuji's safety.

In August, Radio Peking announced, out of the blue, that Colonel Masanobu Tsuji, Japanese member of parliament, had been inexplicably shot by CIA agents in Laos. The US authorities immediately denied the allegation, and Peking refused further information and has never since mentioned the colonel.

Mr Howe now reveals that, early in 1965, a note was delivered to the Japanese consulate in Hong Kong, containing Tsuji's signed and dated identification, which demanded the half-million *yen* ransom for his release from captivity. This demand was sent in duplicate to Tsuji's family – who recognized his signature – at his home address in Tokyo. All efforts by the Japanese consulate to maintain contact with the Chinese who delivered the demand failed. In 1966 a similar ransom demand – but without enclosure from Tsuji – was again delivered to the Japanese consulate – the most discreet diplomatic setup in Hong Kong – but the senders again broke off contact.

The later thorough investigation by the reporter Omori and Japanese agents traced Tsuji from Saigon to Vientiane, where a resident Pathet Lao (communist) official testified that Tsuji had shown him letters of introduction for presentation to leaders of the Pathet Lao insurgent forces at a forward base north-east of the central Plain of Jars. (The Omori report is far more convincing than a secondhand claim by an unknown Chinese interpreter that Tsuji was captured by Pathet Lao guerrillas and shot as a suspected spy in 1965.)

Omori quotes directly a well-known Pathet Lao representative in Vientiane, Tao Sot, who said that Tsuji, dressed in the robes of a Buddhist *bonze*, and under the personal escort of a genuine Buddhist monk (whose brother commanded a Pathet Lao unit in the Viet Vieng area), had delivered his letters of introduction, and had been guided to an airstrip, and then flown in a Russian plane to Hanoi. There, according to Tao Sot, Tsuji had been welcomed by both Ho Chi-minh and General Giap, who had sheltered him on his earlier visit. Tao Sot made the further remarkable – or absurd – claim that Tsuji had later been received in Peking by Mao Tse-tung and had then returned to Hanoi.

Omori, a scrupulously factual reporter, attempts no personal explanation of the motives for this incredible mission, but adds his own firm conviction that Tsuji in 1967 was with the North Vietnam forces in the field.

(On a 1967 assignment in Laos, I visited the then commander of the token force of one hundred Pathet Lao guerrillas in Vientiane – a Colonel Soth Pethrasi. I did not complicate my own inquiries on ceasefire prospects among the Pathet Lao, Russians, North Vietnamese, Chinese and Poles in Vientiane by raising the remote and irrelevant Tsuji issue. But Omori's investigations were well remembered and confirmed at the Hotel Constellation bar, unofficial Vientiane press club; and Colonel Soth's predecessor had been a Tao Sot. Several Buddhist monks were living in the Pathet Lao compound near the rice market.)

Mr Howe's own trusted contacts confirm independently the opinion of my Japanese newspaper and army friends that the Japanese government deliberately withheld inside knowledge of Colonel Tsuji's mission and fate. The Tsuji family, understandably enough, has been reticent even in speculation over the colonel's motives or the mysterious ransom notes.

Only one theory, it seems to me, offers a plausible explanation of the Tsuji mystery.

Tsuji was just curious. He wished simply to study the tactics and operations of the Viet Cong guerrillas on the spot. He wanted to satisfy his own insatiable curiosity, and perhaps to secure additional facts and information to support his argument at home for drastic changes in Japanese army training and planning. He secured semi-official sanction for his approach through his powerful contacts: formal, noncommittal Tokyo letters of introduction, which could do no harm to the Japanese signatories.

Laos was still tolerating the doomed coalition 'government' of Prince Souvanna Phouma (the neutralist and pacifist), 'Red Prince' Souphanovong (the aristocratic Pathet Lao leader), and General Phoumi Nosavan (the rightist army leader). North Vietnam troops were operating only – and of course 'invisibly' – in northern areas of Laos. The cynical Laotian coalition temporarily suited the motley triumvirate, blandly smiling and mutually distrustful, but, like the similar compromise of 1958, it was on the verge of collapse.

The Japanese government would have been mildly interested in any inside report and impressions from Hanoi. The North Vietnamese would not have been uninterested in any firsthand report of events and aspirations in Tokyo; they knew Tsuji's anti-American record, and they recalled his earlier contact with Ho Chi-minh and Giap; they could well have exaggerated his political importance. But there were no significant problems or even straws of consequence in the Hanoi-Tokyo winds. Neither government had anything much to gain, but certainly nothing to lose, from the arrival of a self-appointed and self-interested army colonel whose ageing nostrils simply longed to sniff anew the smell of cordite in the jungle.

Tsuji would never have demeaned himself by aping the spy. But on his personal mission – rash and irresponsible – he could still persuade himself that he was humbly but honourably serving the Emperor, even if he expediently changed his *bonze*'s robes for the uniform of a military 'observer' with the North Vietnamese and Viet Cong forces. He was indeed reportedly sighted once in the jungle by American prisoners of war.

It is inconceivable that Mao saw him, but he could have gone to Peking – as Omori was convinced – and might there have even exchanged Japanese bows with Kinkazu Saionji, that aristocratic Japanese renegade in exile, who had been a convicted member of the Sorge spy-ring in pre-war Tokyo. The bows would, however, have been stiff and Tsuji would not have sought the meeting because he abominated Comrade Saionji as a traitor and consort of communists – Russians, to boot.

The mysterious ransom notes could have been a normal exercise in graft by enterprising operators who abound in Vientiane, Bangkok and Saigon, unfettered by Marxist or patriotic ties.

Anyway, the colonel has vanished. He is probably dead now – despite his loyal friends' wish-fulfilment recollections of his earlier providential escapes. It is a pity: he would have had more interesting and exciting reminiscences for another book. But he would have outlived whatever faint, prospective usefulness his surprised and uncertain hosts might have hopefully anticipated.

One fact is certain. Alive or dead, Colonel Tsuji would have remained to the last a brave and patriotic Japanese, dedicated solely to Japanese independence and resurgence, and steadfastly opposed to us or communist interference alike in Japan's affairs and Japan's future.

CHAPTER 25

The Baritsu Chapter

There is no hard evidence – and only fleeting and fanciful reference for extravagant deduction – that Sherlock Holmes ever visited the Far East. True, his name and influence penetrated, lingered, and lingers, in all universities, libraries, police stations, bath houses, inns and other cultural centres in the Orient where English has been read or heard. Only the blasphemous or the mischievous would challenge his own statement to Watson that he spent a couple of years in Tibet, during the post-Moriarty hiatus of 1891–1894, and was the guest of the Head Lama (not the Dalai Lama) in Lhasa, returning to Lyons via Chinese Turkestan, Basra, Mecca and Omdurman. (Milord Donegal has traced four major expeditions – two English, one French, one American – to Tibet between 1891 and 1894.)

But Holmes, definitely and regrettably, was never sighted east of Lhasa, and he drops no allusion anywhere to any memory of Tokyo, Peking, Hong Kong, Manila, Singapore or Shanghai. (Shanghai, by a curious coincidence that would have amused him, proclaimed its first 'constitution' of 'independence' in 1854, the year of Holmes's birth.) Some ingenious theorists – including the Sydney *savant*, Dr Cyril Pearl – have argued that Holmes's decisive intervention in 'the colossal scandals of Baron Maupertuis and the Netherland Sumatra Company' must have necessitated a personal visit to the East Indies. But in those days authority and responsibility for scandals and colonialism east of Suez was firmly entrenched in European capitals and banking houses; and Holmes – to quote his own reference to Moriarty – always struck at 'the spider in the centre of the web' rather than at the web's 'thousand radiations'. By that same artful reasoning, it could be pretended that Holmes's glib aside about 'the black Formosan corruption', when he convinced Watson that he was dying of 'a coolie disease from Sumatra', meant that he had himself bathed in Taiwan's Sun-Moon Lake and enjoyed an incautious massage at Padang.

The one solitary Japanese word which he ever used – or which was garbled by Watson – does not appear in any Japanese dictionary: *bujitsu* (q.v.). He preferred cocaine to opium. He never ate Chinese food. He had never heard of Japanese *go*.

Yet I saw Japanese translations of his adventures in pre-war Tokyo, and have bought secondhand English translations of *The Short Stories* and *The Hound of the Baskervilles* in the central market-place of Mao's Peking, in a popular store on Karl Marx Avenue in Khabarovsk in 1963, and at a stall off the Shanghai Bund in 1957. (The anglophile Intourist interpreter in Irkutsk told me proudly that he had a complete set of The Master's works in his home; I trust he received safely the membership certificate of the Baritsu Chapter, which I subsequently sent him from Hong Kong.) Most top detectives in 1940 Japan and Occupied Japan had diligently studied Holmes's methods, and many Japanese scholars maintain regular and erudite correspondence with leaders of the Sherlock Holmes Society and the Baker Street Irregulars.

One of the cultural highlights of the Japanese Occupation, indeed, was the foundation, in 1948, of a still-flourishing Tokyo Chapter of the Baker Street Irregulars by Japanese, British, American, Australian and New Zealand students of Sherlock Holmes, his life and times, which culminated in an Oriental tribute to The Master by the public erection of a first Sherlock Holmes plaque in London, five years later.

In view of confused and ignorant misrepresentation, it is useful and desirable to record here the official circumstances of the founding of the Chapter, and also known details of the still unsolved mystery of the plaque's shameful theft and furtive restoration.

The historic founding meeting of the Baritsu Chapter of the Baker Street Irregulars was held at the Shibuya residence of Walter Simmons, Far Eastern representative of *The Chicago Tribune*, on 12 October 1948. Nine of the original twenty-five members have since been called to their reward; others have received honour and preferment in their varied callings; one has been knighted; but all survivors – and later members – although since widely scattered, maintain irregular but affectionate contact, and still rejoice in the good fortune of having been able to participate in the founding of the first and only Far Eastern Sherlock Holmes society.

It was unanimously agreed that the society should be named The Baritsu Chapter, in reverent reference to the use – rather misuse, as later established by the Chapter – of that word by Holmes in *The Adventure of the Empty House*, when, explaining his return from the dead, he credited his escape from Professor Moriarty to his knowledge of '*baritsu*, or the Japanese system of wrestling', which enabled him to hurl the master criminal to destruction in the Reichenbach Fall.

The business of the initial meeting, after a hearty eleven-course Japanese banquet (with suitable quotes on the menu from the Holmes saga for each course), accompanied by an admirable Imperial Nada *saké*, comprised:

(a) Election of a Chief Banto.

(b) The reading by Kenichi Yoshida of a scholarly paper, elucidating a long-standing Holmes mystery, prepared by Yoshida-*san*'s eminent grandfather, the elder statesman, Count Makino (prevented by illness from attending).

(c) A well-reasoned solution of the mystery of Hideki Tojo's suicide attempt, advanced by the late General's leading defence counsel at the war trial, Dr George Blewett.

(d) A firsthand inside account of the detection and arrest of the mass-murderer, Sadamichi Hirasawa, for the poisoning of sixteen bank employees, by his tracker, Detective Tamigoro Igii of Tokyo homicide.

In addition to Count Makino, another notable absentee from this initial meeting was Prime Minister Shigeru Yoshida, who pleaded urgent cabinet business and an appointment with General Douglas MacArthur, Supreme Commander, as reasons for a last minute cancellation of his attendance. A motion by Colonel Compton Pakenham that the honourable member's explanation should be rejected as 'inconclusive, inadequate, unsatisfactory and unsatisfying' was withdrawn, under pressure, following assurances by the Prime Minister's son that his father would attend the next meeting – 'at the expense of any possible governmental or Occupation crises'. (A pledge which was faithfully and happily fulfilled.)

The memorable paper contributed by Count Makino offered a first explanation of the strange word *baritsu*, which had puzzled

Sherlockians since its original appearance in print, and which had been assumed to be another Japanese word for the more familiar *jujitsu*. In point of fact, the word *baritsu* does not exist in the Japanese language, Count Makino pointed out; its misuse in the Holmes story is probably another of Dr Watson's numerous errors as reporter.

The confusion with *jujitsu* is of course obvious (wrote the Japanese statesman-scholar). The word should have been *bujitsu*. What Holmes actually said was: 'I have some knowledge of *bujitsu*, which includes the Japanese system of wrestling'; or perhaps: 'I have some knowledge of *bujitsu*, including especially the Japanese system of wrestling.' *Bujitsu* is the generic Japanese word for the martial arts, which, in addition to *jujitsu*, embrace the study of archery, fencing, spearmanship, pike-thrusting, long and short swordsmanship, military fortifications, and the firing of cannon, muskets and small arms.

Sherlock Holmes's proficiency in all these highly specialized arts is well-known. But, because of his regrettable failure to visit Japan, this proficiency he clearly acquired from London lessons and his voracious reading. We know his weakness for pock-marking the walls of 221B Baker Street with patriotic initials; his knowledge of airguns was at least equal to that of Colonel Sebastian Moran; we have a glimpse of his acquaintance with pike and spear in *The Adventure of Black Peter*, in which he attempts to harpoon the dead pig in Allardyce's butcher's shop. We know also that he was 'a bit of a single-stick expert', while some of his early adventures among the medieval moats, turrets and drawbridges of the London aristocracy would naturally have attracted him to a study of military fortifications.

Only in Japan (concluded Count Makino), do we find one comprehensive science which includes all these studies. Only in Sherlock Holmes do we find a Westerner who combines a notable skill in all of them. For us Japanese, there is intense satisfaction in the foundation of this first Tokyo Chapter of the Baker Street Irregulars, under a name perpetuating (even in error) that complex and subtle Japanese art of self-defence which saved the hero of the West and of the East for further unforgettable adventures.

Arising directly out of that invocation by the late Count – the logic and eloquence of which was unsurpassed even by the Count's contributions to the Versailles Treaty debate – I was later authorized, as Chief Banto of the Baritsu Chapter, to arrange for the erection in London of a first plaque in tribute to Sherlock Holmes. Until then, his memory, inexplicably, had not been formally honoured by his own countrymen, although the names of many lesser historical figures had been publicly enscrolled for posterity.

The natural location for this memorial would, of course, have been the laboratory in St Bartholomew's Hospital, where Dr Watson first met Sherlock Holmes ('you have been in Afghanistan, I perceive'), although the site was hardly public. However, I was rebuffed by a cold and hostile superintendent – bearing a suspicious facial resemblance to Colonel Sebastian Moran – who branded the projected tribute as 'frivolous'.

(It is gratifying to record that, under more civilized hospital administration, an appropriate plaque has since been installed in a laboratory at Bart's, where, the eminent Dr James Edward Holyroyd reports, an old-style lab-stool is also now on display, with Holmes's name and an appropriate date poker-branded on the backrest.)

As an alternative site, I chose a location outside what was then the main entrance to the Criterion Hotel in Piccadilly Circus, where, in 1881, young Dr Stamford encountered Dr Watson by divinely ordained chance over a New Year hangover drink, and took him along to Bart's to meet Sherlock Holmes (then twenty-seven), who was looking for a congenial companion to share rooms with him at 221B Baker Street.

The plaque, an imposing object of heavy oak and the finest Sheffield steel, cost £60. It is gratifying to record that the original and accepted quote was £75, but that, on return, I discovered that a Sherlock Holmes follower was in charge of the creation of the plaque, and had devotedly struck £15 off the quote. It was formally and solemnly unveiled at a televised ceremony by the British Broadcasting Corporation in January 1953. It read simply:

This plaque commemorates the historic meeting early in 1881 at the original Criterion Long Bar of Dr Stamford and Dr John H. Watson, which led to the introduction of Dr Watson to Mr Sherlock Holmes.
Erected by The Baritsu Chapter (Tokyo)
of the Baker Street Irregulars.

It is a shameful and incredible fact that, after a brief period of three years, during which time the plaque had become a celebrated London landmark, it was ravished from the wall on the early morning of Derby Day, 1956, by two or three men, who drove off with it in a car in the general direction of the Café Royal. No clue to the hidden fate of the plaque or the identity of the criminals was ever discovered.

After two personal calls on Scotland Yard and Savile Row police station, I was left in no doubt that the contemporary Lestrades and Gregsons had taken only perfunctory interest in the outrage. Scotland Yard, apologetic but evasive, passed the buck to a Savile Row inspector or superintendent, evasive and blustering. The nocturnal smash-and-grab sacrilege had been obviously dismissed – by stupidity or indifference or worse – as a students' prank.

I am happy to report, however, that the then head porter at the Criterion, an admirable man named Bolger, and Cockney stall-attendants on the pavement outside the hotel, were united in open and indeed indiscreet resentment against police inaction. They agreed – incorrectly, alas, it would now appear – that vandalistic visitors must have been responsible, because, they insisted, no Englishman – criminal or student – would have stolen an historic monument erected to the memory of the national hero of Baker Street. The plaque, they testified, had not been popular with the Piccadilly police because it frequently caused pedestrian congestion – nevertheless, always good-humoured – at the busy corner while visitors took photographs. Even today there are constant inquiries about its whereabouts by world tourists in the old Criterion neighbourhood. (I derived some personal, if petty, satisfaction by embarrassing and impairing the Savile Row cop's goodwill in Fleet Street; I transmitted private word of his torpor and incivility to old press friends engaged on police-round duties, who then systematically harassed him by Maoist guerrilla-like tactics.)

The crime was partly rectified – although the mystery has never been cleared up – by the equivocal recovery of the plaque seven years later. A stranger claimed that he had 'found' the plaque accidentally in an otherwise empty cupboard of a dwelling which he had purchased in Wimbledon. At least it was unharmed. He passed it on to the Sherlock Holmes Society, whose distinguished secretary, Dr Colin Prestige, gratefully offered him guest membership of the Society. The finder never acknowledged Dr Prestige's letter of thanks, and was never heard from again. . . . 'Curious, Holmes,' I remarked. 'Elementary,' my friend shrugged. . . .

PART VI

Travellers' Tales

CHAPTER 26

Escape from Shanghai

Jack Conder crawled under the barbed wire surrounding the Japanese prisoner of war camp at Lunghwa outside Shanghai at midnight on 24 September 1943. A jovial but tough giant from Liverpool, he was wearing khaki trousers and shirt, woollen vest and underpants and rubber-soled shoes, and he was carrying a small attaché case in which he had packed spare socks, shirt and underpants and a grey check jacket, needle and cotton, a Boy Scout knife, a multi-purpose tool, and aspirin and quinine tablets. He also had a handsome gold Waltham watch – a gift from his mother in Scotland – and 600 Shanghai dollars (worth about £5).

Seven months later – on 21 April 1944 – Conder arrived safely in Kweilin, and reported to the British Army Aid Group (BAAG), under the command of Colonel Lindsay Ride, who had himself escaped from the Japanese prison camp in Hong Kong. He was then wearing a Sun Yat Sen uniform, specially tailored to his formidable six foot frame. He still had his attaché case and underwear, plus a Chinese padded robe and a few Chungking dollars; and he carried an impressive document, authorizing his 'safe passage' through enemy lines and demanding 'all assistance necessary' from Chinese guerrillas, officially sealed and chopped by a Chinese general, Chang Pung-fei.

He had managed to traverse about 1,200 miles, through three turbulent Chinese provinces, in 210 days, escaping detection by Japanese army patrols, and death or mishap in continuous fighting between the Japanese occupying forces and Chinese Nationalist and communist forces (united expediently and temporarily in common resistance to the invaders).

Ironically, the official judges at the Kweilin winning post were suspicious of him. A clean finish in the obstacle marathon had been deemed impossible. There were reservations about the champion's performance; surely the enemy had 'allowed' him to pass through; was he a 'ring-in' with Japanese handlers? A steward kept him under surveillance until, at Jack's suggestion, a Shanghai expatriate in Calcutta vouched for him. Then Colonel Ride told him: 'We heard you had escaped. But that was months ago. Where have you been?' 'On the march,' said Jack. 'It's a long way. Have you ever walked it?'

By any standards, it was a memorable flight, which has never yet made prison-escape literature, and which, in retrospect, provokes reflection on those lost opportunities after 1945 for possible continuing Chinese compromise and unity between the Kuomintang Nationalists and the Mao peasants – who were primarily Chinese nationalist revolutionaries, and eventually communists by afterthought, convenience and makeshift adaption.

John Cecil Conder is now the best known foreign-devil barkeep in the Far East, with a flourishing inn and first class Cantonese restaurant in Kowloon. He joined the Shanghai police force on 1 October 1928, aged twenty-one, as a constable, earning 150 *taels* (or the equivalent of £30) a month. He had made an improbable arrival from northern England in 1927 as an army medical corps orderly, specializing in the use of disinfectants, with a British garrison reinforcement for the original Shanghai Defence Force. His army tour of duty ended within a year, but he chose to remain in Shanghai. He quickly learned basic Shanghaiese – his salvation, in escape – and was promoted to probationary sergeant with the celebrated 6,700-man police force. He resigned after a three-year term, and worked first with the Shanghai Gas Coy., and then the old *taipan* firm of Butterfield and Swire, which, among other enterprises, operated thirty-five ocean going and coastal ships out of Shanghai.

The Japanese did not throw him immediately behind barbed wire when they made their initial round-up of 'suspects' after Pearl Harbour. Wearing the red alien armband marked 'B' (for British), he continued with Butterfield and Swire as the Japanese 'liberators' transferred the British company's fleet to their NYK line (and while the Yokohama Specie Bank absorbed the Hong Kong and Shanghai Bank). Jack had certainly qualified as a 'suspect' during the preceding fifteen months, when, under the pistols and noses of the Vichy French cops of the French Concession, he had smoothly organized the defection of at least 500 crew members from French ships, and had daringly smuggled them in Butterfield and Swire tugs, under the guns and binoculars of Japanese naval craft, into B & S ships for escape to Hong Kong. (His associate in this operation was Captain Dewar-Drury, military attaché in the British consulate.)

Jack was publicly slapped in the face once or twice by Japanese army guards, irritated by his neglect of a correct bow or salute when passing, but he exacted impassive retribution by systematically smuggling a treasure trove of 120 bottles of unprocurable Guinness stout from the dusty recesses of the Butterfield & Swire *godown* past the Japanese sentry, whom he did salute punctiliously.

On 15 March 1943, the Japanese *kempei-tai* arrested Conder and put him in the vanguard of prisoners for a new concentration camp at Lunghwa, a former cavalry barracks near the present airfield. This camp eventually accommodated more than 2,000 men, women and children inside a barbed wire perimeter of about three miles. Jack, employed in the kitchen, soon decided that he must make a break. He planned coolly and thoroughly for a couple of months, memorized maps, and innocently patrolled on a dozen occasions the entire length of the eight foot barbed wire fence, which was floodlit at night by blinding electric lights at ten foot intervals. Officially, the lights were turned on at nine every night, but sporadically and inexplicably someone forgot to do this, sometimes correcting the omission later, sometimes leaving them off all night. There was a guard house with an air raid alarm at the camp's single entrance. The Japanese guards, armed with pistols and short swords, dressed in black uniform with yellow buttons, patrolled the large area on bicycles, but gathered at midnight for a coffee break in the guard house, some distance from the four-storey, flat-roofed dormitory building, which overlooked the camp and the ten mile sweep of flat, unsettled countryside. A four foot slit trench had been dug inside the fence along certain 'off-limits' sectors, and rolls of barbed wire were piled outside the fence.

Jack decided that he had to wait for a coincidence of planned and unpredictable circumstances; he would make his break on a moonless night when the guards had omitted to turn on the floodlights; his timetable would begin at the midnight coffee session on the eve of his weekly 'day off', when fellow prisoners in the dormitory would think he was in the kitchen, and fellow workers in the kitchen would think he was in the dormitory, and he would accordingly gain twenty-four hours' grace before discovery.

(Actually, the time of his escape, like his restored point of exit under the wire, was never discovered, because many prisoners, confirming the notorious unreliability of 'eyewitnesses', swore innocently the day after his departure that they had personally seen him on that day – in both the dormitory and the kitchen. He craftily left a note in a book beside his bed, stressing that his escape was not due to illtreatment. The Japanese tried to recover lost face by claiming in the camp that they had shot him as he swam across a river.)

After secret decision and quiet preparation, Jack had to wait six weeks before a black midnight coincided with black fence floodlights. He breathlessly negotiated the four flights of deserted, lighted stairs from the unsuspecting dormitory to the ground floor, and crawled on his belly for 150 yards across the camp sports ground, his eyes on the silhouettes of guards gossiping in the lighted guardroom. It was a cold night with the threat of rain heavy in the dark sky. He crouched for a few minutes in the slit trench beside the wall of the building in which the camp commandant was serenely snoring, then, commending his soul to the aberrant master of the floodlights, used his trusty all-purpose implement to detach half-a-dozen staples binding the lowest strands of barbed wire to the nearest wooden pole, strung each staple on a piece of cord, rolled aside the wire and rolled outside himself. He re-counted each staple as he restored the wire strands, smoothed away all evidence of his presence on the damp soil, and scrambled – scratched and torn – over the next obstacle of three foot high rolls of barbed wire. He could hear, in the black silence, the rumble of a train a mile away on the Shanghai–Hangchow railway line. He reckoned he was clear – only to discover with philosophic resignation that the hidden muddy stream into which he had splashed had become a large odoriferous lake, the level of which rose to his armpits as he gingerly advanced, with his attaché-case held aloft.

Two more surprises awaited him. First, he trod on a living body, which wriggled under his oozing shoe, revealed itself as a lurking pheasant, and flew smack into his face, leaving a wet scatter of feathers on his bruised forehead. Still shaken, he next heard the clatter of an approaching Japanese army truck along the Ming-Hong Road which bordered the camp, but he managed to spreadeagle himself as it passed. Then, soaked and still feathered, he was off, cross country, on the pre-dawn strike, south-west, towards the bank of the river which meandered ahead through the rice paddies. The trodden clay of the raised narrow paths through the fields, he noted, had a curious luminous quality; even so, he blundered along one false track which led to a long promontory jutting into the wide waterway, and had to retrace his steps for two miles before he could press along in a more southerly direction.

At dawn, after having negotiated about ten miles, he prepared gloomily for a fifty-yard swim across the fast-running river. He chastely clad in underpants when a fishing boat hove into sight, was with a solitary Chinese occupant, who nonchalantly accepted the apparition of a near-naked foreign-devil with eccentric ideas of early morning exercise. Jack was rowed across to the far bank, pressed a ten dollar bill into his saviour's hand, bowed, donned his pants and squelched on.

Today, thirty years later, Jack recalls his odyssey with characteristic modesty, an elephant's memory, abiding gratitude for his helpers, and even nostalgia for the hardships and excitement.

At the outset, he foraged for sweet potatoes – he developed a gourmet's preference for those with pinkish rather than yellow skin – but also bought food or cadged handouts at farm houses. He avoided large villages, skirted roads where possible, and ducked into bushes when low-flying Japanese spotter planes swept overhead. Sometimes he was mistaken for a mendicant missionary; generally, however, he was recognized and welcomed as a fugitive from the abominated Japanese soldiers, who infested the countryside in patrols or convoys, accompanied by the equivocal Chinese followers of Wang Ching-wei, the Chinese puppet, who had been Chiang Kai-shek's Number Two but who defected to the Japanese.

Jack encountered a Chinese peasant, bound for distant Chung-king, where he proposed to enlist with Chiang Kai-shek's Nationalist army. They decided to join forces, the Chinese scouting ahead of Jack, who entrusted him with his watch and money as the one less likely to be halted and searched. If either were intercepted, the other, it was agreed, would do his best to escape. They slept where they could – in bushes, hedges, empty outhouses or hayricks. The alliance was roughly broken one morning after they had paid ten dollars to the master of a large junk for river transport to a point near Kashing, where they proposed to cross the railway, turn south and seek contact with guerrillas. The Chinese left to forage before the timetabled departure of the junk at 8 am. He never came back. At noon they took off. Jack, without money or watch, had the first warning signals of a sharp malaria attack and groaningly gulped some quinine tablets.

His luck turned on disembarkation at the next village. The owner of a rice store brushed him off, saying that the Japanese had been there the day before; but the owner of a neighbouring timber store welcomed him, fed him, warned him that roving Japanese agents were disguised as beggars, and thrust 1,000 Shanghai dollars on him. Up the road, he ran slap into an army combat unit, 300 strong, of Japanese officers and Wang Ching-wei troops, waiting at a river wharf. He forced himself to walk casually past, unconcerned and incurious, never looking back but tensed for the challenge or shot in the back that astonishingly never came as the Japanese lined up their Chinese force for embarkation.

At Kashing station, having evaded another patrolling Japanese sentry by crawling at dusk to the railway line, he scrambled across and ended the solitary stage of his escape when he was steered to the farmhouse headquarters of the local Chinese guerrilla force. He had arrived in the village of Sehpah Li-jai (eighteen-Li Bridge), and his host that night was Wang Teh-chi. A dozen tough guerrillas, aged from eighteen to fifty, slept at the farm, some uniformed, bearing a remarkable assortment of ancient and modern weapons, long and short pistols, grenades and even mortars in wooden holsters. Jack had now passed into the care and escort of the Chinese resistance network – the *yu-chih-deh*.

Here he was to remain, hidden, for four months. He formed a close friendship with T. C. Wang, and another Wang – Shih-liang – who was officially the civilian mayor of Kashing, but also an executive boss of the local *yu-chih-deh*. The Japanese, who had a key base at Kashing, never suspected the mayor's double role.

Jack was later introduced formally to the celebrated Nationalist general, Chang Pung-fei, commanding the region's mixed Kuomintang-Maoist forces. General Chang's authority extended over an area larger than Belgium and Holland combined. He was a crack professional graduate of Whampoa military academy, and his forces harassed the Japanese for eight years, blowing up bridges, mining roads, cutting off patrols, and raiding Japanese bases for arms and food supplies. He wore immaculate uniform, carried a sabre, smoked Garrick cigarettes, and was accompanied not only by a trained pack of killer Alsatian dogs, but also – to Jack's astonishment – by a beautiful Chinese woman in elegant *cheongsam*. It must have been his wife, Jack insists today.

Jack's meeting with General Chang was enlivened by the curiosity of a member of the commander's personal bodyguard, who, fascinated by the strange appearance of the first Western foreign-devil he had ever seen, stepped forward, seized Jack's prominent nose and twisted it, vigorously but impersonally, from side to side to establish its authenticity. Jack accepted the attention stoically, but the outraged general struck the bodyguard twice across the stomach with the flat of his drawn sword, and, cursing, drove him from the hut. Later, Jack shared a bottle of *shaoshing* wine with the bodyguard, who was still more impressed by the size of the foreign-devil's nose than the bruises on his own body.

At dinner with a group of guerrillas, brightened by the presence of the beautiful woman, General Chang told Jack that in a recent major clash his *yu-chih-deh* had killed 700 Japanese and Wang Ching-wei followers, and captured several officers. He advised Jack to relax, assured him that escort would now be essential and would be arranged, warned him that Japanese-backed Shanghai currency was no longer negotiable, but promised him that he would be given a handout of 2,000 Chungking dollars. He himself would plot the general direction of the Conder Escape Route, which he hoped – as transpired – would be followed by more British escapers. Jack gratefully protested against a cash handout, but the general remarked: 'England is helping China against Japan, and we Chinese are happy and proud to reciprocate.'

So Jack became literally a giant refreshed at eighteen-Li Bridge, properly fed, reasonably lubricated, cured of malaria. He was popular with everyone. His nose was accepted and respected. There was even a suggestion – not recorded in the history of any other prison break – that he should teach English, part-time, at a local school during his sojourn. He declined, modestly pleading inadequate qualifications.

Then at last he was launched on the perilous forced marches through the embattled heartland of China. He had escort now, but he had no safety. Sometimes he was in the care of communist irregulars; sometimes, Nationalist forces. He avoided ideological discussion. The courage and dedication of the communists and Nationalists did not vary, but notes and written instructions left for him usually disclosed the different political loyalties: the communists addressed him as 'Comrade Conder', the Nationalists as 'Dear Friend Conder'. He gained face at the expense of his feet: there were grave doubts about his ability to keep up with the hard marching guerrillas, but he never lagged; he learned, as he padded his bleeding feet with torn strips from his Chinese robe, that it was fatal to sit down for a snack or a tea break, because the pain in his feet was then intensified.

The southern escape route gradually swung westward, checked and re-routed in emergency by the incessant fighting. The Japanese occupiers were never off guard, far less at ease. 'We had more long cuts than short cuts,' Jack recalls. But at no time does it appear that Jack lost confidence. His own philosophy is 'Excitement is the finest cure for depression.' His common expletive was *'veh-yau-ching*!' – the fatalistic Shanghaiese version of a Western shrug and 'What the hell!'

One dawn, Jack was mystified to hear a second time the strange staccato crow of a cockerel with an individual vocal impediment, which he recalled having first heard when hidden in another hut seven days earlier. The rooster had not followed them. The escort explained that, because of surprise enemy patrols, they had been compelled to double back by a different route to a neighbouring hut in the same village which they had left a week before.

There was one narrow squeak when the escape column ran into a Chinese puppet patrol. That day Jack's strong column included several fugitive Chinese notables. Confronted, each side chose to look the other way and pass without shooting: the guerrillas, because of the importance of their guests; the enemy because they were outnumbered.

For map addicts: after leaving eighteen-Li Bridge, they paused in
Tien Mo-shan, struck through the *shaoshing* (wine-of-the-country)
region of Fuyang, Sinteng and Kienteh, entered Chekiang
province, gave the Japanese military base at Shangjai a wide
berth, met friends at the US outposts of Kanchow and Nantsaung
in Kiangsi, and then, in the home run, reached Kukong in
Kwangtung province and completed the course in relative
comfort by train through Henyang.

One unfortunate human incident – a dialectic misunderstanding,
Jack protests, perchance too much – offered evidence in support of
the popular theory that a man's libido tends to be raised rather
than lowered by danger and excitement. Resting alone in an
outhouse, Jack admired the curves of a young woman who
brought him his frugal supper. In polite conversation, she said
that she was in her early thirties and was unhappily a widow.
Gallant Jack – moved, he insists, by sympathy, and certainly
never by lewd thoughts – hinted that she might be lonely. She
left abruptly. Shortly after, a stern village headman entered to
rebuke the crestfallen Jack, and to warn him against 'improper
conduct'. 'The Shanghai dialect becomes easily misunderstood
as you move south,' Jack explains today.

Later, in Tien Mo-shan, Jack had a more comfortable ten day
sojourn in the luxurious home of Butterfly Wu, glamorous
movie actress, where he slept on the star's own 'Beauty-Rest'
mattress. She had fled from the Japanese – perhaps fortunately,
in view of Jack's dialect handicap. His genial host was a General
Lo Jen, who took Jack one day to inspect the wreckage of a US
Mitchell bomber, which had been shot down after a raid over
Japan.

There was near-disaster on another afternoon, when Jack was
being rushed from a farm under sudden threat from a raiding
Japanese patrol. The waiting escort from the next farm, meeting
them halfway, directed them in panic to go back because another
Japanese patrol had just occupied his village over the hill in a
mopping-up operation (known as *ching-shang*). Advance or retreat
alike seemed doomed. Five hours of daylight remained. There was
no safe cover in the bare grain field, no trees, no shrubbery, not
even a ditch.

But there, in the customary north-eastern corner of the open field, was an ancient family grave – invisible (like Poe's 'purloined letter') because it was conspicuous. 'I shall hide in there,' Jack decided. They forced open one end of the rusty slate-roof of the brick tomb, seven foot long, two foot wide, three foot high. Jack crammed his bulk into the narrow cell, nestling among the crackling bones of the rude Chinese forefather, and reclined, half-sitting, with his chin on his chest. He saluted the empty gaze from the sockets of the skull between his extended feet. The curved roof was hammered back into place against his bowed head, leaving a crevice for ventilation.

And there Jack endured a five hour death-watch, disturbed only by the occasional rustle of scurrying spiders over his limbs and once by the cries of a passing Japanese patrol. He could not avoid breaking some of the skeleton's bones as he shifted his cramped body, but he preserved inviolate the ribs and skull. At sunset a solicitous guard ventured down to thrust him a bowl of rice and a fried egg. When the sepulchre was opened and resurrected Jack stood stiffly erect, dusting off the bones, he had the rare experience of feeling his undigested supper, which had lodged for two hours in his gullet, slide with relief into his stomach, making, as Jack had also done (in Izaak Walton's phrase), 'a quiet passage to a welcome grave'.

'It put me off eggs and rice for a while,' he testifies.

A more seemly and reverent interruption surprised Jack on the eve of a risky dawn dash to a vulnerable rendezvous. A solemn Kuomintang officer aroused him at midnight in his pighouse boudoir and invited him on a secret mission. They penetrated a thick copse, with the noise of gunfire close at hand, and approached a small dark building, which Jack discovered with a shock was an empty Roman Catholic church. His guide, genuflecting, waved Jack to a cushion at the altar rail and asked him to join in a prayer for their safe journey. Chinese Papist and Liverpudlian Protestant knelt side by side with bowed heads for a few minutes, and then, sharing the solace of this strange interlude, crept silently outside, instinctively embraced, and slipped back to the pighouse straw.

Jack Conder still treasures that memory of his escape – and also the happy and appropriate sequel, a year later, at the southern British outpost of Tushan, whence he was to fly ultimately over The Hump to India for paratroop training. Then a commissioned

British army captain, Jack was approached by two Catholic priests, leading a group of thirty-five schoolchildren from a bombed village to a refuge in Kweiyang (230 miles distant by rough dangerous road). The diocese of their Augustinian Order, Jack learned, included the small church in which he had offered his unwonted prayer. Jack himself insisted on driving the leading unlighted truck of the children's convoy that braved the night drive to safety.

Jack Conder still has mementoes of his flight – local 'safe-conduct' passages for stages of the escape; scrawled warnings against night rambles when he was holed up; his Japanese alien identification card; group photographs (including one of him towering amid the class of beaming children who were his putative students) ; and his 1944 Kweilin army health certificate, stamped, plausibly enough, 'Able to withstand hardship.' He failed to trace his friends after communist 'liberation', but was able at least to entertain at dinner in Hong Kong Lo Jen (who had introduced him to Butterfly Wu's lonely bed), when the general passed through to Taipei. He had also been able to express his gratitude to Butterfly Wu, now living in retirement in Hong Kong, for her hospitality *in absentia*.

He managed to locate the former commandant of the Shanghai camp, Hayashi-*san*, now Japanese consul-general in Winnipeg, a couple of years ago, and sent him a polite note, apologizing for his abrupt departure without a *sayonara*. The delighted Hayashi replied in similar vein, and they now exchange Christmas greetings.

But the last newspaper clipping in the Conder escape album is a sad muffled drum:

PEIPING, 17 SEPTEMBER (1946)

The three Nationalist generals executed in Harbin by the Chinese communist forces had been found guilty of being ringleaders of a Kuomintang plot to take over Harbin by an armed uprising inside the city.

The plot was allegedly sponsored by Generalissimo Chiang Kai-shek and General Fu Li-ming, Nationalist commander-in-chief in Manchuria. The uprising was scheduled for August 28, but the plot was discovered two days earlier.

One of the three generals executed after an eight-hour public trial was the legendary Chang Pung-fei (forty-one), who had been in command of guerrilla operations by combined Chinese Nationalist and communist forces against the Japanese south of Shanghai. During the closing months of the Pacific War, as the Japanese withdrew, his headquarters had become an advanced base for British intelligence work.

It is understood that General Chang had been recommended for a high British honour for his services in organizing an escape route for escaped British prisoners from Shanghai.

CHAPTER 27

The Heng Lak Hung

The old and honourable Heng Lak Hung in Bangkok was one of the strangest inns in the world. It bore no name sign. It boasted five thousand permanent boarders, averaged another thousand transients a day, and at a pinch could accommodate eight thousand. Its main entrance was at the rear of a single-front restaurant, open to the rough pavement next to the ancient Buddhist temple on the hot, noisy, bustling New Road in Bangkok's Chinatown. You entered through the restaurant, which did not belong to the inn, which was open round the clock, and where at any time, day and night, there were always Chinese families at the teak tables, gaily splashing their chopsticks in noodles or shark's-fin soup. At the back of this anonymous front, a rickety wooden stairway led steeply to the first of four floors, each of which was a crowded maze of partitioned cubicles, extending above the street-front shops.

It was a cheap but most respectable inn. Room service was obligatory. There was no main dining room on either of the four floors. It was the biggest opium den in the world.

In that rambling, galleried, muted, poppy-scented labyrinth, the five thousand permanent boarders enjoyed an average of ten pipes a night, plus accommodation and a frugal meal, at a cost of about ten to fifteen *baht* (thirty to fifty new pence), less than half their normal day's pay. They used the den as their home, sleeping, eating and (after a fashion) bathing on the premises. They left in the morning for work, returned in the evening, stripped to underpants and slippers, gulped their supper, perhaps gambled and talked for a while, and then, lulled by a couple of hours' unhurried smoking, fell asleep on the plain wooden floors of their cubicles. Virtually the whole of their non-working life was spent in the opium smoke of the Heng Lak Hung.

In 1959, just before it was closed down, I called at the Heng Lak Hung with a Bangkok doctor friend, who took an occasional pipe but who was chiefly interested in a medical study of opium and its effects. He introduced me to the night manager, Mr Chee Fook. Mine host, a stout beaming Chinese, was reverently polishing the eighteen inch wooden opium pipes in a wired recess like an Oriental butler polishing the silver. He was an habitual smoker himself, but had somehow escaped, as some addicts unaccountably do, the characteristic thin, haggard, grey, withered appearance of the typical opium-smoker.

He explained that he was only the humble co-manager. My friend had hinted that I should not press enquiries about the identity of the proprietors. The Bangkok police had for many years devotedly 'protected' the hundred or more legalized opium dens in Bangkok, and there were naturally sympathetic and sensitive liaisons between high police officials and the trade which it would be untactful to probe.

As background, Field Marshal Sarit, Thailand's army dictator, who had seized power in a military *coup* in late 1957, had ordered the closure of all these Bangkok opium dens and the suppression of all opium smoking in Thailand by the end of 1959. This order had infuriated the Bangkok police as much as the trade, but the Marshal had remained obdurate. Some sceptics suggested originally that the Sarit ukase merely masked a reorganization of financial arrangements and affiliations under which the opium trade would pass under the 'protection' of the army. These unworthy suspicions, in the outcome, were completely dispelled.

(There was much amusement at the discomfiture of a senior police official who had not taken the news of the reform seriously. To his bewilderment, he was arrested by Sarit's soldiers as he floated serenely, in the ordinary course of duty, down the Mekong River on a raft in charge of an illicit cargo of ten tons of opium and, despite his outraged threats, was thrown into one of his own establishments.)

The Marshal had evidently resolved to dedicate himself to posterity as an heroic figure of reform and progress. There are many honourable Buddhist precedents for this aspiration. As the last country in the world to permit legalized opium smoking, Thailand had twice promised and twice postponed a ban on the practice. Unhappily, whatever treasure Sarit may have laid up in the Buddhist heaven by at last suppressing opium was more than nullified by the post-mortem discovery of his manifold and mammoth private banking accounts. . . .

'Thailand is a loyal and law-abiding democracy,' Mr Chee pointed out with a straight face, leading us to the first floor of the Heng Lak Hung proper. 'The will of the Marshal is, of course, the wish of the people. But I do not know what we will do with our collection of opium pipes; we have 10,000 and some are worth $100 each; it is the finest collection in the world. They are,' he added pensively, 'very difficult to smuggle.'

I counted an average of three smokers in each of the fifty-odd cubicles we passed before Mr Chee bowed us into an empty one, halfway along the main corridor. He told us there were as many smokers at that time on the three floors above us. 'Smokers form a preference for a certain cubicle on a certain floor, although they are all practically identical,' he said.

There was a heavy, haunting, sweetish, incense-like smell in the long hot passageways. Some of the inmates were already asleep (it was about 9 pm) under the unshaded electric light globes. Others, reclining on their sides, were puffing white clouds of poppy smoke from the long, gleaming pipes, held over the yellow flame of oil lamps. The rows and rows of prone figures – twisted and huddled, naked skeleton limbs asprawl, faces lighted by the tiny tongues of fire, silent or conversing in whispers, sleeping or smoking – were not only unreal but, despite drugged movement and sibilant conversation, seemed unalive.

Some smokers were being massaged by kneeling women. A few, in their cheap cotton underwear, shuffled and drifted up and down the corridors like polite sleepwalkers or dazed ghosts. Some mumbled and nodded sombre secrets to themselves. No-one took any special notice of me as the only visible foreigner on the premises. No one hurried. No one raised his voice. Over all there hung a languorous, hushed, meditative spell that became almost hypnotic.

At one corridor corner six half-naked men were gambling with tiny Chinese playing cards. There was a strange dignity, a grave courtesy, in their shuffling, dealing and handling of the cards. One player turned and looked expressionlessly at, or rather through, me; in the bright light from the dangling electric globe beside his shaved head, I could see that the pupils in his unwinking bloodshot eyes had shrunk to needle-points.

'There is a curious behaviour pattern in gamblers who have
been smoking enough opium to be affected but not enough to fall
asleep,' the doctor told me. 'They actually want to lose rather than
win. Their logic evidently is that an inferior man can win, but one
needs to be a superior man to seek to lose. The smoker has this
instinct for grandiose gestures. Of course, there is a monumental
arrogance and towering sense of superiority behind these
affectations.'

Settled at last in our cubicle, I had six pipes of opium, under the
patient tutelage of Mr Chee; but the first two didn't count
because, overstraining, I puffed too hard, failed to inhale properly
and clumsily extinguished the sizzling opium pill.

The brown sticky opium is squeezed out of a small plastic
container like a free sample, blue toothpaste tube, cooked
tenderly on the tip of a needle in the flame from the glass-
chimneyed lamp, then inserted in the doorknob-shaped (and
sized) bowl on the side of the bamboo pipe-stem. You rest your
head on a blue porcelain 'pillow', place your lips against the
mouthpiece (not around it), tilt the bowl over the lampflame, and
cultivate a deep, easy, rhythmical inhalation which produces a
loud hissing noise and dense smoke.

'Relax, relax,' Mr Chee kept murmuring. 'The true enjoyment
of opium is relaxation, harmony, tranquillity. Your smoking
technique must also be relaxed, serene, effortless.'

You can 'feel' the smoke in your lungs – not as strong as a
Havana cigar, but curiously, fleetingly and delicately stimulating.
One pipe can be smoked in less than two minutes. The opium
makes you thirsty; wraith-like attendants pass continually,
carrying pots of hot tea – never alcohol – to the smokers. Your
sight seems keener and sharper; there is almost an illusion of
second sight. Your brain remains clear, but there are flashes of
lightheaded fantasy in which you find yourself obsessed – as
though in the discovery of a great and hidden truth – with
trivia like the smoothness of the boards on which you are lying,
the texture of the skin of your hand which holds the pipe, or the
warmth of the oil lamp beside your head.

My friend the doctor disposed of four pipes easily, adroitly and
with obvious satisfaction. Mr Chee allowed us to persuade him to
join us, and dealt briskly with six pipes in the manner of a gourmet
sampling the *hors d'œuvres* before the banquet. We conversed

lazily between pipes. Mr Chee was coy about discussing the economics of the Heng Lak Hung (no translatable English meaning), but talked freely of the trade in general. He said that 150 tons of opium entered Bangkok legally each year, worth about 120 million *baht* ($6 million) to the government in excise. A substantial proportion was smuggled profitably to other countries. 'I deeply regret that we did not have Patna opium to give you,' he said. 'That is still the world's best. Ours comes from Laos or the Shan States on the Burma border, where Marshal Sarit's ban will not, alas, be welcomed. Nor do we now get the old popular Dairen variety since Mao Tse-tung took over in China.'

Mr Chee did not know how many confirmed opium smokers there were in Bangkok – far less Thailand. More than 30,000 – mostly Chinese – had then registered as 'addicts', thus securing a six-month postponement of the ban, which had been officially inaugurated at the beginning of 1959. In theory, everyone smoking with us at the Heng Lak Hung that night was therefore an 'addict'. At the expiration of this period of grace, these addicts became eligible for curative treatment at special sanatoriums, which, however, would have accommodation for only 8,000 patients, or the same capacity as the Heng Lak Hung. Clearly, Mr Chee, despite his brave words at greeting, had reservations about the Sarit ban.

He reverted frequently to the problem of his establishment's historic collection of opium pipes, which were (he repeated) worth a small fortune. If he did not expect that opium smoking would be completely suppressed, he was obviously reconciled to a drastic contraction of the trade. 'What can we do with the surplus pipes?' he plaintively asked the doctor and me in turn. The Heng Lak Hung's ten thousand pipes, it seemed, included many made from a shining but rough-grained wood known as 'mountain mandarin', which is reputed to have powerful curative influences over digestive disorders, from which virtually all opium addicts suffer. Other simpler bamboo-stem pipes at the Heng Lak Hung had been fitted with pink ivory mouthpieces, whose colour deepened with smoking over the years.

The six pipes which Mr Chee had consumed in our company, I noted, had not yet visibly blurred or confused his keen business judgment with the characteristic generosities of the drug. He began to make earnest pencilled calculations on an envelope.

The doctor sought a report on my reactions to the opium. With my head resting on the porcelain pillow, I politely expressed deep gratification. Privately, I considered that I would have derived far more enjoyment from six whiskies than from my six pipes. My friend was not fooled.

At first you will naturally think that opium is overrated. Opium is a cultivated taste. And, Western notions to the contrary, talk about opium-smoker's dreams – exotic or terrifying – is mostly nonsense. Whatever the poet says, the poppy opens no 'scarlet purse of dreams'. De Quincey suffered his monstrous dreams because he drank laudanum and ate opium; that is just as barbarous as smoking opium by yourself; if you smoke, you must always smoke in agreeable company.

Nor need a moderate opium smoker necessarily become a hopeless and uncontrollable addict. In the old permissive days, the white bankers and *taipans* in Chinese cities like Shanghai and Hong Kong enjoyed a few pipes of opium once a week or a month in relaxed company in eminently respectable and indeed exclusive surroundings. Those few who became addicts would have become alcoholics had they stuck to liquor.

These unhappy coolies escape from their brutish world over their few pipes here. Opium makes them forget time. Opium makes them forget their troubles. Opium makes them gentler, kinder, happier. They could buy no similar pleasure or escape from reality so cheaply. Maybe they don't live as long as they would without opium. But until life is made more worthwhile for them, that is a relative consideration on which few Westerners are competent to pass judgment. To paraphrase Lenin, opium is the religion of these people – the people without hope.

The Bangkok coolies would run amok as drunks – could they afford liquor. When the opium ban applies, they will probably turn to heroin in secret. And that is the killer. Crude, violent.

Outside, I felt a sudden heady exhilaration and a pleasing detached sense of superiority as I halted for a moment in the eruption of noise and traffic along New Road. The neon lights surely looked brighter, sharper, more elegant. The hot wind from the river seemed cooler and even refreshing. I knew that if I chose suddenly to raise my hand and walk across the crowded road, the vehicles would obediently halt for me. I shook Mr Chee's limp hand perhaps too heartily. I had a gregarious impulse to step forward and shake hands in lordly condescension with a group of passersby. I realized that I had no idea what time it was, and was surprised to find myself chuckling over this ignorance.

'You will doze off, remembering a pleasant day, and will sleep peacefully without dreams,' said the doctor, leading me to a taxi; 'and so will they' – nodding at two sweating pedicab drivers, who were slipping inside the Heng Lak Hung – 'doze off, forgetting an unpleasant day, and sleep peacefully without nightmares.'

Opium has now been officially *verboten* in Bangkok and Thailand for a decade and the historic Heng Lak Hung is today broken up into shops and apartments and a dying amputation of the inn itself. No-one seems to know the fate of the polished pipes.

But the opium still comes down the old trail from the fields where poppies are shining in the Shan States of Burma, northern Thailand and Laos. General Ne Win's socialist-military autocracy in Rangoon is coming to administrative terms with the militant Shans by indulgently getting to windward to escape the scent of the *Papaver somniferum* cultivated illegally on Burmese soil. A tough force of Nationalist Chinese soldiers – around three thousand survivors of Chiang Kai-shek's old and once honourable 93rd Division – have remained in the jungle hills bordering Laos and Thailand, after getting out of Yunnan province when the Communists 'liberated' China. They have 'married' into the wild country, rejected repatriation to Taiwan (where they have been disowned), and they and their descendants now grow opium and impose typically Chinese tribute on opium passing through their territory. Frequently there are pitched battles between the adherents of the old 93rd boys – now ethnically registered as 'Haw' tribesmen – and the Shan growers and Thai agents who try to bypass the Chinese middlemen. It is a long and hazardous trail, either from Laos via the Mekong to Cambodia, or through northern Thailand and lovely Chingmei to Bangkok, and then the final sea lap to Hong Kong. But the risks are rewarding and occasional losses are compensated. Opium is the essential base for heroin. An ounce of heroin in Tokyo, Los Angeles, San Francisco or Seattle is worth more than ten times its price f.o.b. Hong Kong.

There is not the slightest evidence to support recurrent charges that the Chinese communists are in the opium business – either capitalistically, to grab some foreign exchange, or spiritually, to debauch the non-revolutionary world. That is an attractive theory, but it just doesn't stand up. The North Vietnamese comrades, however, are under reasonable suspicion. They have traditional links with the racial minority groups which try to maintain uneasy coexistence along the frontiers of Laos, Burma and Thailand.

Chiang Kai-shek, it is often forgotten, not only shared Mao Tse-tung's revulsion against the 'foreign mud', but laid down in the early thirties the draconic Opium Suppression Plan as part of his New Life Movement. He could not then take action against the unspeakable Japanese military, who were growing and selling opium – and its deadlier by-products – and organizing mass distribution outside areas which had escaped their tyrannical occupation, to raise revenue and encourage addiction. So Chiang struck at his own people. A first offender went to a health clinic for care and rehabilitation; if he drifted back to the opium habit and was caught, he was shot.

There are no reliable statistics on the spread of heroin in Bangkok since the pipe-lights went out in the Heng Lak Hung and other old opium divans – to use the fashionable term. But if the more secret heroin habit hasn't jumped, especially in an Asian boom city reflecting military spending, Bangkok is a miraculous exception to test a universal rule.

CHAPTER 28

Sayonara to James Bond

I had the honour of accompanying my friend, the late Ian Fleming, on his second and last tour of Japan. He was seeking local colour, factual detail, spiritual inspiration and carnal folklore for the twelfth – and, alas, penultimate – James Bond volume, *You Only Live Twice*. I filled the humble role of valet-comrade to Fleming-*san*. The third member of our evangelic group was the late Torao ('Tiger') Saito, distinguished Japanese editor, photographer and architect – who, like myself, has been shamefully lampooned in the book.

Our odyssey – which was the most instructive, enjoyable, crowded, leisurely, lively and hilarious trip I ever made in thirteen long and happy years of residence in Japan – was ideally timed amid the gorgeous colours of a late autumn. It spread luxuriantly over two weeks. We travelled by car, steamer, train, hydrofoil, funicular, sedan chair and riverboat, stayed at Western-style hotels and lonely inns, purified ourselves at the Grand Shrines of Ise, crossed the Inland Sea, paid reverence to the great Japanese poet Basho (a sort of poor Oriental's Shakespeare) at one of his innumerable birthplaces, concentrated on *saké*, lay long together and argued ideologically in hot-spring baths, survived two mild earthquake shocks, narrowly avoided violence with a group of foreigners in the dining car of the night express from Kyushu to Tokyo, met one of Tokyo's leading gangster bosses (murdered six months later), and drank turtle blood at a *sayonara* banquet with respectful members of Japan's new secret police.

Tiger and I also had the privilege of studying at firsthand Fleming's technique of precise and meticulous investigation for the background and action of a James Bond adventure.

It has now occurred to me, in sentimental retrospect, that the itinerary which Fleming requested in broad outline, and which Tiger and I sought to fulfil in detail, could well be a recommended route for other enterprising holiday visitors. Ian's original letter to me – we had travelled together previously in Hong Kong, Macao and Japan – ran in part:

Dear Dikko:

I have it in mind that James Bond's next adventure shall be in Japan, and though I have been reading up some excellent books on that excellent country, notably by James Kirkup and Fosco Maraini, I find that I can't get any further without coming back and taking another look myself. . . . After perhaps a couple of days in Tokyo, I would like us to take the most luxurious modern train down south to the Inland Sea and beyond to whatever bizarre corner of Japan you and Tiger can think up. I have in mind somewhere like Fukuoka. I would also like to see pearl-girls diving – my heroine will be a beautiful *ama* girl who has learned to speak English working on an underwater film in Hollywood and hot baths, a live volcano for suicides, and any terrifying manifestation of the horrific in Japan. . . . There will be a mad foreigner in an old Japanese castle, and it will be James Bond's task to bring him to book, with the help of Tiger, who will be transformed into the head of the Japanese secret service. You, Dikko, will be Australia's secret service chief in Tokyo.

The James Bond itinerary which Tiger and I finally drew up, and which, with one exception, we warmly recommend to visitors to Japan, was as follows.

Early morning express from Tokyo to Gamagori (first-class hotel); hydrofoil to Mikimoto's pearl fisheries; thence car, via Grand Shrines of Ise, Matsuzaka and Nijo *Jin-ya* (house of secret corridors and sudden death), to Kyoto (with special inspection of the ancient Shimbara bordello, which is now classified as 'a national treasure'); from Kobe, all-day steamship to Beppu (rather vulgar, but amusing and lascivious); to Mount Aso, where there is a live volcano and a good hotel; then to Fukuoka (anticlimactic, Nagasaki would have been better). Finally, late night express back to Tokyo (good dining car, with excellent *sashimi*, *kabbayaki*, *sushi*, and plenty of *saké*).

Fleming had a consuming admiration for Japanese simplicity, although he never really cared for eating and sleeping on the *tatami* (floor mats). He himself wore throughout our rambles a dark blue suit of light texture (with cuffed sleeves), blue shirts (without cuffs or even long sleeves), a jaunty polka-dot bow tie and moccasins, and carried an expensive and arrogant shooting stick. He and I made the mistake of bearing large suitcases on the trip. Tiger carried only a change of linen in an overnight bag. Every Japanese inn gives you a crisp *yukata* to wear while your shirt is laundered, and in which you may eat and promenade handsomely. Sealed toothpaste, toothbrush and razor await you in your bathroom.

We achieved a near-miracle for three men in their middle years, travelling together in unbroken company for two weeks: we never quarrelled once. This happy phenomenon may be partly explained by the fact that, despite casual indulgence, we never once suffered a hangover – separately or *en masse*. Credit here does not derive only from our instinctive temperance, Japanese *shibui* (or urbanity), or the heady sea and mountain air that refreshed most of our travel. We adhered faithfully to *saké* at dinner and as the night shadows enfolded us – an alcoholic stratagem which we recommend unhesitatingly to all travellers in Japan.

Tiger and I soon adjusted ourselves to Fleming's working technique. He organized his day-to-day work on a flexible time-table, from which he hated to depart but to which he never became a slave. Generally, the day was given over to travel, to observation, to inquiries. Each evening he withdrew with a civil bow for an hour or two before dinner, while he recorded his impressions of the day and drew up questions and anticipations for the following day. He made his notes in pinballed longhand in softcover padbooks. He never doodled on this ruminatory coverall, which was always clearly, precisely and even elegantly recorded. This solitary exercise was prudently lubricated by a reasonable admixture of bourbon whisky – reasonable, because his supply, which he carried in his suitcase, lasted him throughout our pilgrimage.

I asked him did he really prefer bourbon to Scotch. He offered an abstruse personal theory, which would have intrigued his medical advisers, that the reaction of the cardiac muscles to bourbon was less harmful than to Scotch. 'The muscles *expand* under bourbon, Dikko, but they *contract* under Scotch,' he told me, spreading and bunching his long fingers.

This ingenious theory was also an alibi for his cigarette smoking. He was not supposed, I knew, to smoke heavily, but he was constantly screwing his Bondian cigarettes into a long holder. He protested, deadpan, that the non-Scotch-like influence which bourbon exercised on his cardiac muscles also tended to correct ill-effects from nicotine.

'In other words,' I argued, 'the more bourbon you drink and the more cigarettes you smoke, the better for your heart?'

'Come, come, Dikko,' he replied, 'a little commonsense please. You are not writing a news story for *The Lancet*.'

Fleming's curiosity was insatiable. He never minded asking naïve questions. . . . 'What happens to all the cherries from the Japanese cherry-trees?' (There are no cherries; the trees produce only blossom.) Like all good conversationalists, he was a good listener. He crackled with ideas. He offered Tiger three immediate and inspired titles for a Dr No-like hotel which Tiger designed for an island in the Inland Sea; next day he had forgotten his suggestions and began to improvise once more until Tiger reminded him of his earlier titles.

His abiding passion for detailed accuracy and precision in the Bond adventures was exemplified daily. He pushed gently through the crowd of sightseers watching the Japanese girls dive for pearls at Mikimoto's island and, clinically but tenderly, placed one hand on her bare shoulder as she emerged. 'You must *touch* to get the precise texture of wet feminine skin,' he explained, adding absently that wet Oriental skin certainly had a different feel from Caucasian. 'Negroid? I cannot say,' he answered Tiger's waspish query rather sharply.

He sipped our steaming bath water with pursed lips at Mount Aso to determine whether there was a salt base: virtually none.

He insisted that we inspect on the spot the provincial Kyushu police station which is one scene of Bond's skullduggery in *You Only Live Twice*. We took tea with the perplexed local police inspector, who never really understood Tiger's explanations and, after Fleming's searching questions and voluminous notetaking, was left, I still feel, with the haunting fear that we were actually Interpol cops investigating a fantastic local crime which had escaped his attention.

I thought I had stolen a march on him at our Gamagori hotel. I was down earliest and discovered that a long table had been set, at 7 am, for a lavish and very correct and stuffy Western-style banquet, with, alas, coloured glasses for the plonk, in the hotel's main dining room. I made puzzled inquiries. 'Did you notice,' I then asked Ian, when he arrived, 'that the Japanese give these lessons in Western-style dining and etiquette?' 'Of course,' he replied, adding: 'What interested me – did you notice, Dikko? – was that they are teaching the students to use both hands for knife and fork, and rejecting the American transfer of fork to right hand after surgery?' Of course, I hadn't noticed.

In Fukuoka, he confirmed detachedly with a hot match end that *fugu* – the deadly but delicious Japanese blowfish – does temporarily deaden the lips of the eater. He took over the hard brush used to massage the beer-fattened cattle at Matzusaka, and himself spat copious mouthfuls of *shochu* in authentic style over the back of the delighted animal before rubbing the fiery Japanese gin-spirit deeply into the flesh – thereby helping to 'marble' the fat through the meat. 'A poor vintage year,' was his verdict on the *shochu*: 'Better for a cow's rump than a gentleman's belly.'

He provoked an animated discussion with the sports editor of *The Asahi* and other Tokyo newsmen by his perverted preoccupation with the intricate method and theory of wrapping the *sumo* wrestlers' protective groin girdles before battle; this debate was conducted in a corner of the Tokyo American Club's lounge, and I fear that raised voices, excited explanation and explicit gestures by the disputants stimulated wild surmise among shocked elderly members, straining and peering from a distance.

He checked the number of *tatami* bedrooms in the ancient Shimbara brothel in Kyoto's Gion district, and worked out how many *ronin* could have eaten in the great ground-floor kitchen, their swords beside them, while their *daimyo* lords feasted, roistered and wenched in the echoing shadows upstairs. (The bordello curator, obviously shaken, told him that his estimate was precise.) He inquired into ancient toilet procedure in the rooms of niquity above – apparently facilitated by a wheeled framework structure which could carry twenty thunder-mugs on one run – and was impressed by the thinness of the faded-paper, sliding *shoji* which separated the bedrooms. 'No place for drunken military leaders and assassins to discuss plans with their light-o'-loves,' he remarked with a severity which Bond's boss, M, would have applauded.

The three of us spent a strange, prickly couple of hours, exploring the dark secrets of the evil Nijo *Jin-ya*, in a Kyoto suburb, curiously ignored by visitors. On reflection, maybe the authorities don't encourage *gaijin*. Tiger took us there. This is

one of the most sinister and haunting houses I have ever entered.
Since that visit, I have never felt quite at ease in an unfamiliar,
Japanese-style building if I do not know my hosts well. Even
Fleming was shaken. 'I wouldn't dare write this for Bond,' he
said, as Tiger slid back a panel opening from a hidden attic on
tiled rooftops. 'There must be some show of plausibility.'

Outwardly, the Nijo *Jin-ya* was a kind of pocket-size inn for
VIP *daimyo*, visiting the old court at Kyoto in the treacherous
days when an emperor was never sure of the loyalty of nobles
coming to pay him homage. Today it looks like a modest, one-
storey villa built in conventional Edo-style. There were originally
eight *jin-ya* – or guest-houses. There is only this one left. It is
called Nijo because it is close to the Nijo palace – indeed one of
its small hidden windows has been designed to command an
unbroken view across the low roofs of the old days to a similar
spy-hole in the palace, so that lantern signals could be exchanged.

But the diabolic Hitchcock architect concealed two secret
storeys in the tiled roof and riddled the house with trapdoors,
false walls and ceilings, sliding panels, a listening-post and a
death-drop from one of the secret storeys to a hidden chamber
located, conveniently and amusingly, behind a simple Shinto
shrine, invoking long life, trust and happiness, which faces the
modest entry at street level.

The boards of the narrow corridor leading from the entrance
were specially built to squeak and keep squeaking – as they still
do – under the lightest pressure. The Japanese called this sort of
burglar alarm 'a nightingale floor', calculated to wake the
heaviest, *saké*-rotten slumberer in the main guest room. (This
device is, of course, noted by every *gaijin* visiting the Nijo
palace.) But in the back corridor, leading to the Nijo *Jin-ya*
kitchen, a snugly fitting section of the low ceiling pulls down,
smoothly and silently, under the pressure of one knowledgeable
finger, and becomes a stairway to the secret two-storied accommodation above. Here is a world of fantasy: no 'nightingale
floors' here, only spy-holes and an acoustic chamber which can
pick up the slightest whisper in the VIP's room below. One secret
room, which the closest examination from the ground outside
cannot detect, could accommodate twenty men, lying at ease.
Two lofty, hidden, unlighted corridors crisscross the *jin-ya*
proper below. One corridor has a sharp, dog's-leg turn: a man,

pursued, who knew the layout could slip with a grin into a niche; his unsuspecting pursuer, or any intruder pressing along the blacked-out main corridor, fell down the yawning elephant-trap to break his neck, legs or back on the stone floor behind the Shinto shrine. It is all very ingenious – and terrifying.

Fleming was impressed by the Japanese stratagem of a 'nightingale floor' in a useless location. 'Reassured needlessly below,' he remarked; 'therefore doubly vulnerable above.'

When Ian was devising the poetical Japanese aphorism for the book's title, *You Only Live Twice*, Tiger and I besought him to attribute it directly to the poet Basho. 'Consider how many of our intellectuals will pretend they remember the sham quote,' Tiger argued. 'You will leave a *jin-ya* boobytrap for all our phoney professors.'

'No, no, I cannot do that,' said Ian. 'It will have to be attributed: "after Basho".'

His first composition – and I still think the best – was:

> You only live twice:
> Once when you are born,
> And once when you are about to die.

(You can read for yourself his eventual selection.)

Only once did I fancy that Fleming was ill at ease during our journey. We had chosen a modest but superlative restaurant in the Shima peninsula (a stone's throw – if you know where to throw the stone – from Mikimoto's island ferry), distinguished for lobster and *sashimi* (raw fish). Our large lobsters were only partly severed, so that each beady-eyed head, with waving tentacles and groping claws, began slowly to edge from the plate and to clutch blindly at us as our chopsticks probed the succulent content of the trailing crimson body.

'By God, it's still alive!' cried Fleming, defensively interposing his chopsticks between his wrist and the clutching antenna of his pulsating meal.

'No, no,' said Tiger, pinning down his own restive victim. 'It's just flesh – I mean, fresh.'

'Only *rigor mortis* setting in,' I agreed with a full mouth. Some sentimentalists affect to discover a blind galvanic reproach in the writhings of a parboiled lobster, but I prefer to believe that, like a Strasbourg goose suffering slow death to enlarge its liver, it is enjoying an ecstacy of satisfaction at happy delivery and in fulfilment of its destiny.'

'No doubt, no doubt,' Fleming responded, rallying pluckily with Bondo-*san* realism. 'We only live twice.' And he fell to decisively. But it did seem to me that he gulped his *saké* heavily and averted his eyes from the still shuddering head of his meal.

As readers of his *From Russia With Love* will recall, Fleming was fascinated by the shape and appearance of the backs of men's heads. He claimed that he could assess character from the back of the head – just as he allegedly found sex appeal in the back of a girl's knee when she was wearing the Chinese *cheongsam*. (He could also halt all conversation at any *geisha* party by telling the girls' fortunes from a study of their palms.)

Our near brush with violence in the Kyushu night express dining car, and its strange sequel at Tokyo station, arose from his intolerant dissection of a bulky Bavarian with a gross neck and thick unshorn hair pressing mattily below his sweated collar, who sat incautiously at the next table, with his back to us. He was joined by two ferret-like *gaijin* of eastern Teutonic appearance. Tiger had retired.

'Look at the back of that man's head, Dikko,' Fleming declaimed, as the express roared through the Kammon undersea tunnel and our empty *saké* decanters tinkled together on the swaying table. 'There is no self-respecting barber in all Piccadilly who would condescend to bring scissors to that abominable fleece. He should be handed over to your Australian shearers – with or without dip. Consider how his greasy mane laps to his shoulder-blades. The man is a debauched scoundrel, self-convicted by the hairy snarl on the back of his neck. He should be tied in a cattle truck.'

I guess it sounds pretty strong in retrospect. The wretched hirsute traveller, aware dimly that he was under disapproval from the rear but unable to swerve around in his Japanese-style chair, communed uneasily with his embarrassed colleagues, who were facing us but avoiding Fleming's stern eyes. A timid man, I was apprehensive of the outcome; but Fleming arose at last with Bondian disdain and moved languidly past the furtive, silent and puzzled table. He surveyed the group with open contempt, shrugged and passed on. I was forced to conform. I can still see their tense, angry, frightened masks.

Next morning, Fleming, in a mood for mischief, sighted the hairy man on arrival at the Tokyo terminal and the end of our mission. He was getting out quietly enough, but recoiled as he met Fleming's gaze and glared around him like a hunted beast. Fleming compressed his lips, brandished his shooting-stick, and walked to the nearest railway policeman, who saluted him.

'Where may I buy choice seaweed?' Fleming inquired, pointing his stick deliberately, as it seemed, at the hairy man – now a desperate shaggy stag at bay. Tiger translated. The policeman bowed deeply and peered, pointing, along the platform towards the station arcade. The hairy man suddenly broke into an anxious shamble, carrying his own luggage, brushing aside porters, glancing back over his shoulder, disappearing fearfully down the crowded stairway.

It could have been the opening of a new Bond adventure. I still wonder who the unhappy fellow was, what his sins were, what he had in his luggage, who the devil he thought we were, whether he has yet had his hair cut. Fleming watched his flight, expressionless. 'You see, Tiger, Dikko,' was all he said. We did see and we went, brooding, towards the shopping arcade, where we may – for all I now remember – have bought some edible seaweed.

Ian confessed a strange secret ambition to Tiger and me at our last meal together in the Prunier restaurant at the Marunouchi Kaikan on the moat opposite the double entrance to the Imperial Palace. He there established an all-time record in Tiger's and my awed experience by devouring in rapid succession four one-dozen plates of the full-bodied Hiroshima oysters, washed down by an encouraging flagon or two of *saké*. 'My last chance at these,' he agreed, as Tiger and I moved from our first dozen to a more conventional variety. His taste, as always, was sensitive and selective: by some Japanese miracle, the Hiroshima oyster, like the carrot-sized Japanese strawberry, loses no savour in corpulence.

His ambition? He wanted, simply and innocently, to pass through the Panama Canal. 'I'd like to see how the thing works,' was his only explanation. But he was deadly serious. Neither Tiger nor I had the wit at the time to realize *why*. But we pointed out to him that he could easily gratify his perverted aspiration by taking a freighter from Yokohama or Kobe, writing *You Only*

Live Twice on the uninterrupted Pacific voyage, examining the
Heath-Robinson gadgets of the Panama Canal, and then finding
his way by sea or air directly to his Jamaica sanctuary.

'Let your secretary and your correspondence, your debts,
paternity suits and libel actions await your dignified emergence in
Jamaica, after you have indulged your Panamanian ecstasies,'
was our reasonable advice.

'Do you think I would ever worry about those butterfly wings?'
Fleming replied with spirit. 'The office and my secretary can go to
hell. But I must go to Ulster for Christmas – to my lovely warm
family in an unlovely freezing fortress. This is our curious
pommy nonconformist custom. You Japanese and Australians
don't understand the affectionate family tyranny in darkest
Belfast at Christmas. We are the only well-informed lemmings: we
really know where we are headed and why.'

So the three of us went to our last farewell at Haneda airport.

Only later did Tiger and I realize that, of course, Ian wanted to
pass through Panama for on-spot detail and colour so that he
could make the canal the scene of the last James Bond story. He
knew then that he had at the most a couple of years and a final
Bond adventure ahead. How right he was in sniffing an offbeat
plot and setting in Panama for that *sayonara* to 007. The indifferent
Man With The Golden Gun could have been *Man In The Golden
Canal* or just *Panama Crisis*. Fleming's genius for imaginative
gadgeteering would have reached its climax in a simple man's
guide to the manipulation of locks by oceans instead of by
keys.

But he went – correctly – to Ulster. Ulster – surely – should
have come to him.

At our Haneda *sayonara*, Ian turned to Tiger and, with a bow and
an embrace, handed him his cherished shooting stick which had
aroused such envious attention during our travels.

'No, no,' said Tiger.

'Yes, yes, old friend,' said Ian. 'We are only as good as our
friends.'

It was the right curtain-call. I only hope that Ian knew that
Tiger and I knew and felt the same as he did. We never saw him
again.

Morning cold:
The voices of travellers
Leaving the inn.

BASHO (1644-1694)

CHAPTER 29

Midnight Noises in a Temple Garden
(BY ROBERT LASHER)

Utumporn Pisai is the first place where I ever actually looked for a ghost. Like people everywhere in Thailand, the farmers of this remote village in the north-east are convinced believers in spooks. Certainly Utumporn Pisai has more than its share.

Travelling around with teams of Thai officials in the years when I was an up-country man for the US Information Service, we were always hearing about the spirit of this tree, the ghost of that house, or the restless spectre of any place associated with tragedy or evildoing. If one were to credit all the stories, Thailand must outdo Ireland per capita (or occasionally per decapita, for some of these ghosts were said to be headless) in the number of its resident wraiths. In Utumporn Pisai it was, of all places, a vegetable garden that was haunted.

We first heard of Utumporn Pisai's troubled garden while gathered under the acid gleam of a Coleman lantern on the front porch of the village headman's house the night of our arrival. An old man, his grizzle wrapped in a bright sarong, told us about it – with confirmation and interpolations from other village elders. Long ago, it seemed, an old man had been murdered at the base of an ancient Cambodian temple ruin at the place now tilled as a communal garden – but tilled and visited only by day. No-one would go there after sundown.

At one time, they said, the garden had also been the site of a clay pot factory, and the crumbling kilns and broken shards could still be found around the edges of the garden patch. Of the Cambodian ruins only a single stone tower remained, a relic of the days when Utumporn Pisai had been part of the Khmer empire some seven hundred years before. Old ruins seem to accumulate supernatural tales, and this contributed to the villagers' awe of the spot. Yes, the villagers said, strange things happened there in the dark of the night.

Pressed for details, another of the elders, a crinkled gnome of a man crouched by the porch railing, told of footsteps of unseen people. Sometimes, he went on, large clay pots would appear and jump and dance about of themselves. But it was the old ghost, white-visaged, long-haired and malevolently fiery-eyed, who was dreaded most. But who had seen these things since everyone was afraid to go to the garden after dark? It was explained that a boy once had lost his way there returning home, and that several times in the past farmers had dared the place to find strayed farm animals as evening shadows were falling. These were the witnesses who had passed along the legend.

Doubtless the choking local brew which we shared inflamed the visions of great galumphing genie jars and of dragon-eyed old men, blending with the faces of the villagers under the flickering light, which filled my mind as I faded off to sleep on a straw mat on the headman's floor that night. In the morning, with the bright sun searing my eyes, I felt, along with the hangover, renewing scepticism, and as we talked about it over a Thai breakfast of raw eggs, I told my team colleagues I intended to visit the garden that night. Not one of them, university educated men though they were, would even consider accompanying me. The villagers also, when they heard of my plan, thought I was plain crazy; but, after all, I was a foreigner. I was particularly pleased, then, when one of the two local policemen – assigned to protect us during our stay – offered to go with me. We agreed to remain in the garden one hour. The more I thought about it during the day, the more ridiculous the village tales seemed. Dancing pots, ha, ha.

The policeman and a colleague picked me up in their jeep at midnight and drove to the head of the path leading to the garden. The hour was not chosen for its witchy associations but because that was when the police got off duty. It was a typical tropical night – hot, still, clear and, as it happened, moonless. I carried a flashlight, as well as mosquito repellent, a small bottle of hair-of-the-dog from the night before, and a small clay Buddhist amulet – presents from a couple of the villagers. Each in its way was supposed to help me safely through the dangers of the garden. What I looked forward most to having, however, I had to do without. At this last minute, my police friend declined to go further with me than the head of the path. He and his friend said that it was better they stay behind to guard the jeep, although they probably were the only two men in the area who knew how to drive it.

With my flashlight I found my way down a steep bank closely thicketed with brush and trees which walled off the garden from the road. In two or three minutes I emerged on level ground, furrowed and planted, prosaically enough, with corn, beans and squash. On the far side, a dark tower rose, behind which – as I had been told, and as bullfrog croaks confirmed – lay a swamp. I crossed to the tower, swung my light up its worn and weathered carvings, then around the garden itself, perhaps half an acre in size. I turned off the light, deciding to make this my vantage point.

I sat on the eroded lower step but didn't remain long, thinking that a loose stone might crash down. Walking a few feet away, I leaned against a large coconut tree until I imagined coconuts falling on my head. Finally I took up a spot in the centre of the garden, switching off my light, the better to get accustomed to the dark, the better to conserve the batteries.

For ten minutes frog choruses, crickets and other less familiar jungle insect sounds were all I heard. This, I thought, was mostly going to be a bore as I re-slathered myself with repellent. Then I heard the footsteps.

Ah, the policeman has decided to join me after all, I thought. Flashing the light towards the path, I saw nothing and the sound stopped. Puzzled, I switched off the light, listening. The footfalls began again. Could it be a stray water buffalo? It sounded too human for that, and also decidedly stealthy. I managed to hold out about thirty seconds before using my light again, turning it in a full circle round the garden. Nothing was there, and so long as I kept the light going there were no footfalls.

Somehow the tropic night seemed less warm as the gooseflesh crept up my arms. I reached for the old man's booze bottle in my hip pocket, but memory of my headache stopped me. I forced myself to flick off the light. For three or four minutes it was quiet before the footsteps began again.

Now they were behind me on the other side of the garden. Staring hard, I managed to keep the light off for a moment or two. Even though accustomed to the faint star glow, all I could see were cornstalks. Still the steps continued, closer and moving in a wide circle around me. Now and then I could hear the snap of a twig. There had to be something there – something natural – not fifty feet away. I shone my light again. Results were the same. I moved around the garden, poking my light in dark corners. Still nothing. I dismissed thoughts of practical jokes. The villagers, and even my fellow team members, were too genuinely afraid of this place. In darkness, the steps resumed, this time closer.

Now I could hear dry earth crunching underfoot, and the whisper of weeds and plants brushing against clothing. Again I couldn't resist the light, but once more saw and heard nothing – for which I was beginning to feel grateful. A glance at my watch: still forty minutes to go. Repeated several more times, the steps always kept advancing until they seemed no more than ten feet away. I would have given a lot to be back under the cosy light on the headman's porch. Then they stopped.

Five, maybe ten minutes passed in darkness. Not a sound. But it was a different sort of silence. It came to me that even the bullfrogs and insects had stopped singing. This, too, was un-nerving in a way. My eyes ached as I stared deeply in all directions. Gradually I relaxed and even considered taking a swig of the liquor, but I didn't, wishing it were scotch. Half an hour had now inched by.

I jumped – so I almost dropped the flashlight. This was some-thing entirely different – a heavy and reverberating thud on the ground near the tower. A stone had fallen from the ruin, I thought, feeling grateful I'd moved away from it. Almost immediately there was another heavy thump. This time it came from the other side of the garden.

No anti-aircraft searchlight could have locked on to that sound faster than my flashlight beam. There was nothing to see. Light still on, I took a swig of the burning brew, gagging as it went down. The reassuring effect of the liquor was quickly counteracted by the sound, and vibration underfoot, of a third, a fourth and a fifth resounding whump. By now I was keeping my flashlight on. These were the 'dancing pots' I'd been promised.

After a pause, with fifteen minutes still to go in that now thoroughly scary garden, the thumping began again. Now it stepped up its tempo, becoming almost continuous, the ground shaking under my feet. All my disbelief gone, I probably would have run had I thought of it.

Then, as suddenly, it stopped. The thumps and reverberations died away to the same total silence of a few minutes before. Suddenly a cricket chirped loudly at my feet. I jumped galvanically. A frog gurgled from the swamp, coming up to a great groan, and all the natural sounds of a humid tropic night resumed their haphazard orchestration. It reminded me of an audience at the end of a show. Or was it simply an intermission?

I was not about to wait and see. My time was up, and I headed for the path. I couldn't find the entrance to it in the dense wall of brush and had a panicky feeling that I might have to spend the night there, dodging wild-eyed old men while great pots dashed themselves at me. Under a low branch, I finally found the opening. I paused then for a last unlighted look back at the garden and over at the old looming tower. Impulsively, I called out, 'May you rest in peace.' But as I climbed back up the path, I realized how crazy that was: what Thai ghost could be expected to understand English?

My policemen were waiting, huddled together under a blanket in the jeep. They reproached me for being five minutes late, saying they had begun to think I would never come back. After all, they were in charge of our security in Utumporn Pisai.

By morning I was regretting not having seen the ghosts. I was sure, however, that something not natural, or at least not understood by the sciences of today, lived in that garden. I remain convinced of that, and have gone on to other looks – and 'listens' – at haunted places. These experiences have confirmed my conviction. My Western scepticism about the supernatural has never recovered from the Utumporn Pisai experience.

The villagers were eager to hear my story, but were not the least surprised by it. It only confirmed what they already knew. Nor did they think it strange that I had not seen the ghost or the pots. As the old man in the bright sarong put it, 'I think the ghost did not show himself because you are a foreigner and he felt shy.'

CHAPTER 30

Old Hands' 'Last Supper'

This chapter is, literally, a collector's item.

The best reporters' stories are seldom printed. They are told, in relaxed and contagious, aggressive or defensive, sentimental, sceptical or name-dropping mood, at any spiritual gathering of Old Hands.

Bob Miller, latterly the United Press despot in Pearl Harbour and the Pacific, and Donald Wise, London *Daily Mirror* teaser of hornets' nests, who turned his back on the blackamoor democracies of Africa for the livelier scenes of Asia, gave me this idea of a 'Last Supper' of Old Far Eastern Hands. Miller taught me originally the difference between Patna and Burma opium in Vientiane. Wise, in Singapore's Cockpit Hotel, in the remote era of John Ridley, coined, pre-lunch, the original Wise Law: 'In the Country of The Long Soft, the Man With The Half-Hard is King.' Each of them told me a story that made me blench nervously. After all these years, I still brooded: could such things be? Then I began to recall similar stories from other Far Eastern reporters, each reflecting, by implication if not by direct illustration, the problems, challenges, surprises and contradictions besetting the labours of foreign-devil reporters out of the Orient.

So I sent a circular to a random selection of old friends and Old Hands, asking them to visualize this improbable grand reunion. 'We have all been out here too long,' I reminded them. 'But we meet together now all too seldom. Give us a favourite Last Supper story, mate.'

The response was pretty good, I think. I forbore from asking several other old friends because I know they are engaged in prodding their memories for their own personal revelations, and who am I to try to pinch rare Peking duck from their poised chopsticks?

One thing is certain: you couldn't summon a livelier band of better friends together for a livelier dinner anywhere, anytime, anyhow.

Well, now, gentlemen – no ladies, you will note – shall we begin? Roughly in chronological order – but roughly, for sure.

NOEL MONKS R.I.P.

I got my first close-up of the Far East, secondhand, in London, long before my years and home with Marjorie in the old Gloucester Hotel in Hong Kong, and in Korea and Japan. A US delegate to the Economic Conference of 1933 told me the story. It seemed too good to be true – or too true to be good. But who could have invented it? After a while out there, it became reasonable and natural enough.

This US representative had to meet a group of Japanese delegates for a pre-conference discussion on the agenda. The US and Japanese delegates were staying in the same London hotel. My friend came down, dressed in informal lounge suit, to find the three Japanese waiting – all dressed formally in striped pants and cutaways. They arose, bowing blandly. He was shaken. 'Forgive me,' he said, inventing quickly. 'I'm just back from the embassy, just looked in on my way to my room, a Washington phone-call, *etcetera*, down in a few minutes.'

He raced upstairs, changed – cursing – into formal clothes, shot down to the assembly suite, tugging at his tight collar, brushing back his dishevelled hair.

Yes – you are right – there were the three Japanese delegates, still waiting, still bland, still polite – but now wearing informal lounge suits.

JOHN GUNTHER R.I.P.

I recall two stories of Old Japan from that redoubtable reporter, Junius B. Wood, now alas deceased, who found news all over the world for our *alma mater*, *The Chicago Daily News*, decade after hearty decade.

He wrote one letter to his boss in Chicago from Tokyo in the thirties, in which he said parenthetically, 'You may never get this – the Japs have taken to opening and stopping mail.' In due course the letter came back to him from the Tokyo post office, with a pencilled ring around his words and the solemn marginal inscription: 'It is quite untrue that we ever open mail.'

I believe that it was Junius, too, who told the anecdote about the Tokyo father – in the Kwantung army days – who thought that he would vastly please his son (in geography class) by buying him a globe. But the boy burst into tears, on sight of the gift, with the reproach: 'I want a globe with only Japan on it.'

A. B. JAMIESON

I remember coming back to Japan from Europe via the trans-Siberian railway in 1936. You could then shorten the last stages of that marathon trek by coming down through Manchuria and Korea, which were both then under Japanese dominance. But you needed more than a Japanese visa because of the fiction that Manchukuo – as it was then called – was an independent country.

Armed with both a Manchukuo visa and a knowledge of Japanese, I anticipated little delay at the frontier station of Manchuli. There were only nine passengers left when we had passed the last Soviet checkpoint. All but one had the necessary visa: he was an amiable Dutchman, whose business credentials were impeccable; in answer to his rather worried questions, I assured him that I foresaw no trouble provided he had at least two passport photos. We both smiled when he produced three.

He was not smiling when I saw him an hour later in a bleak room, facing three stern Japanese officials. I had been summoned to help him in an unexpected dilemma: a new regulation required the production of four photographs. He had only the three which he had shown me – but also a picture of his family, including himself. He had asked whether this might not be accepted. The officials had said no. Could I help in any way? They seemed to be ready to order him back on to the train to Russia.

I asked, with seemly deference, whether I might be allowed to act as counsel and interpreter for my fellow passenger, and, after sharp scrutiny of all the forms which I had filled in, permission was granted. The following conversation ensued:

Could the family photograph not be accepted in view of the passenger's hurried departure and his business interests in Japan?

No; that is quite impossible. We require a photograph of the passenger alone, and not of other people. He will have to leave Manchuli on the return Russian train, procure another photograph, and re-enter at the end of the week.

But he is going to Japan on urgent business; besides he is a strong anti-communist, and it would be very distressing for him to have to go back into Russia.

Then, to avoid such distress, he must provide us with one more likeness of himself.

After a hurried conference between the offending Dutchman and myself, the conversation resumed.

He appreciates the scrupulous way in which you carry out your duty, and has asked whether you might not accept the likeness if it were removed by razor or scissors from the family group photograph.

But that would be a most regrettable act. We have heard that foreigners have a special attachment to their wives. Also there is a male child in the photograph, who is presumably his heir.

But this man is in quite a desperate situation. He will write and explain to his wife what has occurred, and on his return to Holland another and better photograph will be taken.

Would you please ask him to explain why the photograph would be better. He has his wife in the photograph, and also his son.

He tells me that it will be better because by the time the new photograph is taken, his wife will have borne the baby that she is expecting. They are devoted to their first son and are praying for a second son. Could you not allow him under the circumstances to cut the old photograph?

There was whispered discussion among the officials, and the senior then pronounced: 'We are not prepared to witness destruction of a family photograph, but we have some sympathy for the situation in which this passenger finds himself. He may retire into the next room and, should he be able to return with a likeness of himself, we will accept it even if it may not be quite the regulation size. But please make haste because the delayed departure of your train is a matter of embarrassment to us all.'

So we left five minutes later, after congratulating the three satisfied officials on their sincerity.

ROBERT SHAPLEN

For me, and I think for others who shared the experience, the weirdest and most exciting year I ever spent was the year immediately after World War II. No 'trip' taken on psychedelic drugs today by anyone thirty years younger than myself could be as fascinatingly full of romantic adventure, wild discovery, and sheer sensation or shock as the trips I took between mid-August 1945, when I went into Japan from Okinawa, and mid-August 1946, when I returned from racially ravaged Calcutta 'across the hump' to my then-home in Shanghai.

I had come 'up the line' from Australia and into the Philippines as a war correspondent with the late General Douglas MacArthur, a man for whom, notwithstanding his tremendous ego, I retain profound respect both as a military leader and as an individual with a powerful, far-soaring intellect. Having sloshed through the mud of New Guinea and countless other islands, and finally into Manila after savage street fighting, I had gone back to New York for a rest from my combined duties as *Newsweek*'s Pacific war correspondent and publisher of its new Manila edition. When the war suddenly ended, I was back on Okinawa, getting ready for what we all expected would be the forthcoming invasion of Japan.

That August night, when the word came from Emperor Hirohito, the Okinawan skies were filled with anti-aircraft tracers, celebrating the news of the surrender. No Fourth of July ever equalled that display. A few days later, a lone, white, two-engined plane floated down on to the island, bearing the Japanese emissaries, bowing stiffly, who had come to discuss preparations for our 'peaceful' invasion of their defeated homeland.

When we landed at Atsugi airstrip, I and two others, Howard Handleman, then of INS, and Howard Pyle, then of NBC and later Governor of Arizona, decided we would go first to Yokohama and the naval base of Yokosuka. Tokyo was supposed to be off-limits anyway, though most of the correspondents disobeyed orders and took cars or trains to the capital. (MacArthur had warned us to hold off until he got troops and tanks into Tokyo, in case there was any diehard *kamikaze* resistance. There wasn't, so the press took over the old Imperial Hotel until the brass kicked us out.)

My first and lasting impression of Japan was one of silent stares; and having been *kamikazi-ed* several times during the war, I decided that passive resistance could be worse. As we rode through the lush Japanese countryside bathed in a soft mist, not a peasant in the fields so much as looked up at us. And as we drove across the square in Yokohama, it was even more frustrating and frightening: not one Japanese among the thousands milling about raised an eye or a hand. The word apparently was out – ignore the conquerors. I have never felt so lonely and unprotected in my life.

By the time we got to Tokyo, two days later, it was different, but not much. I remember the man who conducted us through the Japanese Diet. No, we couldn't see this room – it was the Emperor's private chambers; nor that one – it was reserved for members of the Court. The girl attendants in the department stores were only slightly more civil. Up-country, it was better. With Bob Reuben (Reuters), I went to Kyoto, the lovely ancient capital. We thought we would be the first two Americans to get there, and we were – from 'outside'. But several dozen American prisoners of war, having been released from their nearby camp by their guards, had beaten us to it by simply boarding a train to Kyoto, where they had commandeered the Miyako Hotel and were revelling in soft beds, *saké* and sin. The *geisha* were delightful, but the shops were almost empty. The owners of the local department store were apologetic over the lack of goods but served us a delicious soup – delicious until I realized that it was full of live ants, a local delicacy. I drank it anyway, and then went to a classic tea-drinking ceremony, *sans* ants.

After the surrender aboard the *Missouri*, I stayed in Japan another couple of weeks and went to Okinawa, to cover the us return to China. We landed with the marines in Tientsin harbour and went up-river to the city in small amphibious craft. What a different reception! It was staged – ordered by Chiang Kai-shek – but still impressive. The shores were lined with thousands of shouting people waving Kuomintang flags, and I had the feeling that they would have been happy to see us even without the command performance. Tientsin was wide open: it was hard to choose at first betwen the bottles of White Label or the bodies of the White Russian girls proffering them, but in those days I was still capable of enjoying both simultaneously.

By train next to Peking, that most magnificent of cities. The Wagon-Lits Hotel. The soft, beautiful, cobble-stoned streets, the palaces and gardens, greens and reds, and the ancient alleys and byways. The street-cries, the markets. This is where I wanted to live and write that novel, I decided right off; but all of Asia beckoned, and the rumbles of the war to come in China were already beginning to be heard.

Down the coast with the late Admiral Dan Barbey, that most lovable of admirals, to Cheefoo, on the southern edge of the Gulf of Chihli. A major decision: should we put our marines ashore to occupy the port, or should we let the communists stay there? They had already raced ahead to seize it and most of the Shantung peninsula. We walked through the hilly little town. More silent stares, but communist ones. Frightened ones from the White Russian citizens, who didn't know what would happen to them and who hadn't left in time – many were later killed. Back to the ship, and a bull-session with Barbey. Ultimately it was decided not to land – a factor that undoubtedly enabled the communists to consolidate their hold on North China more rapidly. But that wouldn't have made much difference anyway in the final outcome of the civil war.

In the larger port of Tsingtao, we had a fine meal and I bought a bottle of Scotch which someone snitched when I laid it in the grass to play softball with a bunch of marines. By flying boat the next hungover day to Shanghai, to land in the middle of the Yangtze-poo. No place I have ever seen was like Shanghai after the war. A city that played its own pulse-throb constantly in its ear – and loved it. Bold, booming, blatant, blasé, beautiful. Sleek black sedans and sleek women of all colours, nationalities and inclinations seemed to emerge overnight. The old international settlements, virtually intact. Rickshaws, sampans, and people, people, people. Shanghai was the potpourri of cities, the most cosmopolitan place, including Shanghai, I have ever known. Unbelievably delicious food, Chinese and European. The Broadway Mansions, Japanese-built, adjacent to the old Japanese section, overlooking Soochow Creek. Most of the correspondents lived there, incestuously. At midnight conferences, we watched and listened to that fascinating man, Chou En-lai, the communist 'delegate' to Nanking, speaking in Chinese through an interpreter and pretending he didn't understand English. At dawn, we watched the Chinese go through their slow-motion callisthenics on the lawns below. Then a knock on the door one afternoon – a friend from *The New York Times* to tell me my father was dead.

Manchuria, and the 'truce teams', which were supposed to stop the spreading fighting. One communist officer, one Kuomintang officer, and one frustrated American officer to a team. Mukden, and its huge, empty hotel. The Fushun peninsula, and its great open-faced mine. Our jeep stuck in the mud, and a band of singing communist soldiers, marching by, helped to push it out, and continued, singing, on their way. The gradual realization over a period of months that, despite the efforts of that most eminent of eminent Americans I have met, George C. Marshall, the communists were going to win the war. Beyond corruption and inefficiency, sheer social dislocation had shaken the whole Kuomintang structure when the Japanese had invaded the country in the late thirties. Once they had moved west, to Chungking, the Chinese Nationalists would never re-establish themselves in the east, where they had built their earlier base of entrenched power.

Hong Kong. City-port of some 600,000 (now four million), basking in its silvery mixture of sun and water. Begging youngsters in the streets of Kowloon: 'No momma, no poppa, no money, no flight pay.' A fantastic, thirty-course banquet given by the southern warlord, Chang Fa-kwei, in return for a medal some American friends of mine in the Office of Strategic Services had given him for helping plan the invasion of southern China that never took place. Afterwards, an emergency appendectomy, performed by a British naval surgeon, and ten days of convalescence, time to think, in a quiet room in Queen Mary Hospital, overlooking Hong Kong's outer harbour and the approaches to Macao.

Saigon. The tree-lined streets and yellow stucco buildings put up by the French: one of the few things the colonial French ever did well was build good cities. The Hotel Continental, that lovely old hostelry, with its vast rooms and sidewalk wicker tables. The tables are gone now, but one of the few things in Saigon that hasn't changed, twenty-five years later, is the Continental. Ho Chi-Minh and the Vietminh were names that meant nothing then. Ho was in Fontainebleau that summer, vainly trying to negotiate with the French to avoid the war that began a few months later and that would cost the French the empire they refused to believe they had already lost. And the bitter brutal war that would lead to the American involvement, and more bitterness and brutality, when the French had left.

Bangkok, burning in the sun. Golden, emerald temples, Buddhas everywhere, floating flower markets, a nation untouched by the war because it had found the way to peace through accommodation and opportunism. . . . Rangoon, sullen after the long, dirty war of its own theatre, and already in the throes of its own endless revolution. A shabby city, then as now, but, like Bangkok, another great place in those days to buy rubies and other gems for a hundredth of today's price.

Calcutta. I arrived there on 16 August 1946, exactly a year after the war had officially ended. Direct Action Day, it was called, signalling the renewal of the racial bloodbath between the Hindus and the Muslims that had already started and that would ultimately lead to the partitioning of all India – and to more hostility and bloodshed. In all my years abroad, during World War II and later in Korea and Vietnam (and Malaya and the Philippines), I have never seen such sheer bloody brutality as I witnessed in those five days in Calcutta. Six thousand people murdering each other in cold blood. We Westerners were 'mere' spectators. We roamed the streets in police vans, helplessly watching the Hindus and Muslims mutilate one another with long knives, scald one another to death with pots of boiling water thrown out of windows, along with pots of filth. Dead sacred cows, their stomachs also cut open, lying bloated in the fly-filled streets. Long wooden *lathis* breaking skulls, spilling brains across the sidewalks. The lobby of the Hotel Imperial, a haven for the Europeans, drinking tea, speaking softly, while the keening and the killing continued beyond the swinging glass doors. And there was a girl there, who later became a communist and died in Peking, with whom I managed to share moments when I wasn't watching death. Sex and violence – the two themes that intermingled during that first post-war year – came to a climax in Calcutta.

When I got back to Shanghai, the war was already spreading throughout China, and the sense and shape of Asia for decades to come was forming. A few months later, when I interviewed Mao Tse-tung in Yenan, more than the handwriting was on the wall of its caves. The calligraphy of China's future was already communist.

SYDNEY BROOKES

There is a good deal of evidence on the side of those prolific Japanese critics who say that most foreigners in Tokyo are crazy.

ean only foreign newsmen. There must be some-
. . . ut a foreign minority community that complains so
. . . ys put so stoutly.

. . . city in the world outside the English-speaking
. . . as so many English-language newspapers. There are
five, and each day foreign residents fill them with criticism of the
city, its inhabitants and customs. There are many foreigners'
clubs, and these too are full of members discussing the faults of
Tokyo and the troubles they have met. On the face of it, they must
be crazy to stay in Tokyo. But what is visible or audible is not
everything. If there is any reason for this, it must lie in the fact
that the foreigners love Tokyo. It is their village, and they cannot
bear to see anything wrong with it. The noise they make is the
whine of the perfectionist – annoying when repeated too often,
but in its way a tribute to the loved one.

Tokyo, as a whole, is probably the least attractive of the world's
big cities. It is dusty and noisy; its smog is poisonous; its design
and architecture irretrievably hopeless. The English-language
papers are a sort of parish pump, round which the gossips gather
morning and night to discuss the affairs of their neighbours.

The foreigner is usually cut off from normalcy; that is, from
the normalcy that is life in Japan, speaking and reading Japanese
and seeing Japan through Japanese eyes. Even the foreigner with
the time and capacity to study Japanese is often, I think, vaguely
resistant to the idea of competence in the language, perhaps for
fear it might lead him to spiritual intricacies. He may be an
expatriate physically. But he wants his soul to stay home.

Staunch in this village spirit, the foreigners in Tokyo, despite
protestations otherwise, are immensely proud of their situation.
. . . They are not only proud of 'their' city, but also of their
performance of having, after some years, mastered some of
its complexities. They can find their way about more or less,
and carry out esoteric discussions about getting from there to
here.

In the hotels that absorb tourists, the foreign resident assumes
a superior air. Like the Japanese, he thinks the visitors are
strange, and look strange. They are long and garrulous and old,
and have beaked noses and high-pitched voices. Noticing these
peculiarities (but not in himself), the foreign resident identifies
himself with his city and its attitude to strangers.

He can go home, self-satisfied, secure behind the walls that keep out life, discomfort and eleven million neighbours – and write another letter to the editor.

FRANK ROBERTSON

In March 1947, with Chou En-lai's blessing, I was flown (in an American Air Force plane) to Yenan, the communist fastness since October 1935, when what remained of the force of 90,000 who had set out on the tortuous 6,000-mile Long March one year earlier had arrived at that remote and impoverished Shensi village in the far north-west. It had been not so much a march as an almost unceasing series of running battles.

That March was a crucial time for the communists, for they were preparing to retreat from their hallowed base – now always spoken of in China as a 'sacred place', like Mao's birthplace – farther back into the hills. General Marshall's vigorous and statesmanlike efforts to bring Nationalists and communists together had failed, and in Sian, the one-time capital of China to the south, a major offensive against Yenan was being prepared. In a few days Chou En-lai and his negotiating teams from Nanking, Peking and two Manchurian cities would arrive in Yenan to join the retreat.

Yet the communists in Yenan were quite buoyant as they loaded their camels and mule carts. The day after I arrived the vanguard of officials came in from Nanking. Several I had known there asked me to take charge of a suitcase of radio spare parts which the Nationalists had tried to confiscate at the Nanking airport, but finally had allowed to be given into the safe-keeping of a colonel on General Marshall's neutral staff. 'What shall I do with it?' I asked. 'Just keep it for us. We'll be back before long.' The loading for the retreat went on all around us. The communists were as sure as the grave.

Chairman Mao remained invisible, but I met Liu Shao-chi, then honoured, and many other members of the hierarchy. General Lin Piao was away in Manchuria with his New Fourth Army, preparing the first really decisive communist offensive. I had dined with him there a few months earlier, a quiet, confident man, but unfortunately for me the other guest was the late, formidable Anna Louise Strong, a rather domineering lady who seemed to think her hosts would be offended if ever she stopped talking in that great muscular voice of hers.

So I had little opportunity to question at length Chairman Mao's one-time heir, but he left a strong impression: a slight, even frail figure, clearly possessed (to my inexperienced eye) of daring, burning determination and imagination. (And thoroughness. Almost two years later I sneaked through the lines outside walled Peking and met him again. He knew that General Fu Tso-yi was about to surrender the city, yet his carpenters were still at work preparing hundreds of scaling ladders the height of Peking's massive ramparts, each fitted with a roller at the top.)

True to their concept of not confiscating peasants' property, the communists had not occupied the mud-hut village of Yenan, but had settled along the narrow, adjoining valley, hemmed in by steep cliffs of *loess* soil. Light, porous and dry, *loess* is easily worked, so that the new inhabitants could burrow into the cliffs quite easily. They were not the mysterious caves of fond school-boy imagining, but scooped-out rooms to serve mainly as air-raid shelters or strongholds for party archives. By the time I reached Yenan most of the famous 'caves' had attached living quarters of mud and stone, or timber, projecting into the valley.

It was in such a cave-annexe that I dined with Chu Teh, then commander-in-chief of the scattered armed forces, his charming wife, and several Central Committee members. We sat at the usual round table in a spartan room furnished with a couple of battered wooden filing cabinets and several equally battered trunks. Chu Teh, then sixty-one, was ruddy, stocky and jovial, with the appearance of a prosperous farmer who found life good. He laughed much, usually explosively.

The fiery sorghum spirit *pai kan'erh* (literally 'dry white' – a major understatement, since in emergencies it has been known to propel motor vehicles) was poured prodigally. In due course it emboldened me to ask my host where he directed his far-flung forces from; they were spread over much of China, usually grouped in what the communists called border areas.

'From this room,' he said, grinning hugely.

I said I had spent all of World War II in the South-West Pacific, and even at divisional level, once the battlefield situation permitted, the headquarters was filled with earnest men bent over desks or shouting into telephones, the walls covered with overlaid maps discreetly shrouded, and the air loud with the clack of radio operators' keys. How did Chu manage?

He gave a great hoot of laughter, slapped a sturdy thigh with delight, and answered: 'Twice a year I send out a directive to all my field commanders: "Advance victoriously on all fronts." ' An exaggeration no doubt, but not as much as one might think, for the distant commanders did have a great deal of autonomy.

Before I took off some days later from the uneven, dusty little airstrip on the valley floor, Chu Teh gave me a large *laissez-passer* to all communist areas, stamped with his seal, measuring fully four by six inches. This, and nothing else, was stolen from my wallet two months later, presumably by a Nationalist agent. From that time, in Nationalist eyes, I became a communist. And not too long passed before my communist friends, perhaps as the result of several articles I wrote in *The Christian Science Monitor*, let it be known that they regarded me, for what little I counted in the scheme of things, as a Nationalist sympathizer.

Trying to steer a middle journalistic course in a conflict as massive as that which convulsed all Chinese was an interesting experience; but it also was damned frustrating to be regarded with suspicion by both sides. As a newspaperman, I could not advance victoriously on any front at all, really.

CARL MYDANS

Looking back over the tragedies of Asia in the past years, we often remember the small bright breaks in the general mood of disaster. Maybe this is because we needed them so much, just to see us through – and still need them, to cover up the dark memories.

I remember a time in August 1950, near the end of the second month of the Korean war, when everything was going badly. North Korean tanks had broken through the main defences above Taegu, and we were getting ready to abandon the refugee-packed city. For the last two days I had been photographing the ancient walled town, making the kind of hard-eyed record we so often did of how a city looks and lives before the enemy smashes into it, and how we respond, after he has occupied it, blowing it up around him to deny him the comfort of victory.

Now, very nearly done, I stopped to scribble my last notes in my notebook, using the hood of a parked jeep for a desk. Then I changed film, slung my musette bag of cameras over my shoulder, and went off, looking for a hitch to the airstrip. Something was missing. I felt in my pocket for the notebook, scrabbled through the musette book, searched my pockets again. I had an unused duplicate book. But the one with all my notes – all my captions, roll by roll, frame by frame, of two days' shooting – was gone. I had to ship my story as soon as I could get to the airstrip, and now all the background I had written, all those captions – lost! It struck me as something awful, a real tragedy.

I began to run back towards the jeep. For days, all around the city, the big guns had been firing, and there had been a steady, penetrating staccato of machine-gunning. The overtone had hung over me everywhere I went, colouring whatever I saw and giving a special urgency to everything I did. Now, suddenly, I no longer heard it. I was looking for a notebook.

The jeep was gone when I got back there. I was searching along the roadway when a small boy came up to me. 'Hello, GI,' he said. 'What you do?' Perhaps he was eight. He wore a pair of shabbily cut-down American army fatigue pants and his shirt was fashioned from a US army mosquito net.

'I've lost a notebook,' I said. He stood looking at me, not understanding. 'Like this,' I added, and I produced the duplicate from my camera bag. He was clearly the product of some transient American camp unit, quick to learn a few words of English, and quick to fill the gaps with his wits. He joined me, searching earnestly along the roadway.

A Korean military policeman saw us and came over. 'I'm looking for a notebook,' I said again. He didn't understand me either, but the boy ran up and, reaching for the blank book I was holding, gave it to the MP, shouting a lot of things up at him in a high, imperative tone. I marvelled at the boy's poise and his eight-year-old authority. I don't know what he said, but it had an electric effect on the policeman, who began to stop people along the street and to question them and press them into the search, flourishing my notebook for all to see and yelling instructions. Soon we had a circle of people milling around us, talking rapidly to one another and to me. I understood none of it.

Then I saw the boy again. 'Okay!' he yelled. 'Okay, GI!' And he signalled me to follow him. So we all surged forward, everybody in high spirits now, laughing and jostling as though we were playing a game. We turned up a narrow, dusty street and then through a thin, littered alley into a small, rubbish-strewn quadrangle, formed by four two-storey, age-stained, wooden houses. People pointed up at one of them, and a woman who had thrust open her shuttered window to see what the noise was all about slammed it shut again.

Led by the boy and the MP, I went into the dark entry and up the steep ladder-like steps. The crowd minded its manners and waited outside. The room was tiny and in disorder. A woman dressed in Korean white stood in it, her mouth open in astonishment. Behind her, two little boys, maybe five and six, jostled each other for the protection of her skirts. Baskets and bundles and the oddments of clothing that make up the contents of a poor Korean's home cluttered the room. And there, on a pallet on the floor, we saw the notebook, and beside it the written pages which had been torn out and discarded into a crumpled heap. What the little boys wanted was just a notebook to draw in, and they were delighted when we gave them the new one in a swap for the old. The woman still stood open-mouthed as I thanked her profusely for my mutilated notebook and the crumpled pages of my notes.

When we came down the crowd was still waiting. I waved the retrieved notebook and they laughed and patted me on the back as though I were a winner – a hero. The MP fetched his jeep and, with the boy sitting beside me, glowing with pride, we left the waving crowd and set out for the airstrip. And somewhere along the way, suddenly, I heard the artillery again, and the machine-gun fire, and the war.

And I realized that for all those people – and for me too – the notebook had given us a moment's chance to forget, a break in the foreboding and the knowledge of disaster close at hand. It had been fun.

GEORGE THOMAS FOLSTER R.I.P.

I saw this son-of-a-bitch Japanese politician down at Tokyo airport that grey morning in late 1951, when MacArthur, ordered home by Truman, was quitting. I knew he hated MacArthur's guts. I watched him. He bowed deeply as he shook hands. MacArthur showed no surprise, accepted his good wishes and sympathy with dignity and gratitude.

I couldn't help it. I sidled over to the s-o-b later, as we were watching the plane take off. I asked him bluntly why he had gone out of his way to farewell his great hate.

He looked at me with surprise – and a certain pity. I'll swear he wasn't putting on an act. He explained, patiently and carefully: 'All come to admire the cherry trees when they are in bloom, but they are truly kind who visit them when the blossoms have fallen.'

ROBERT C. MILLER

A new foreign embassy had been established. Nationality, year and names shall be changed to protect the guilty. J, the bachelor arrival, would be the major domo, as well as titular incumbent, in a handsome mission residence until his ambassador arrived. J liked the look of that soft, lazy, dusty, curly amalgam of villages called Vientiane. (Oden Meeker first noted the curls: 'Everything in Laos seems peaceful and nicely curly: the rooftops and the lottery tickets, the long serpent balustrades that lead up to the pagodas, the water buffaloes' horns and the carts that the beasts pull, the heavy flatirons with the curlicue, cast iron roosters sitting on them, and the Lao language itself. On a typewriter keyboard, the symbols @ and ? are the most Lao-looking things I can find.')

J, a tall, handsome, randy, fair-haired fellow, soon found the curly Laotian girl he proposed to install as his housekeeper. Housekeeping was of secondary importance: he wanted to learn the language the best way. He found her, with quick intuition after a lucky first choice, in Vientiane's Number One bordello, down on the river past the slaughterhouse and its black muster of buzzards in the tall trees. She was a typical, supple Laotian beauty, with soft eyes, hot lips, black hair bunched in a gold chain behind her left ear, slim waist wrapped in the gold-embroidered, midi-length cotton sarong (felicitously called *sin*).

He effected a satisfactory, three-way financial arrangement to buy her out from the fat madam, pay her a fixed income, and endow her with a handsome gratuity when he departed, or if, improbably, his friend the ambassador, due in six months, frowned on the setup. It was agreed virtuously that she should, of course, cease to be on call, and J departed, happily but foolishly, to Bangkok to complete some unfinished personal and diplomatic business. He returned in two days to discover, to his shocked rage, that his deputy, B, a tall, handsome, randy, black-haired fellow, who had arrived in Vientiane as he left, had enjoyed his putative housekeeper's favours on his first social call at the bordello.

The madam, who had not cleared B's visa for entry into the house, and the girl, who had welcomed B, were alike aghast at the revelation. 'She thought it was you,' the madam kept on explaining to the disgusted J, as he cancelled the agreement and tramped away, disillusioned, past the slaughterhouse and under the hooded gaze of the attentive buzzards.

The innocent girl shrugged off the shock of her failed release from the bordello contract with true Laotian philosophy. 'All those fat, red-faced foreign-devils with the big noses look the same to me,' she explained.

JACQUES MARCUSE

Do I really think Panditji – we used to call him that before he insisted on the more commonplace *Sri* Nehru – was, in truth, a great man? Well, yes, I suppose so.

I liked Jawaharlal Nehru as a person: he wasn't all one piece; he had *les défauts de ses qualités*, being a man of faith rather than judgment, of vision rather than farsight. And, of course, a statesman – but never a politician. And that is already not so bad.

When Nehru died in 1964, I was in Peking. The Indian *chargé d'affaires* told me, which I again heard many a time in New Delhi, that the shattering of his Chinese illusions had done much to precipitate his death. It did not surprise me.

Remember him at Bandung, in 1955, arm in arm with Chou En-lai, when the Five Principles of Peaceful Co-Existence – of which he, Nehru, was the sole author – were all the craze? A second Afro-Asian conference was due to follow a few years later, to cement and build on the cornerstone that was supposed to have been laid. It never took place, of course, and it is odd to reflect that, of all the special correspondents who covered Bandung, only a few honestly believed in the future of Afro-Asian solidarity. But Nehru – and perhaps Nehru alone – was sincere. He was always sincere: it was his weakness as well as his strength. What was it he said to us then? 'This is the dawn of an era of peace and understanding.' Can't you still hear him say it? Amazing.

In 1960 came the Delhi Sino-Indian conference on Tibet and Chou En-lai's press conference at Katmandu, on the way back, when he bitterly criticized Nehru, whom he had embraced at Palam airport the day before. It was the beginning of a betrayal, and Nehru was deeply hurt, for he had trusted Chou, and it had been his mistake, neither his first nor his last, but a particularly painful one. It rankled.

Mind you, it was a typical Nehru mistake, and he didn't lose an inch in moral stature for making it. It was the mistake of misplaced trust and illspent generosity. The world remembers Nehru as an outstanding thinker: the importance of sheer wishfulness in his process of thought has never been sufficiently emphasized. The fact is that he was an incurable optimist. It was an asset in a way: it kept him going through the darkest hours of his career and he was never known to despair. But he was overdoing it. To him, optimism had become an instrument of national policy. He was almost American in that respect.

I can give you a striking example of that. But we shall have to go back quite a few years.

Late in 1946, I was about to leave India, where I had been based for quite a long time, and I went to see Nehru to say goodbye and also for a last interview. He was then living with relations in, I think, Curzon Road in New Delhi. He was his usual affable self, and there he sat, cross-legged on a low sofa in his *khaddar* cap and the inevitable rose blossom gracing his breast. (I had covered the two Simla conferences where the independence of India had been haggled out and I had fresh memories of the last one and of Nehru riding his piebald horse up and down the Mall on his way to the Vice-Regal Lodge and back, full of hope and irritation.)

We – mostly Nehru – talked for over two hours. As I was going, he walked with me to the door, put a gentle hand on my arm and said: 'Marcuse, there are three things I want you to remember. One, India will never be a Dominion. Two, there will never be a Pakistan. Three, when the British go, there will be no more communal trouble in India.'

I asked him whether this was on the record, and he said it was.

After a long holiday in France, I found myself on my way to

China – once more – in August of the following year. Actually, I landed at Karachi on the 16th of that month – having missed the independence celebrations by twenty-four hours. Karachi was a new and peaceful capital, so very peaceful that in the main square (the name of which escapes me, but it must have been called the Maidan), there still stood a life-size statue of Mahatma Gandhi, complete with real steel-rimmed spectacles which, I was told, would be piously replaced as soon as they became rusty.

It was after a few days in new Pakistan's new capital – I was in no particular hurry – that I heard of the 'murder trains', running in blood rather than on time, by which one could still make the journey to Delhi. Murder trains they were, and I know because I took one of them. I'll spare you the gory details. The only other foreigner on the train was a young British major, whose sole concern was not to be late for his wedding at Meerut. Every time the murderers, who were actually travelling with us, pulled the communication-cord and brought us to a stop in order to drag their already half-dead victims from the carriages on to the permanent way, there to finish them off, his only comment was: 'I hope they'll be fined for it. In England, it would cost them five pounds a go.' We finally reached Delhi station.

Very soon, the Delhi riots – remember them? – got under way, the bloodiest perhaps of all the massacres India had seen since the Great Mutiny. One day, when I was watching Moslem shops being looted in Connaught Place, I saw Nehru, never cowed in any way, driving up in a car and setting about the plunderers with a formidable *lathi*.

When things had quietened down, I asked for an interview with Nehru. It was nice to see him again, unchanged despite his Prime Ministership, legs crossed, Gandhi cap, rose blossom and all, and urbane as ever.

India had become a Dominion, there was a Pakistan, and communal trouble was breaking all its past records. I hadn't the heart, of course, to remind Nehru of his three predictions. At the same time, I couldn't put them out of my mind and, as I asked the usual questions, I felt acutely embarrassed. Not he, though. For, after a while, he gave me one of his charming smiles and abruptly said: 'You remember, Marcuse, what I told you? No Dominion. No Pakistan. No . . .'

He broke off there and we were both silent for several seconds.

You could have heard a fly fly, as the French say. And then he added: 'Wasn't I wrong?'

There was, I thought, more than a touch of greatness there.

DENNIS BLOODWORTH

'Here lies the fool that tried to hurry the East,' they say of our copy, but in fact we manage to tell a remarkable amount of truth, considering that we are painfully torn between two qualities of time – the priceless stuff jealously hoarded by our editors in the impatient West, and the cheap, throwaway variety of the bureaucrats in the eternal East. And how beautifully this formula for mental frenzy worked on Saturday, 30 November 1957, the day Darul Islam terrorists rained hand grenades on President Sukarno outside the Tjikini School in Djakarta, but succeeded only in murdering the women and children as they emerged with him in the late afternoon.

Blissfully ignorant, James Wilde and I were most ill-advisedly throwing a joint party for about twenty-five people that evening in the glorified garage which, thanks to his hospitality, we shared whenever I was in Djakarta. 'Glad you didn't have to cancel the party on account of the Tjikini business,' remarked the last guest to arrive casually. He turned away to look for a drink, but Jim grabbed his shoulder and swung him around again. 'What Tjikini business?' he demanded, blue eyes and nose and teeth suddenly sharp with professional suspicion. The young diplomat told him.

Jim was working for AP then, and competing against three international agencies; in London, the front page of the first edition of my own paper was just being made up. Jim and I were out of the party and into his Land-Rover in twenty seconds flat, leaving twenty-five astonished guests somewhere behind in the haze to give themselves a good time. It was already after nine in the evening, dark and raining. The city was full of troops and armoured cars; roads were cordoned off as police hunted for the assassins. We dodged about in a desperate quest for detail. The main cable office was already closed. At the subsidiary night bureau we fell on the typewriters and began banging out copy for dear life. Mine was cleared to London by 2 am, Sunday morning, and I collapsed with a bottle of Coca Cola.

Within limits, Jim's first fine frenzy began approaching panic when kind colleagues told him that the rival *Agence France Presse* correspondent had sent the story at least six hours ahead of him, and had beaten all others. Jim then rushed to hand over his cables at the transmission desk, to be informed by a friendly, smiling little Indonesian that, under a new ruling, he would have to pay cash, as he had not settled his collect account at the end of the previous month.

Going through our pockets with trembling fingers, we found we needed thousands of *rupiahs* more if Jim were to file at all. We tumbled off into the night, followed by a yawn and a warning from the counter that the office would close within an hour and a half. Through pelting rain and obtuse army checkpoints, we reached the AP office, dashed up its rickety wooden staircase and into Jim's room, and charged at the safe in which he kept his coat. I glanced at my watch and reassured him that we could make it – just as he shook out his last pocket and discovered he had left the safe key in another suit at home on the other side of the sprawling city.

Outside it was darker, wetter, more than ever crammed with tripping soldiers demanding identity papers by torchlight and then holding them sideways. After a lifetime of agony we found the key, returned to the office, grabbed several bricks of *rupiahs* from the safe, and hurtled back over slippery roads to the cable office to find it just shutting. At first, the slow-moving Javanese on duty refused to take the copy, saying it was too late anyway, but a second look at Jim's shark-like countenance, the taut skin and flesh streaming back from the predatory nose as if he were in a wind-tunnel, made him change his mind. Jim frantically counted the money, while the man laboriously counted the words, and then we left. It was 4 am – perhaps nine hours after AFP had filed their story.

Much later that day we rose to hear that a cable had arrived from Jim's head office. He opened it with shaking hand to read: 'Congratulations . . . world beat . . . Sukarno assassination attempt.' The *Agence France Presse* story had been held up by a technical hitch after reaching Amsterdam for onward transmission. Other reporters had been non-starters. We had risked throwing a party; they had risked going away for the weekend to the hills, and had not been in Djakarta at all.

But the episode had aged Jim more than it aged Sukarno.

DONALD WISE

I fell in love, mildly, with Madam Nhu – the late President'
sister-in-law – one sultry afternoon in early 1962, just after I ha
given her a one-man demonstration of the 'Twist' in her Gia Lon;
palace in Saigon. She made a remark to me which, for basi
wisdom and worldliness, cannot be beaten in my book, and ha
caused me no mysterious wonderings about the Far East since

At the time of my audience with her, Madam had exacerbate
Vietnamese-American feelings by stating that, since America
soldiers had come to Vietnam to 'dance with death, not wit
Vietnamese girls', she would allow no public dancing. In shor
she passed death sentence on the dance of the day – the Twist.

One of my early questions to her was to ask what she ha
against it. She replied that she had never seen it, at which point
upped like a cobra and, before stunned palace guards, gave he
the treatment. 'It's not sexy; you don't touch your partner,' I sai
unctuously. 'You don't have to touch your partner to be disgust
ing,' she replied witheringly.

Realizing I had set the dance back perhaps ten years, I decide
to needle her further. Shortly before she had moved from th
second to the first floor of her palace, without use of either li
or stairs, when a dissident pilot bombed it from the air. She wa
wearing a fringe over a scar on her forehead and continuall
fidgeted it with her fingers. Was that scar due to the fact, I aske
politely, that she insisted on putting make-up on her vain prett
face before it was fully healed; and that as a result she had g
some sort of poisoning? Rubbish, she blazed, and I felt that I ha
got her to the point when she might make some outrageou
remark.

She did, repeating the one about suitable partners for GI's, an
then turning to the evils of communism as a whole. I would kno
nothing about Asia or communism in Asia, she said, as I wa
neither Asian nor experienced in Asia or communism. People lik
me and the world in general were soft on communists and feare
to use tough methods against them. The only way you coul
convert a real communist was with a bullet in the head. Hanger
on, the undecided, had to be dealt with just as firmly. N
advantage must be missed, no opportunity left unseized, to har
them. Economically, financially, every which way must be used

a means of attacking them. Even natural disasters – like famine – must be used.

'Monsieur,' she asked in a moment of French, 'what do you do when your enemy is hungry?'

'?'.

'You kick him in the stomach, monsieur,' she replied, tapping me lightly on the forearm with her fan.

It felt like the thud of a rifle butt.

Then she offered me something cool to sip. The invitation rang like the tramp of the firing squad.

But I have been her slave ever since.

DENIS WARNER

It is not as well known as it ought to be that the source of all the evils that afflicted South Vietnam in 1963 was the decision made by the late President Ngo Dinh Diem and his brothers to beautify the ancestral tombs at Hue with an artificial lake. Careless workmen cut the vein of a dragon resting quietly in the ground and began the series of appalling misfortunes that destroyed the family and threatened the land.

When he heard the news about the dragon, brother Nhu sought a fortune-teller's advice and was told that he would retain power throughout his life, a prediction that was as reassuring as it was correct. On the male side of the family, only the clerical office of Archbishop Thuc was proof against the dragon's magic.

I am sorry about this long-winded introduction, but the background is necessary, I think, to understand the climate, as it were, of my tale, which concerns Madam Nhu's young brother, Tran Van Khiem.

My friendship with him dated back to the mid-fifties and the days of the battles between the sects and Diem. Khiem was then the palace press officer, and I can remember him, his eyes flashing with indignation, telling some of our more gullible colleagues of the human bones and bits of government uniform he had found in the tiger's cage outside the bedroom of Le Van Bien, the Binh Xuyen leader, on the Arroya Chinois. The story got wide distribution and helped the innocent abroad to understand the difference between Good and Evil in Saigon.

Professionally and socially, we saw a lot of each other as the years went by. In the last tragic but comic days of the Diem régime, Khiem was privy to many of the family secrets, and, through him, so was I. Together, we tried to persuade the Americans that the Nhu family really did plan to crack down on the Buddhists – we could even name the date – but, in the face of Nhu's bland denials (and with that damned dragon working against the family), no one would believe us.

Khiem went into prison after the *coup*, and his prospects seemed pretty gloomy. His mother, Madam Tran Van Chuong, a highly sophisticated woman, who for years had watched South Vietnam's interests at the United Nations, flew out from Washington to intercede on his behalf, and I told those officials who would listen that Khiem was a good man and had not been running the secret police. I left Saigon after promising his mother to return if he was called before the Revolutionary Court.

Her cable to my chicken farm at Mount Eliza in Australia came late one Friday afternoon. Khiem was to go before the Court on Monday morning. To save his life, I should be in Saigon before noon. The banks and the Vietnamese embassy in Canberra had closed for the weekend, and I had neither money nor visa, but by an unusual combination of good luck and co-operation, I got to Saigon just before noon on Monday, armed with my files and the statements that I was prepared to swear before the Court.

I phoned Madam Chuong from the airport. She urged me not to go to the Court, but instead to get a taxi to the Majestic Hotel, where she was staying. I could feel the relief in her tone when I spoke to her, and I worried as the taxi crept through the lunchtime traffic whether I had not raised her hopes too high. My 'evidence' was pretty slim.

I hurtled into her presence. I was an explosion of questions. Where was the Court sitting? Where were her lawyers? Where was her car? Had she a *précis* of the charges against her son? Could we see him first? For how long? Madam Chuong calmed me. 'Khiem has not been called before the Court,' she said. 'Now that you are here, all is well. There is no longer any need – you understand? – to worry.'

I had just finished a long journey. I was tired, and I could not understand.

'Let me explain,' said Madam Chuong patiently. 'Last Thursday I went to a fortune-teller – the very best here. He said that I was

n trouble, that my son's life was in great danger. He could be
aved only if a close friend who lived far away could reach Saigon
y noon the following Monday.'

And so she had sent off the cable to me in Australia. And I had
esponded. So all was well. It was, too. The Court action, as
redicted, was abandoned. Khiem was released from prison after
ome months, and finally was allowed to leave the country and
oin his parents in Washington.

Me? I bought a book on astrology, and am now better equipped
o be a reporter in South-East Asia.

JAMES CAMERON

was sitting down to a glass of ale with the Prime Minister when
1 walked Ho Chi Minh. I reckon that is as good an intro as any
mall story deserves.

The point is that I had no reason to believe I should ever see
Io Chi-Minh; indeed I had every reason to believe otherwise.
t had been God's own job getting into Hanoi anyhow. This was
efore the journalistic package-tours; in 1965, Hanoi, for a non-
om Westerner, was as accessible as the moon. However, such
as the notorious innocence and purity of my heart that I fluked
; and naturally the first thing I did before unpacking my socks
as to ask for a brief *pourparler* with the President, the legendary
Incle Ho. And he said no. It was a very un-Oriental response;
1ere were no maybe's, or don't ring us we'll ring you; he
ategorically said that he would not find it convenient to receive
1e at any part of my stay, be it short or long. I can take a hint.

For the first fully paid-up *kwai-lo* correspondent to enter North
ietnam for twelve years, professional life was not, as you might
1y, a bed of roses. The North Vietnamese were, as ever, charm
1d courtesy itself, but they could not have been more watchful
ad I been an attested sex-maniac in a Bunny Club. I was, as it
appens, making a film; no film in the world had every shot so
1gerly and vigilantly supervised. The problems of free expression
ere akin to those, I imagine, of trying to make a blue movie in
1e Vatican.

Nevertheless, I travelled hopefully. And after a few weeks I
as agreeably and cordially asked to partake of a drop with the
rime Minister of the People's Republic, Mr Pham Van Dong,

with whom many years before I had formed a tenuous acquain‑
tanceship during the long-forgotten Indo-Chinese conference i‑
Geneva. For several hours we conducted the familiar dialectica‑
and conversational sparring match customary to such occasions‑
and it was during the height, or depth, of this dialogue that th‑
door opened and in came Uncle Ho himself, padding noiselessl‑
about in the clumsy, practical sandals everyone wears in Hano‑
made of old automobile tyres. He wore a rather modish versio‑
of the official, high-collar uniform, in fawn. He was laughing lik‑
a drain at my surprise. Manifestly his only compulsion wa‑
curiosity; having diplomatically denied me, he nonetheless fe‑
obliged to see what manner of imperialist running-dog ha‑
managed to make the Presidential Palace in the end.

The conversation is unimportant; there were no revelation‑
'I don't propose to talk politics,' said Uncle Ho. 'You've had thre‑
hours of that with my Mr Pham Van Dong; that ought to b‑
enough even for you. Tell me,' said this strange old man, like a‑
impish Chinese ivory miniature, 'what does the Haymarket loo‑
like now?'

(Long years ago, one recalled, he had endured part of h‑
education as a pastrycook at the Carlton under, of all peopl‑
Escoffier.)

'You wouldn't know it now,' I said; and he replied: 'I wouldn‑
know anything now. I've got used to being an old revolutionar‑
for whom nothing remains the same. Let us drink a few glasse‑
of beer and be frivolous. Let us be daring and try to spea‑
English. As you can imagine, I get few opportunities thes‑
days.'

We tried, but he was very rusty; it was easier to return t‑
French. I asked him where he got the American cigarettes h‑
chain-smoked incessantly, and he said: 'I do not discuss sta‑
secrets.'

By and by he wearied of our banal talk and sprang to his fee‑
it was necessary to take a promenade to the estate; we wandere‑
around the rosebeds and exchanged blossoms; we ran about an‑
slapped each other on the back and exchanged elaborate civilitie‑
The court photographer was summoned up from somewhere ‑
other, and we were recorded in a multitude of extravaga‑
attitudes of *bonhomie*. We finished the evening in what can only b‑
described as a blaze of amity. And all the time at the back of n‑

mind was the reflection: Well, it has been tough going with the comrades up to now, but this is the breakthrough; after all this I can surely ask what I like.

So by and by I romped back to my hotel, erstwhile the old French Metropole, now the Tavern of Reunification. I was full of euphoria; from now on, I thought, I can get to work.

In the lobby were two friends from the Foreign Office with a bleak *pro-forma* from the Government to the effect that my stay in North Vietnam had run its course, that my presence in Hanoi was no longer desirable, and that I must leave the country without fail at six the following morning.

It is not the easiest system in the world to understand.

ALEX JOSEY

Not only does an old man's memory-computer work more slowly as the calendar slips away, but somehow the value of the stories seems to change.

For example, my encounter with President Sukarno outside his bedroom in Merdeka Palace was once a prized memory. We had a breakfast appointment. I wandered alone down a corridor. Sukarno suddenly appeared from one of the bedrooms. He approached me, hand outstretched. We were shaking hands when his bedroom door opened again, and into the corridor stepped a beautiful, young and shapely European woman. I stared, astonished. Sukarno looked at me, turned and saw the girl. He was visibly annoyed. Then he smiled at me and said: 'I know what you are thinking. That she's my girl friend. Aha! All you journalists are the same. She is not.' I shook my head and said brightly: 'Mr President, at this hour of the morning I am incapable of thought.' Sukarno, never lost for an explanation, said: 'She is a furniture designer. I want a new bedroom suite.' By then members of his Court had appeared. Sukarno pointed to one official. 'She's his wife,' he said briefly. The man looked astonished. We moved on to the verandah for breakfast. Sukarno had solved another problem. . . .

Prince Sihanouk on one occasion was about to pin a decoration on my chest. 'But you've got one already,' he remembered. I murmured that he had indeed made me an Officer of the Order on my previous visit to Phnom Penh. 'Then I shall promote you to Commander,' he exclaimed happily, and dangled another badge around my neck. . . .

In Peking, in 1956, David Chipp, then Reuter's man in Peking, and I unexpectedly encountered Chairman Mao Tse-tung and President Liu Shao-chi in the Forbidden City. We conversed in Chinese, and my mangled Mandarin (all six phrases) made Mao's belly wobble with laughter. 'I made Chairman Mao laugh,' I cabled *The Sunday Citizen*. I dined off that anecdote for years. . . .

In Manila, in the 1960s, I interviewed Sheikh Azahari, the organizer of the abortive Brunei revolt, and later that evening met Osmena, his wealthy financial backer. Osmena considered Azahari a dubious investment: 'What's he doing here? He should be in Brunei. He's a bum. What sort of a revolutionary is he? He's more interested in women than the revolution.' Osmena also thought that I was an envoy from Tunku Abdul Rahman, trying on behalf of the Tunku to find out how much Osmena wanted to call off the whole thing. I gave Osmena my word that I wasn't. He insisted I was, because, he said, he knew that I had played golf with the Tunku the week before. He whispered in my ear the number of millions the Tunku would have to pay – 'American dollars, I mean; not Malayan dollars' – and begged me to give the message to the Tunku without delay. Meanwhile, would I like to meet two hot-stuff Cuban stripteasers? Two! Well, to cut a long story short, I did agree in the end to tell the Tunku. I told him from the front page of the following morning's *Straits Times*. . . .

Suddenly, overnight, late in the 1960s, Singapore was gripped with fear. Men walked with eyes downcast. *Koro*, that dread disease, had struck the island republic. In the dawn of yet another day, a half-demented Chinese had hammered on the door of his doctor's house, sobbing that his penis was disappearing. That which nature had intended to be outstanding was retreating, entering his own body. What the hell was happening? The medico, a modern man, loftily explained to reporters that the man's acute shrinkage was probably due to a sudden drop in temperature, a theory to which most of us might subscribe. But not the older Chinese: they would have none of it. This, they insisted, was a well-known Chinese ailment, described in detail in the *Annals*. Certain treatment, and herbs, would have to be prescribed. There were other cures, too. The pages of the local papers were full of them. The ladies kept silent. Until, at last, some Malay girl

creamed and ran about, moaning, as they fainted right away in
the arms of their teachers, that their nipples were suddenly turning
inwards. One school for big girls had to be closed – seriously –
because of the hysteria.

Interesting place, the Orient. . . .

STANLEY KARNOW

How much does a Westerner really learn about the Orient over
the years? How deeply can we penetrate to an understanding of
Asians? Or do we only skim the surface of the Far East, never
actually probing and feeling and comprehending its depths?

These are the questions I asked myself as I left Asia after more
than a decade as a correspondent in the region. And, if I had
acquired knowledge rather than wisdom, I took consolation in an
anecdote related by Daniel Vare, the sensitive and talented Italian
diplomat-writer who lived in Peking for nearly forty years prior
to World War II.

In his delightful *Novels of Yeh Ching*, quasi-fictitious memoirs
of his life in Peking, Vare relates his efforts to write an account of
a minister in the Imperial Ming Court who sought to protest
against a reform promulgated by the Emperor.

As Vare wrote the story, the minister outlined his objections to
the reform in a Memorial and obtained an audience with the
Emperor in order to present his case in person. But, in approaching the steps of the palace, the minister committed suicide in order
to emphasize his protest.

A few days after finishing his story, Vare recounts, he showed
it to his Chinese teacher. The teacher frowned and shook his
head.

'This is a ridiculously implausible tale,' he said. 'Only the
Emperor, the Empress and the imperial concubines are permitted
to commit suicide inside the palace grounds. Commoners such as
the minister must, according to etiquette, commit suicide at the
foot of the Western Hills. Therefore, the Emperor would not
have even so much as glanced at the minister's Memorial – if,
indeed, the minister had actually been ignorant enough to have
violated Court etiquette.'

Shattered by that critique, Vare asked his Chinese teacher to
suggest a plot that could be written into a similar story. The

teacher thought for a few moments, and came forth with the following story:

Once upon a time there was a celebrated scholar who visited an aristocratic family every week and was given a bowl of sugared turnips as a mark of esteem. But one week when he arrived for his visit, the sugared turnips were absent. The scholar took this to signify that he had fallen from grace. He went to the foot of the Western Hills and committed suicide.

'There,' said the Chinese teacher, 'is a good tale you can write.'

'But,' replied Vare, 'if I write that story, nobody in the West will believe it.'

'And if you write *your* story,' countered the teacher, 'nobody in China will believe it.'

So, recalling that anecdote, I quit the Orient with the confidence that I had not been alone in my ignorance. For the East is a university in which one is never awarded a degree.

CHAPTER 31

Fanfare of Chopsticks

Confucius eats nothing out of season. He does not eat what has not
been properly cut. He does not eat what is too ripe or too green.
He does not eat without the proper sauce. He does not eat more of the
meat than of the vegetables. He does not restrict the amount of his
wine, but he does not let it befuddle him. He does not partake of wine
and dried meats which have been purchased at a store. He does not re-
use food seasoned with ginger, but he does not eat too much of it. . . .
Whenever his bowl was filled at a feast, he would blush and rise to
thank his host – *The Sayings of Confucius*.

Chinese food is the one magnificent unifying solace for all foreign-
devil expatriates in the Far East. Whatever their lost inheritance,
pawned birthright and rejected patrimony, they have at least eaten
in exile as they could never have eaten at home. All those Old
Hands, tape recorded at the Last Supper in the previous chapter,
would never have contemplated any such reunion except at a
Chinese banquet. There would have been dispute over individual
dishes – or even regional variety in the menu – but there would
have been universal insistence, with a fanfare of chopsticks, upon
irresistible Chinese food.

Myths about Chinese food are as abundant, adhesive and spurious
as bores at an official Chinese communist party banquet. There is,
for example, the tedious myth: 'One hour after a Chinese meal
you want another meal.' Perhaps a Western gourmand who
customarily on cheeseburgers feeds and drinks the milk of Bass
will feel unbloated after the manifold variety of *dim-sum* lunch. But
anyone who treated himself to a normal Chinese dinner, built
round, say, Szechwan smoked duck and steamed bread, and later
complained of premature hunger would be an abominably valiant
trencherman. The Chinese do not stuff their bellies today for
tomorrow's ache, but they know the best stuffing and flavours for
most bellies – today and tomorrow.

Most of the myths, of course, raise venerable but hopeful heads above the mirages of virility and seduction. These we may skir with heightened colour and averted eye, noting only that the viands and sauces of reputed restoration or stimulation are happily, always a delight to the palate, on the short run, even if unhappily, they disappoint the libido, on the long stand. The mythical elixirs include not only rhinoceros horn, birds' nest soup monkeys' brains and 'gold-and-silver flowers' – those esoteric standbys and stand-ups – but also such familiar staples as 'drunken shrimps', snapping turtle, eels-and-garlic, snake-blood, and of course aconite, that sturdy, long-lasting plant-friend.

Another overblown myth is the legendary banquet menu of the ancient Imperial Palace. The cherished gourmet extravagances of the Royal Viands Room (or Imperial Kitchen) must be repudiated in large measure. 'The emperors' feasts were made in heaven maybe,' says my friend, Master Sanjia Wu of the National Palace Museum in Taipei, 'but much of the food didn't get eaten, and some of it wasn't fit to eat – on earth or anywhere.'

The legend has persisted that Chinese emperors always gorge heroically on three-hundred-course meals each day. Precise archives in the National Palace Museum indicate, however, that relative austerity usually prevailed. The awe-inspiring banquets of a hundred courses and more included a majority of stale dishes provided only to give the appearance of an imperial feast. Attending eunuchs had the priority task of steering the fingers and chopsticks of drunken or indiscreet diners away from these Dead Sea fruit courses.

To express his gratitude for promotion, an official of the Southern Sung Dynasty once offered the emperor a 180-course banquet, but more than half the dishes were dried, honey preserved or fresh fruit. Only sixty-three fresh meat and vegetable dishes appeared on the groaning table. 'Considering that banquet given for Louis XIV in similar circumstances included 168 dishes, not counting dessert,' Master Wu points out sternly 'the Chinese offering showed considerable gastronomic restraint.

Pu Yi, the sad, last non-Marxist emperor of China, who came to the throne aged two in 1908, and who served as a cardboard front-man for the Japanese and a brainwashed convert for the Chinese communists, was allowed to record by his Maoist master that the imperial cuisine was 'flowery without substance, show without virility, elaborate without taste, and lacking in nutritional value.'

However, the myth of the Chinese imperial banquet does receive fleeting, cynical support from the following historic menu of the birthday dinner of the Empress-Dowager in 1861. It is pleasing to note that she gave instructions, first, that the birthday repast (served at 3 pm in the Pavilion of Heavenly Memory) was to be 'kept simple' in harmony with the conventional mourning for the emperor's recent death in equivocal circumstances; but, secondly, that swallow's nest – with its reputed encouragement of fertility and virility – should dominate the banquet. (Her new favourite was at table.) The menu:

Two chafing-dish courses –
  Julienne of pork with spinach
  Salted vegetables
Four large platters –

  Julienne of white duck meat with swallow's nest
  Three delicious chicken with swallow's nest
  Eight sublime duck with swallow's nest
  Ten flavour julienne of chicken with swallow's nest

Four medium platters –
  Swallow's nest with julienne of pork
  Fresh shrimp balls
  Braised duck kidneys
  Bèche-de-mer

Six dishes –
  Swallow's nest sautéed with julienned roast duck
  Puréed chicken with mashed turnips
  Julienne of pork sautéed with shark's fins
  Duck with bean sauce
  Salted vegetables
  Julienne of pork with egg

'The art of Chinese cooking,' says Master James Wei, Taipei gourmet and prince of hospitality, 'is to make the meat taste like vegetables and the vegetables taste like meat, without either the meat or the vegetables losing their original texture.'

That is the simplified Wei Law. It has added and poignant interest now, because, in exile Chinese opinion on Taiwan, the splendid heritage of Chinese cuisine is being slowly suffocated by ideology. Always an optimist, I am rashly confident that the art of cooking will resist or evade the farmyard strictures of the communist régime. But it cannot be denied that, if you are an ordinary Chinese today, you are being demonstrably disloyal to Chairman Mao and revolutionary ideals by eating bountifully, discerningly and with relish. If you salute the poet Li Po, drunkenly but happily drowning as he tried to embrace the moon's reflection in a lotus pond, you are a vicious revisionist. Still I cannot accept that Chinese love of good food – like Chinese love of women and of gambling – will be indefinitely submerged and finally drowned in alien dogma and unnatural servitude.

But Master Wei and other Nationalist exiles point out that traditional Chinese kitchen apprenticeship – paralleled by patient French kitchen training – is now vanishing in the communes, where cooks are being encouraged to simplify mass-produced menus in dismal party-line cafeterias. Visitors to China and lucky urban residents enjoy of course preferential menu treatment and greater variety in rationed food in city hotels and dining rooms, but in rural areas the party hero is the kitchen-chef recently acclaimed in Tientsin for discovering thirty different ways of preparing the sweet potato. When the ancient kitchen apprenticeship is lost, the Taipei sceptics demand, how can the savoury torch be handed on? When the master Chinese cooks ascend the dragon, can *chop suey* and sweet potatoes, *chow mein* and noodles be far behind?

Master Wei, as generous as he is seasoned, threw a banquet for me in Taipei as a guide to an instalment of my visionary Last Supper. He summoned seven other guests – all Han, mature and discerning diners of 'unbounded stomach' – but, to his chagrin, could organize only four master cooks, at two days' notice, to prepare his nine courses. He made it clear that he adhered to the Erasmus table roll-call: no more than nine.

The banquet was prepared to support his thesis: that there are still five major schools of regional Chinese cooking – not four, as some heretics now pretend to argue. He lists them as: Canton, Foochow-Fukien (including the coastal area), Shantung (including Peking and the north), Szechwan, and Honan. (The simplifying heretics seek to incorporate Honan with Shantung, Peking and the north.)

He rejected, politely but firmly, my innocent suggestion that the Foochow or coastal school might be classified under the generic label 'Shanghai'.

'Shanghai has – or had – many acceptable restaurants like the Sun Ya on Nanking Road,' he conceded, amidst a murmur of approval from his Han guests. 'But food or dishes of its own offering – none, pah, none! The one common and unique claim for each of the five schools which I have listed is that any respectable restaurant in each zone can – rather, could – offer its patrons on demand on any night more than one hundred different courses prepared from local products.' He brooded, then added: 'I would say, more precisely, at least 108 different courses.'

His Han guests approved more vociferously; the warm, encouraging *Shaoshing* wine was circulating.

Master Wei, essentially a fair and reasonable man, temporized. 'I would praise Shanghai because the best *Shaoshing* wine once came from spring water on a hill on the outskirts of Shanghai,' he recalled. The company reverently toasted the spring. 'Of course we have excellent water here also. You must drink *Shaoshing* at blood temperature,' he continued, with a bow and a swallow. 'When cold, reject. Drink with full heart and open throat. Remember that over-indulgence brings neither headache nor thirst in the morning. Remember, also, that, while Confucius, a diner of moderation, argued that the meat a man ate should not be enough to make his breath smell of meat rather than rice, he imposed no limit on wine consumption, so long as the diner "did not become disorderly".'

The company drank to Confucius.

I ventured to promulgate my own personal preference for light dry Western wine with Chinese food. There was only qualified tolerance of this bastardization, and I detected glances of disapproval when I reported the growing popularity of Beaujolais among Cantonese in Hong Kong restaurants. However, inflamed by the *Shaoshing*, I insisted that Western wine with Chinese food, in my opinion, was 'the second best way in which West meets East'. Master Wei, with adroit compromise, diverted my minority opinion to majority acceptance, and then unanimous agreement, with a non-segregation toast to 'the best way in which West meets East'.

Meanwhile, the four admirable cold *hors d'œuvres* – 'drunken' chicken, pigs' kidney, mutton and tiny clams – had been plucked by nine pairs of chopsticks, and the delicate Shantung fish with wine had been followed by the Szechwan hot-peppered chicken, the magnificent Hunan *tofu* or curd (frozen for eight hours, cooked for twelve), the dazzling, jewel-like Hupeh meatballs, the roast Cantonese sucking-pig (of which, of course, only the skin was eaten), the Lanchow steamed dumplings, the Foochow fish soup, and the lotus-root sweet.

'We could have had Szechwan smoked duck,' Master Wei, ever the unsatisfied perfectionist, brooded. 'Or Honan sweet-and-sour carp. Or Peking duck. Or monkey-head – we are having difficulty in getting supplies of monkey-head, which, as you well know, is a special kind of mushroom, tastier, I believe, than French truffles.'

An elderly general from Peking hailed Master Wei's reference to Honan sweet-and-sour carp, and, amidst general applause, saluted our host for his insistence that Honan cooking should not be merged with the Peking-Shantung school.

'Let Shantung cherish its steamed bread and dumplings, its Peking duck and its barbecued meat,' he declared. 'Foochow, Fukien and the coast have their red soy sauce and their soups and seafood; Szechwan boasts incomparable smoked duck and hot peppers; Canton has *dim-sum* and a range of dishes as rich and varied in flavours as the legacy in recipes brought by exiled cooks from the Imperial Palace. But we stand firm on separation for Honan and its Yellow-river carp!'

He then recited a celebrated poem:

> Out in the garden in the moonlight,
> Our servant is scraping a golden carp with so
>   much vigour the scales fly everywhere –
> Perhaps they go as high as heaven.
> The beautiful stars up there might be the scales of our fish.

We drank to the carp. And then to the stars.

'Which special dish did you prefer tonight, sir?' I asked the oldest diner at the table, a gentle professor whose life lies behind him in the communist Peking University.

'May I echo the excellent riposte of your Master Thoreau to that question?' he replied, with a box and out-thrust chopsticks. 'The dish I liked, and like, the best here is, as Thoreau said, the nearest.'

The company toasted Thoreau.

The four cooks were paraded and, bowing, joined in a common toast. The pretty girl waitresses were summoned and, bowing, accepted another toast.

'I must apologize,' Master Wei told us, formally and conventionally, 'for a most indifferent meal.'

CHAPTER 32

The Betrayal of Comrade X

This is an unworthy and even scurrilous episode, but I do no
take up my typewriter with a heavy or sluggish hand to record it
It is, indeed, an appropriate Asian memory on which to close thes
disjointed recollections. Here, after all, is rough but deviou
justice, Oriental in essence if Occidental in initiative, justice whicl
was seen to have been done as betrayal, but how or by whom only
a few knew or suspected – and these did not include the betrayec
one. As he brewed, so did he drink.

The names, the time and the place must be disguised to protec
the guilty. It could have happened in Djakarta or Phnom Penh
Rangoon or Vientiane, or even Bangkok or Tokyo. It had to be a
place where the foreign-devil correspondents had contact with th
diplomatic representatives of either Peking or Moscow or both
We shall not say where. Or when – except that the context wil
show that it happened after the Soviet army rescued Czecho
slovakia from the tyranny of the Czech people.

The newspaperman, an affable and mellow but formidabl
figure, does not now rove the Far East. I shall give no clue to hi
continuing affiliations, and I shall portray him as an Englishman
not because he is necessarily of Fleet Street, but because, to m
anyway, as an honest, bluff Australian, the English remain th
world's most enigmatic race, shaming the alleged inscrutables o
the East. We shall call him Dudley.

His victim was a sterling, high-ranking party man, but we wil
not say whether he hailed from Moscow or Peking, or whether h
was an accredited correspondent like the eminent Victor Loui
or the late Richard Sorge, or a career diplomat like the eminen
Comrade Chi or the late Madam Kung Peng. We shall call hin
Comrade X, Moscow Ying or Peking Yang, as you like it.*

* The error would be understandable, but Dudley must not be confused with th
late Dr H. N., an 'adviser' and not a newspaper correspondent, who once skilfull
and cruelly 'organized' the abrupt recall of a top communist party observer at pre

Dudley had the opening lines in the First Act of this strange three-act play in – we shall say falsely – the bar of the Million Elephants in Vientiane, overlooking the muddy Mekong.

'Richard, I shall have to do something about this bastard, Comrade X,' he told me with what appeared to be genuine regret.

I was impressed. Dudley seldom used bad language.

'It is not because he has thrown down a straight story which I wrote and tried to embarrass me with our fellows here and at home – and the French and Poles here,' Dudley hastened to explain. 'Nor because he just called me a liar to my face. But I learn that he has thrust a party knife into old Y's back and had him recalled in disgrace to some Siberia.' (Comrade Y was an agreeable old party hack in the same embassy, faithful, but human and amiably self-indulgent in liquor.)

I shared Dudley's resentment over old Y's fate, but was baffled by his threat.

'If I can help you to break Comrade X's neck, I am yours to command, Dudley,' I said. 'Just as he would happily break your or my neck. But what the hell can we do?'

He ordered two more Gibsons. 'I shall have him recalled,' he said simply. I gaped. And then we were joined by other foreign devils. (We were covering some blown-up party 'summit conference' and could bank on Page 1 or 2 for a week or so.)

So ended Act I. Act II opened, without warning, in a foreign embassy two days later, when a 'foreign adviser' asked me casually whether I had seen Comrade X lately. I said I hadn't, and didn't expect or want to see him. 'Watch him,' my companion told me; 'could be a story.'

That night after dinner my diplomat host – of an officially 'neutral' country – took me on one side: 'You get up to their embassy; what's with Comrade X?' I had now been alerted even if I still knew nothing. 'Maybe only gossip,' I ventured, 'but you can't tell with those bastards of course.' 'You're right,' he said, obviously still probing. 'We both think the same about X, I know, but strange things are happening. Y has been recalled, you know.'

Next night, the 'summit' pygmies threw a formal reception.

Korean war negotiations on the border by brushing close to him with conspicuous inadvertence on two separate occasions and whispering in his ear: 'Good-day, comrade; how are you?'

Comrade X, a gross scoundrel with a con-man's laugh, usually strode grandly from group to group at these gatherings, but this night he was clearly ill at ease and even on guard and tried to stick close to his ambassador's side.

'What's this story about Comrade X and his drunken outburst over Prague?' was the almost invariable opening query by eager and puzzled correspondents. Dudley was partly informed but wholly sceptical. 'I heard some of the details, but the story sounds improbable,' he would submit, reasonable and objective as always. 'Even if X disapproved of the Soviet takeover, he would be too smart and too pro-X to be openly and idealistically anti-Red Army, don't you agree? I think Bertie' – (one of the two top imperialist ambassadors) – 'was badly informed and thinking too wishfully yesterday.'

By this time, even I – because of my fortuitous Act I fill-in – was awake, but Dudley's undercover operation, however smooth, could only discomfit Comrade X fleetingly and briefly. The man was too solidly entrenched.

The rumours persisted spasmodically over the next two days and Comrade X appeared in public only with a bodyguard of respectable and respectful embassy runners. Then the conference ended, and we correspondent birds of passage sought our home perches. Act II ended as an anticlimax. I never even saw Dudley to say goodbye; he retreated a day earlier – despondently, I was sure.

Act III was delayed for more than a month. Then Dudley, in transit, sauntered into Jack Conder's bar in Hong Kong. 'Well met, Richard,' he said with uncharacteristic self-satisfaction. 'Have you heard? The bastard X has been recalled. Whimpering, I promise you. May he rot in his party hell.'

I was astonished – chiefly because Dudley seemed to be connecting the bastard's downfall with that first ripple of cocktail gossip – now remote in time and place.

'You underestimate the evil of the enemy,' Dudley explained patiently. 'Surely you do not believe that I rested my offensive on that opening whiff of grapeshot? The second operational stage was simple infiltration by telephone and airmail – all conducted by proxy. The final stage was expedient and inevitable betrayal inside the home front. Against the communist enemy in such skirmishes, one must carefully plan the second stage – which varies tactically, of course, according to problem and terrain – but in the third stage one only waits confidently for the reflex strike by the zealous comrade resolved to demonstrate his superior loyalty and grab his superior's post.'

Well, how had Dudley infiltrated?

'Elementary, my dear Richard. In this case, I simply arranged, first, for a friend, who speaks that Asian language, to phone the embassy, and, identifying himself – or was it herself? – as "Overseas Telephone Calls", to request the private number of Comrade X for a booked incoming call from Washington – or was it London? No doubt there were feverish checks with "Overseas Telephone Calls". No doubt official suspicion mounted with every denial.

'Secondly, old and trusted friends at widely separated Western capitals airmailed straightforward messages of personal goodwill – no more than two each week – to Comrade X, each brief message incorporating the same agreed numeral as a date or an obscure reference. I fancy twelve was the mystical number – because, I now recall, I left the capital on the 12th.

'Of course, dear X was already under dark surmise because known "advisers" in certain embassies, scenting a possible defection, were constantly rolling their eyes and nodding their heads whenever they glimpsed him in public.'

'I don't believe it,' I faltered, strangely frightened.

Dudley shrugged. 'Your incredulity reflects your naïvety. You have been working in the Far East for three decades. You have been meeting sincere party representatives most of that time. You have reported purges and counter-purges. Yet you still don't realize that for every Comrade X, who can eliminate a Comrade Y, there is always a Comrade Z, who is waiting – if insensibly – to eliminate Comrade X in the name of party loyalty.

'Whatever their racial and "revolutionary" rifts, the Moscow and Peking comrades are united in this intra-party distrust, factional conspiracy, and putative self-betrayal.'

It is a good point. Would you say Comrade X was a Russian or a Chinese party boss?

Index